AN OCEAN TO CROSS

*Daring the Atlantic,
Claiming a New Life*

LIZ FORDRED

WITH SUSIE BLACKMUN

INTERNATIONAL MARINE / McGRAW-HILL
Camden, Maine • New York • San Francisco • Washington, D.C.
Auckland • Bogotá • Caracas • Lisbon • London • Madrid • Mexico City
Milan • Montreal • New Delhi • San Juan • Singapore • Sydney • Tokyo • Toronto

International Marine
A Division of The McGraw-Hill Companies
www.internationalmarine.com

10 9 8 7 6 5 4 3 2 1

Library of Congress Cataloging-in-Publication Data
Fordred, Liz.
    An ocean to cross : daring the Atlantic, claiming a new life / Liz Fordred
  with Susie Blackmun.
        p.   cm.
    ISBN 0-07-135504-9 (alk. paper)
    1. Fordred, Liz—Journeys—Atlantic Ocean. 2. Usikusiku (Yacht).
3. Voyages and travels. 4. Paraplegics—Zimbabwe—Travel. I. Blackmun, Susie.
II. Title.
G475.F72 2000
910'.91631—dc21   00-044899

Printed on 55# Sebago by R.R. Donnelley, Crawfordsville, IN
Design by Dede Cummings Designs, photo layouts by Shannon Thomas
Production management and page layout by Janet Robbins
Edited by Jonathan Eaton and Patricia Sterling
Maps by Susan Carlson/Publishers' Art
Boat Plan by Jim Sollers

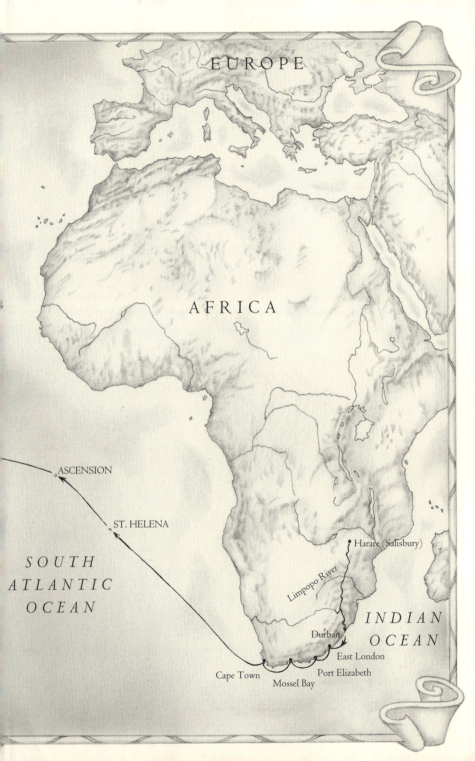

EUROPE

AFRICA

ASCENSION

ST. HELENA

Harare (Salisbury)

SOUTH
ATLANTIC
OCEAN

Limpopo River

INDIAN
OCEAN

Durban

East London

Port Elizabeth

Cape Town

Mossel Bay

AN OCEAN TO CROSS

To Pete
for your deep love and understanding,
for teaching me,
and for holding me steady while also giving
me my rein.
I love you.

To Mom
for blessing me with unconditional love.
And for not holding us back
but instead allowing us to spirit you along on
our adventure
into a new and fulfilling life.
May I be half the mother you are.

Contents

Illustrations can be found on pages VIII, 59, 155-156, 173-174, 207-208, 257

Maps can be found on the endpapers and pages 60 and 226

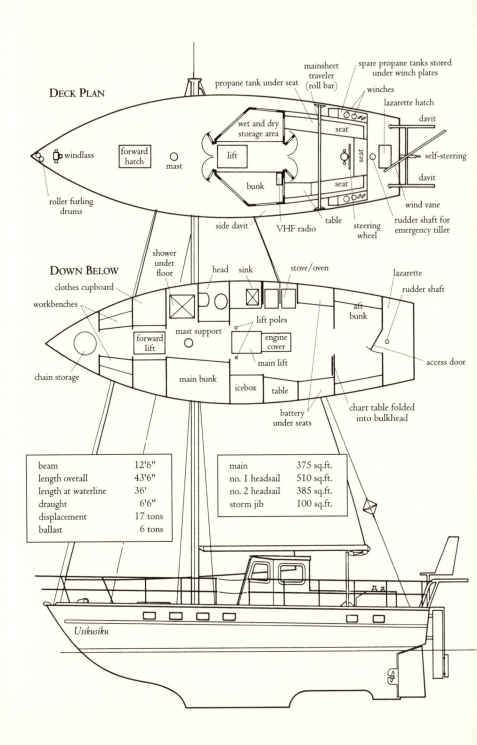

DECK PLAN

windlass
forward hatch
mast
roller furling drums
side davit
VHF radio
propane tank under seat
mainsheet traveler (roll bar)
spare propane tanks stored under winch plates
winches
lazarette hatch
davit
self-steering
davit
wind vane
rudder shaft for emergency tiller
steering wheel
table
seat
seat
seat
seat
wet and dry storage area
lift
bunk

DOWN BELOW

clothes cupboard
workbenches
chain storage
shower under floor
head
sink
stove/oven
lazarette
rudder shaft
forward lift
mast support
lift poles
engine cover
main lift
aft bunk
access door
main bunk
icebox
table
battery under seats
chart table folded into bulkhead

beam	12'6"
length overall	43'6"
length at waterline	36'
draught	6'6"
displacement	17 tons
ballast	6 tons

main	375 sq.ft.
no. 1 headsail	510 sq.ft.
no. 2 headsail	385 sq.ft.
storm jib	100 sq.ft.

Usikusiku

Prologue

B ETTER WAKE UP, PETE. It's about to pour." For the last hour we'd been sailing toward lightning so horrific it seemed alive. Some bolts drilled into the water with furious pulsations. Others streaked down to the horizon and then shot off horizontally. I'd never seen such lightning before.

"Furl the sails, Liz," Pete said, even before stirring from his nest in the cockpit. How stupid of me! We were running before the wind with twin headsails poled out, but I'd been so engrossed in watching the approaching spectacle I hadn't thought to reduce sail. While Pete tossed gear from the cockpit into the deckhouse, I eased the starboard headsail sheet and winched in the furling line until the sail was half its original size. Before I could get to the port winch, the first squall was upon us, and Pete had to tail for me while I furled that headsail all the way in.

"What the devil's happening, Pete?" I grunted as I put my shoulders into the task. "An hour ago I was thinking this was our best passage ever." I'd been lulled half to sleep by the gentle downwind ride through the Bahamas, mesmerized by the moon's reflection upon a calm sea and the gurgle and swish of water against *Usikusiku*'s hull. Now the wind was increasing at an alarming rate.

Pete scrutinized the ominous cloud bank that had wiped out the moon and was seriously working on the stars. "Looks nasty. I hope it won't last more than a couple of hours."

A terrific gust slammed into us. The mast vibrated. *Usikusiku* shuddered and heeled over hard, and the rigging screeched like an out-of-tune instrument. Pete and I furled the starboard headsail again, this time all the way. In minutes we'd gone from full sail to bare poles. Then the same squall line that had brought the wind dropped its wet load upon us. We scrambled into our foul-weather jackets, a mostly useless exercise because rain and sea spray drove horizontally, streaming down our necks and crawling up our sleeves. Yuck! I hated the feel of wet, salty rubber against my bare skin.

I disconnected the self-steering and took the wheel. In order to keep us pointed dead downwind I had to watch the self-steering vane, but whenever I looked back toward it, needles sandblasted my skin and forced my eyes shut. How could mere water hurt so much? I turned to ask Pete for help. Where was he? He'd been next to me just a minute ago! Then, through the torrential, driving rain I caught a glimpse of him—still right next to me. I reached out and touched his arm; in this six-year adventure there was no place for the thought of finishing alone.

Usikusiku charged through the now starless night. "Look at the wind generator!" Pete shouted over the deafening din of wind, waves, and rigging. "It's right off the scale!" In 30 knots of wind, Pete's homemade device trickled a quarter of an amp, max, into the batteries. Now it was pegged at one amp. I pictured the metal propeller taking flight and giving one of us a slice on its way past. "Is it safe?" I yelled back. "It looks like it's going to fly off!" Since everything Pete made was twice as strong as necessary, I deserved the dirty look he threw my way.

The full violence of the storm engulfed us. The wind escalated until it sucked the air from our lungs, making us fight just to inhale. Waves piled up around the boat, and their crests blew off into the blackness. Then that awful lightning moved in, igniting the spume-filled air around us. Some bolts stabbed into the sea so close we heard the water sizzle and saw it turn a gorgeous, glowing jade.

We were scared—not with paralyzing, shake-in-your-seaboots terror but with an adrenaline surge we had to channel into actions that would keep us alive. We'd often talked about what would happen in a survival storm. Would *Usikusiku* hold together? Would we make the right decisions? Most crucial of all, could we physically handle the challenge? We'd always been confident we could and had meticulously planned for all eventualities. Still, I could hear the echoes of our many skeptics: "Paraplegics? Sailing? Never! They shouldn't be allowed to go!" We'd never conceded them a moment's victory—in fact, the criticism had actually spurred us on—but at times like this, when I was cold, wet, and scared, I wondered why the hell I was here.

Steering required absolute concentration because the wind direction fluctuated wildly, and *Usikusiku* responded sluggishly. Three hours later the wind decreased a little, which was good, and settled upon one direction, which wasn't good: it had swung around to the southwest, which meant we no longer could make a straight course down the Northwest Providence Channel. We'd have to put up some sail. "Time to get the poles down," said Pete. I smiled weakly, a futile attempt to mask my concern. I lifted the cockpit seat and grabbed a safety harness. Pete put it on without protest, struggling to keep his balance while he raised his arms and dropped the harness over them. "Be careful," I couldn't resist saying as he clipped himself in and adjusted the straps.

Because we'd built the deckhouse extra wide to accommodate our wheelchairs in port, Pete went through it rather than around it, closing both sets of double doors behind him. With each wave that thrust *Usikusiku* skyward, he held on and waited for the subsequent plunge. When the deck dropped out from under him, he used the momentary loss of gravity to slide on his bottom along the slippery surface until the boat slammed into the wave trough and halted his progress. Clouds of sea spray blocked my view of him through the deckhouse windows. I was never comfortable when Pete was on the foredeck. What if he should go overboard? Of course we'd planned and practiced a crew-overboard procedure, but would we be able to execute it in these conditions? I gave myself a mental slap to stop this lapse into the negative, a state I refused to enter. I just had to trust the harness and everything it was connected to, including Pete's savvy.

Once both of the 18-foot running poles had slowly slid up the mast, I could begin to relax. Even after 8,000 miles of sailing, it still amazed me how Pete had worked everything out, down to the tiniest details, way back during the designing and building stage of our boat. And before we'd sailed a single mile, he'd obviously practiced in his mind how he'd perform each maneuver.

"Well done!" I said when he heaved himself onto the cockpit seat next to me. He was winded from his effort. Paralyzed from midchest down, and without stomach or back muscles, both of us had to do almost everything with our arms. But we had an abundance of strength in those arms now; in fact, our entire bodies were a far cry from the condition they'd been in when we were confined to hospital beds back home in Rhodesia. Wheelchairs might be permanent fixtures in our lives, but we were having an adventure most people only dream about.

The Accident

FROM THE TIME I COULD WALK I had loved animals, especially horses. As a kid I'd hung around Mr. and Mrs. Butters's stables for hours, willing to do any kind of work just to be near anything that resembled a horse. We couldn't afford riding lessons, but if I mucked out stalls, cleaned tack (saddles and bridles), and ran errands, Mrs. Butters occasionally rewarded me with a ride. The more I helped, the more I rode. I guess I learned quickly, because when I was about ten I began helping her teach, although I really didn't have the patience for it. I wanted to be on the horse myself, not instructing someone else who was up there.

I drove my sister Joan crazy with my smell of horse and dog. She was ultrafeminine and kept her frilly bedroom immaculate; you couldn't even sit on her bed lest you wrinkle it. I, on the other hand, would return from riding and flop on my bed while still in my dirty clothes and boots. I'd grope under the pillow for a can of condensed milk that Mom had left there as a treat, snuggle against Comrade, my white German Shepherd, and settle back with a book.

"How can you stand the smell of yourself?" Joan would ask in disgust.

"What smell?" I'd answer, smug about irritating my older sister.

When I was eleven or twelve, Jenny Bowden offered to coach me if, in return, I'd exercise her horse, Fantasy. Jenny, whose mother worked with mine, was one of Rhodesia's top riders. Fantasy was a handful, but then so was I, which may have been why we made a good match. When I wasn't riding the feisty little mare, I read to her. I'd have slept in her stall had Mom not made me come home at night.

After several months of riding Fantasy, plenty long enough for me to fall deeply in love, someone bought her. I was inconsolable —until the new owner brought her back. Yahoo! Was it because of the seditious thoughts I'd whispered in her ear that Fantasy bit, kicked, and behaved in an unladylike manner? I certainly thought so, unaware she'd been sold and returned three times before. After all, *I* had no such problems with her. I could crawl between her legs, kiss her muzzle, even put my fingers in her mouth. Realizing that I was perhaps the only person who'd ever want Fantasy, Mrs. Bowden offered Mom a good deal.

We could little afford a horse. My brother James had already left home. Joan still lived with us but was on an apprentice hair-dresser's salary. Dad was an alcoholic and drank whatever he earned, which left Mom to support the family with her income as a bookkeeper. Somehow, though, she did it. She bought Fantasy.

At first I tried keeping the horse at our home in Salisbury (now Harare), but she refused to stay. She could open anything, including the stable door. She'd nudge the top bolt with her muzzle until it slid out, then kick the door to loosen the bottom bolt. "She's gone," Dad would say, shaking me awake. In the velvety dawn we'd drive down the road toward Jenny's house until we spotted Fantasy ambling along, her blanket trailing behind her. She let me catch her exactly once. From then on, knowing what was coming, she'd break into a trot, throwing an occasional glance back to make sure I didn't get too close. I swear she even grinned. Fantasy was my horse and knew it and, I think, even liked it, but she made it clear where she was going to live. After a half-dozen escapes I succumbed to her stronger will (and to the neighbors' reminders that the local zoning laws required three acres for a horse, rather than our one acre) and boarded her at Jenny's.

I couldn't have grown up in a better setting for indulging my passion for riding. In the late 1950s and early 1960s, Southern Rhodesia—a landlocked, Montana-sized area in south-central Africa—was still a British colony. Framed by the Limpopo River to the south and the great Zambezi River to the north, this picturesque land was one of the last parts of Africa settled by Europeans. Only a century earlier, the missionary-explorer David Livingstone had been the first white man to set eyes on the Zambezi's spectacular Victoria Falls. The indigenous people called it *Mosi-oa-Tunya*, "Smoke That Thunders," because of its deafening noise and the cloud of spray that can be seen from as far as forty miles away. Livingstone's tales generated interest among English-speaking missionaries, gold prospectors, hunters, and adventurers, but the real push toward settlement came from Cecil John Rhodes, the South African gold and diamond magnate who founded DeBeers. Rhodes envisioned an empire, a British presence that would offset the growing power of the Germans in southwest Africa and the Boers in the Transvaal. He founded the British South Africa Company, to which Queen Victoria gave a Royal Charter to explore and annex territory. At Rhodes's insistence it was self-governing.

In 1890 a wagon train of settlers and British South Africa Police set out from the British Cape Colony on an arduous trek north into uncharted territory. After traversing hundreds of miles of bush, several large rivers, and rough, rocky terrain, they emerged onto the beautiful open space of the highveld. Upon this mile-high plateau they established a fort they named Victoria, for the Queen, and then went on to found Fort Salisbury and hoist the Union Jack there.

Tales about the temperate climate, plentiful game, and sparse population of what soon became known as Southern Rhodesia lured thousands of mainly British settlers north. In school we were taught that Rhodesia was an empty land when the white Europeans settled it. In actuality, an estimated quarter-million people lived there: on the central plateau and in the mountainous woodlands of the east roamed various nomadic tribes collectively known as the Mashona, of Bantu origins; in the semiarid southwest were the Matabele, of Zulu origins. But tribes weren't married to specific tracts of land; they moved about. The Matabele, in particular, had only recently moved in. Europeans had been in South Africa for 350 years, and trekboers were roaming through Rhodesia long before the Matabele came.

In 1923, BSA Company rule ended, and the British government asked the now 37,000 colonials to choose between joining the Union of South Africa as a fifth province or becoming a British colony with "limited self-government." The white residents opted for quasi independence. My paternal grandfather, a Scotsman, and grandmother, an English Jew born in South Africa, were already there. Having heard of the opportunities in Southern Rhodesia, they'd come north shortly after their marriage, and my dad was born in Fort Victoria, which is now called Masvingo. Mom arrived in Salisbury as an infant. The daughter of a Greek and a Swede, she was born on a British-registered vessel in South African waters, which made her British. I guess all this makes me a mongrel, but as far as I'm concerned, I'm Rhodesian through and through.

By the time I came along, in 1953, Southern Rhodesia was the jewel of Africa, with a solid infrastructure and a thriving economy based on farming, mining, and industry. The white population had leveled out at around 200,000 and, as was the norm in small British colonies, ran the government and owned most of the farms and businesses. The vast majority of the Africans, as we called the blacks, were still uneducated and lived primitively, as subsistence farmers. Those in the cities worked in industry or as domestic servants, although some owned small businesses. Their families were large, with many children, sometimes from several wives. Girl babies were preferred because they brought a *lobolo*, or bride price, from prospective husbands; often it was paid in cattle, which were a sign of wealth.

This push for children, coupled with improvements in health and hygiene, had given Rhodesia the highest rate of population increase in the world. With blacks numbering three to four million, African labor was so plentiful and cheap that nearly all white families could afford servants. Even ordinary people like us had a "houseboy" and a "garden boy." Many servants stayed with their white employers for decades and became an extension of the family. When my mother no longer needed Amos, who was with us when I was growing up, my brother James took him into his business, where Amos remains today.

For most of my childhood, life in many ways was idyllic. After all, with our two servants doing the chores, I had plenty of time for riding. Fantasy and I rode in cross-country events and in gymkhanas, those equestrian-centered days of sport peculiar to the British colonies. We even won a special shield for "Courage, Endeavor and Achievement"—or rather I won it for handling a horse everyone in the community knew had a terrible temperament. Fantasy was as stubborn as I. If she didn't want to go out on any given day, I did a lot of walking around the pasture before I caught her. When not training or competing, I explored the countryside with my best friend Sue, while my dog Comrade and her dog Lassie trailed behind us. In the summer we often headed bareback to the quarries and rode the horses into the water. Fantasy loved swimming so much it was hard to get her out.

By sixteen I was bored with school. I was impatient to begin my life yet despondent about my options, because for everything conected with animals you had to be male or go to school for a million years. If I wanted to be anything, it was a vet, but I didn't want to be ancient by the time I got there. I wanted to work with animals *now*. Just when I was at my lowest, Mary and Wally Herbert offered me the chance of a lifetime, a two-and-a-half-year apprenticeship in veterinary nursing, kennel administration, and grooming dogs to show standard. I worked hard and learned all I could. Eventually I managed their grooming shop in town and moved into a room behind their house, which was about thirteen miles south of Salisbury and more country than urban.

Best of all, Mary let me take over the schooling of her horse, Chaka. Wally marked out a dressage area and built me a set of jumps, and Mary paid for me to have lessons with a well-known dressage teacher. Chaka was not yet the powerful animal he would become; he was young and goofy-looking, his muscles not yet fully developed. Still, I welcomed the opportunity to ride a big horse because I was a big girl and had already outgrown my beloved Fantasy. Animals were my life and horses my passion. So in addition to running the shop twelve hours a day, I rode Chaka both before and after work, driving relentlessly toward the perfection required for dressage and show jumping.

Although I enjoyed competition in the ring, I far preferred getting wet and muddy while tearing around on cross-country courses. Much of the bush around Salisbury had been cleared by farmers earlier in the century, but parts of the Rhodesian countryside were untouched and magnificent. Clumps of msasa trees peppered the sweeping grasslands of the highveld. Ridges, rocky outcrops called *kopjes,* and *vlei* (valleys), hazy in the distance, changed color throughout the day. If I found a fallen tree, I'd check carefully for nearby holes and then go for the jump—the higher the better. I spent every spare minute riding, relishing the freedom of being one with my horse, accompanied only by

Comrade and perhaps Mary or Sue. It was a narrow, solitary existence, but I loved it. It took a life-altering event to slow me down enough to notice the tremendous kindness and thoughtfulness in people.

I remember the day of my accident vividly, although I try not to revisit it. I was eighteen. We were preparing for the Meikles International Horse Trials, a three-phase event that entailed dressage, show jumping, and cross-country riding. This was the first time I'd had a horse capable of entering it, so Chaka and I had been training hard, trying to improve our standard. After more than two years of hard riding, Chaka was a different horse from the one I'd started with; he'd become a credit to the great Zulu chief after whom he'd been named.

To ready him for the trials and make sure he was fit enough, I entered a paper chase, a rugged, three-part cross-country event. For some reason, though, I was not in a good frame of mind when I loaded Chaka into the horse box for the ride to Countess Dabrosky's farm, where the paper chase was to take place. I felt gloomy without knowing why. Could it have been a premonition?

A wide swath had been cut through the tall, golden grass to mark the course, which included gullies and ridges and jumps over brush piles, heavy logs, and stone walls. A paper chase wasn't a race but a fitness trial. Nobody won. You could choose between high and low jumps or skip the jumps altogether if you rode a young horse. You could have a grueling run or stop when you or your horse got tired. It was an elegant, very British affair, with everyone decked out in formal riding apparel—white or camel-colored jodhpurs, high leather boots, dark blazers, and black-velvet-covered riding helmets. Horses' coats gleamed. Manes and tails were brushed, braided, and beribboned. It was much like the fox hunts you see in English films, minus the fox and dogs.

I offloaded Chaka, saddled up, and joined the other riders who had gathered to drink the traditional glass of sherry. Then we mounted our horses, and at the high-pitched hooting of a horn the paper chase was on.

The riding dispersed my feeling of gloom; it returned briefly after the first leg of the course, but during the second leg I immersed myself not just in the ride but in the extraordinary beauty of the countryside. I almost felt like leaving the course and taking off on my own into the bush. At the lunch break I joined my friends for a quick sandwich and then set off on the third and final leg of the paper chase.

A jump. Chaka stumbles. I sail over his head, landing on my face while my body carries on over me.

A crowd. Panic. Terrible worry on Mary's face and in the voices around me.

I'm picked up. I scream and pass out.

I'm in the back seat of a Land Rover. "Stop! Take me out! Get this rock out of my back!" They stop the car and turn me on my side.

During the thirty-mile ride to Salisbury Central Hospital, I have no bracing or support. For the first ten or fifteen minutes, before we reach the main road, we bounce over unpaved farm roads. The pain is a searing ball of fire in my back. Sometimes, mercifully, I lose consciousness, but when I resurface the pain is worse than before.

"Cut her jodhpurs." The words penetrate the fog of agony that enshrouds me.

"No!" I've just had those jodhpurs tailor-made! What will I wear next time I go riding?

The emergency room nurses actually slit the seams.

They roll me onto my side. More pain. Someone injects my spine with radiopaque dye, then I'm wheeled off to X-ray and the excruciating transfer to a hard, cold table. They tip it this way and that to move the dye around. The pain is unbearable, even worse than in the Land Rover. I scream and cry.

"Try not to scream. It will be all right."

Easy for them to say! I black out.

A week of haze; I must have been sedated. Now and again I'm aware of strangers in white, floating past. Sometimes I smell the lovely, familiar scent of Mom's perfume, and I know she is there.

At last I come to. Bags of blood and saline hang from stands at the foot of my bed, but it takes time to realize they're connected to me, dripping fluids into the veins in my legs. What the hell is going on? I slowly become aware of my body, or rather I become aware that I don't seem to have one. The first thing that alarms me isn't the lack of feeling in my legs; it's that I can't feel my chest—it's as if my breasts have gone. How terrible! I have no breasts!

To prevent pressure points that could turn into bedsores, the nurses turned me every two hours, but I couldn't tolerate lying on my back so all they could do was roll me back and forth, from one side to the other. When I was lying on my left side, my face bothered me because the entire left side—forehead, cheek, chin, and neck—had been scraped raw in the fall. It took weeks and weeks to heal.

One of the strangers in white turned out to be Professor Lawrence Levy, a neurosurgeon who pricked me with pins I couldn't feel. This didn't worry me in the least. Did I know I was paralyzed? I didn't want to think about it, so I didn't even admit to myself that I couldn't feel anything. Nothing was wrong with me I couldn't fix, given time.

I'd reacted similarly when I was fifteen and Dad had died suddenly of pneumonia. My feelings about him were so conflicted that to escape the reality, I headed straight off to field hockey practice, then wondered why I felt no joy when I was chosen team captain. Dad and I had never seen eye to eye, but rather than tiptoe around him, as the rest of the family did, I answered back and inevitably set him off. His alcoholism made it impossible for me to respect him, even though I knew it was a disease and not willful behavior. Not until I reached adulthood did I understand that he'd probably stood little chance of a normal life. He was descended from generations of male alcoholics, and he carried emotional scars from going off at sixteen (he lied about his age) to World War II, where he was exposed to more death than any person should have to witness. As a child and teenager, though, I was too young to pity him. Instead, I'm ashamed to admit, I hated him and I was relieved when he died. Maybe we could get on our feet now, I thought, and Mom would be better off. Yet he was my father and I loved him. His death only added to my adolescent turmoil.

I can see now that my intense involvement with animals, throughout childhood, may have been an effort to avoid human relationships. Because a parent had disappointed me, deep down I must have assumed that all people would do the same. Animals, by contrast, were uncomplicated. You didn't simultaneously love and hate them, nor did they hurt you. Having learned to hide my feelings even from myself, I guess you could say I was in denial about my paralysis. Still, I've always been an optimist who sees the glass as way more than half full, and if not, I will just fill it up. Whatever the reason, I was a cheery patient, cracking jokes across the ward. I wasn't faking it. I honestly felt that way.

Five weeks went by before I was forced to confront the severity of my injury. The night before I left the hospital for a rehabilitation center, Professor Levy came by to announce his verdict. "The parts of you that have no feeling will not regain it," he said. I guess he had to hit me hard in order to break through my walls.

"You're wrong. I have feeling just above my left knee."

He took out his pin. "Close your eyes."

"Ha!" I said. I had feeling in a patch the size of a quarter.

"You should not be able to feel that. You will not walk again. You're going to be in a wheelchair for the rest of your life." I could see the pain in his eyes; I wouldn't have had his job for anything.

"No, I'm not. You've got it all wrong."

"You've completely severed your spinal cord between vertebrae T4 and T5. This is the area between your shoulder blades, and you are paralyzed from that region down. You have one of the worst dislocations I've ever seen."

After Professor Levy had gone, I cried for what I had so stupidly lost, but the tears dried within minutes. I *was* going to prove them all wrong.

Rehab

MOM AND MY COUSIN PAULINE, who was a nurse, went on a reconnaissance mission to Saint Giles Medical Rehabilitation Centre. It was very pleasant, they assured me. I'd have my own room and access to the patio outside it.

I dreaded it. This change meant facing the next step of my life, and it wasn't the step I'd planned. The ambulance ride, though, opened my eyes. Seeing the outside world again was like being reborn. Cars still drove on roads! Grass and trees—what a joy! The sun beating through the small window was warm on my arms and face, and I wanted the ride to go on and on, not come to a halt three miles later at Saint Giles, where a new worry awaited. I was wearing a standard hospital gown, far too short and split down the back. My legs had already started to have spasm, which is common with upper thoracic spinal injuries, and mine was growing more ferocious by the day. Usually my legs straightened, but sometimes they kicked about. My own familiar nurses had put me on the stretcher, but who was going to take me off? The ambulance crew were men. All I needed was for my legs to start kicking and for the covers and gown to fly off, forcing me to make a flailing, naked entrance into Saint Giles.

The ambulance driver slid me out into sunlight so dazzling that at first I couldn't see. Then I made out an attractive blond woman walking out to meet me. She was Jennette Trow, the head nurse, and even from a distance I felt her warmth, the kind that radiates from within and envelops everyone around. She must have sensed my concern about my wayward legs, because she kept me decent while I was wheeled into the building and lifted onto my new bed. I was grateful for that.

Alone in my room, I gazed through French doors to the patio and the carpet of grass beyond. Oh, how I longed to feel that green springiness under my feet! Roll in it! Feel its prickles against my skin!

An elderly man wandered in. "Hello," I greeted him cheerfully. "Gone, gone, Monday Jesus," he said. In fact, that's all he said, repeatedly. I didn't know how to respond. In walked another chap who at least helloed me back, but an emptiness in his eyes suggested he wasn't quite right, either. Dear God! Was this a mental institution? Had I damaged not just my back but my head as well? At last a good-looking guy in a wheelchair rolled in, and he sounded normal. "Am I going mad?" I asked. "No," he said— Gone-Gone had a speech defect caused by three strokes; the other man had a head injury from a car accident. Oh boy, what next?

Even though my spasm stimulated my circulation enough to prevent bedsores, the nurses continued the hospital routine of turning me, like a steak on a grill, every two hours. Colleen Kemp, my physical therapist, continued passive movements to keep my legs from atrophying. Then, for the first time in six weeks, I was allowed to sit up, and with apprehension I began to learn what I could do.

I'd been donated a wheelchair. Heaven forbid—me in a wheelchair! Oh, dear God, please no! For a week it sat reproachfully in a corner of my room while I refused to look at it. One day my brother James lowered himself into it. "Do you mind?" he asked.

"No, go ahead."

He wheeled out the door, zipped up and down the passageway, spun around a couple of times, zoomed back into my room, and said, "This is not too bad, you know. You can do quite a lot in this."

I began to accept it—not because I acknowledged the permanence of my "condition" but because I was fed up with being in bed. I'd briefly tasted the sun on my skin, and I wanted to get going. If that meant sitting on wheels for a while, so be it.

My bed was cranked up to 45 degrees for a couple of hours to prepare my body for being upright again. Then Colleen, nurse Sandy Brown, and physical therapist George Turnbull lifted me out and placed me in the wheelchair with pillows all around. How bizarre it seemed! Where was my body? I could see it but had no sensation of it. I felt lightheaded and nauseated. Colleen tipped the chair back until I felt better, then gradually set it down. She took me for a short walk (although I'm sure she didn't use that word), then brought me back to bed. I was exhausted.

The early days of being a paraplegic are a roller coaster of emotions. There are times of hope versus times of despondency, of striving versus failure, of elation versus tears and tantrums. My world had been knocked upside down and I had to start the long climb upward to find out who I was and what I had left. Regaining independence—the ultimate goal of rehabilitation—was the hardest thing of all. Nevertheless, I was at Saint Giles to get better, and that's what I would do. Only one track led out the door to freedom, and I got on it with the single-mindedness that has marked me since birth. Like a toddler, I had to start from scratch with simple tasks: dressing, bathing, picking things up off the floor. They were incredibly frustrating, but each small success brought tremendous satisfaction, coupled with the realization I could go on to try harder things.

Saint Giles was filled with the most wonderful staff. Nurse Sandy Brown, in particular, intuitively knew whether to cheer you up with her dry wit or leave you alone to work through your inner pain and frustration. Sometimes her mere presence was enough to get you back on the climb up that long hill to emotional and physical well-being. John, her husband, was like a cool breeze from an outside world we all once knew, and when he visited the six of us in the ward, he treated us like normal people.

My spasm had gone quite mad. My stomach jumped nonstop, day and night, and I wasn't sure whether my passive movements consisted of Colleen's exercising my legs or the spasm's exercising Colleen. My legs became so strong that if you put your hand between my knees, they clamped together so hard you'd never get free; I had to strap them to my wheelchair with two-inch webbing, which they sometimes broke. I actually could stand when my legs were in spasm, although it was likely to release without warning and dump me on the floor. All this muscular madness was a bother, but at least it kept my legs from atrophying, and eventually I learned to use it to my advantage. Fed up with having to be lifted onto the physical therapy bench, I developed a method of getting there myself. I shoved off from the chair with my arms, which caused my legs to shoot straight out in spasm. My hips followed suit, snapping me upright like a wooden soldier, and my upper body's forward motion launched me toward the bench. Voilà, I was on it! Most of the time, anyway.

I refused to have rails on my bed, even though I sometimes woke up in midair because my legs had decided on their own to take a walk—we had a definite communication problem. I'd instinctively grab the mattress as I went, not that it softened my fall, since I was the first of us to land. The African night nurses would rush in and lift the mattress, expecting to find me injured, only to find me laughing so hard they had trouble getting me up. It was as if there were two of us: I was merely a spectator to what my legs did, except they got the rest of me in trouble. The nurses and I had many a good laugh at their antics. When I was put into the bath, if my legs didn't want to bathe or if the water was too hot for their liking, they climbed out and hung over the side. I just had to make sure my hips didn't straighten too, as then I'd be blowing bubbles. These kinds of scenes really appealed to my sense of humor.

After several visits, Professor Levy diagnosed me with Wallenberg's syndrome: I could move nothing on my left side, but the quarter-sized patch above my left knee, where I'd been able to feel Professor Levy's pin, was hypersensitive—a mere touch felt as if you'd whacked me with a cactus. On my right side I had absolutely zero feeling, but wonder of wonders, I could move that leg slightly if I was lying down and my spasm relaxed. With such a high dislocation, my back and stomach muscles should have been nonexistent and sitting virtually impossible, but I had surprisingly good balance. Colleen and George would feel my abdomen as I lifted my right knee. They never told me what they thought. Was it leg muscles? Hip flexors? I suspected they thought I was using my spasm, but I could feel a message going through that leg as in no other part of my body. I found I could even move my big toe. It wasn't useful for anything, but I felt I could have swung from the highest tree.

My first trip out of the rehab center came three or four months after the accident, when Charl, my former boyfriend, strolled in and announced he was taking me for a ride. Ignoring my protests, he pushed me outside, scooped me up, and plopped me in his beach buggy. Even though he didn't seem to care that I was in a wheelchair and had a bag of wee hanging from me, I was horrified.

First he took me to the Herberts' place and drove right up to the paddock. I called out to Chaka, who came to the fence at the sound of my voice. Tears ran in rivers down my cheeks as memories flooded over me: the freedom of riding Chaka through the bush, the power of his body moving beneath me, the friendliness of his nudges, the warmth of his mouth when he sucked on my fingers. *Oh, God! I'd lost all this!* I thought my heart would break. I pulled myself together when the Herberts came out of the house, although seeing them wasn't any easier: Mary and I bravely tried to make conversation, while Wally stood aside in quiet agony. More memories swirled around, of training and competition, of rides with Mary and Sue. I'd had two and a half years of fun with Charl, too, lots of it in the beach buggy. *What had I done to myself?*

Then Charl took me to see Mom. Her face, so happy to see me out and about, got my tears going again. She'd already had enough hardship in her life, I thought, without another heartache to face. How could I have done this to her? Her smile faltered, and I saw my own pain and loss reflected in her eyes.

As agonizing as this outing was, it demonstrated that although I might have changed, the same world was out there. Eventually I'd have to face it.

For a long time I didn't talk with Sue or Mary about the accident. I knew they were upset (I can feel their pain even now), and I didn't want them to feel worse. Months went by before I asked them which jump I'd fallen on. I was stunned to learn it was an easy hedge; considering the consequences, it should have been a six-foot wall! The ground was smooth and free of holes. So what had happened? No one who had been there knew, and I remembered nothing. Mary and I could only surmise that Chaka was tired and dropped a shoulder; Mary had come off him before, without reason. Nor did I find out why no one called an ambulance. Were they afraid I'd die of shock before it got there? And why wasn't I braced before I was moved? Didn't anyone realize I might have a spinal injury?

Why didn't I dig for details? I still don't know. Maybe I didn't want to dwell on my mess-up. Maybe I didn't want anyone to see my agony. Maybe *I* didn't want to see my agony, since most of the time I couldn't acknowledge even to myself that I was hurting.

I never experienced much of the anger or bitterness about my fate that so many paraplegics go through. I had one period of deep depression when I just wanted to be left alone, but because mourning my loss was a normal part of the recovery process, everyone let me grieve. After a week of that, I sensed that when you get yourself down in a hole there's only you to get yourself out of it, so I pulled myself up. At times I felt strong enough to pull others up as well. My sister Joan had a really tough time accepting what had happened to me. "I wish it had been me, not you," she sobbed one day. "You enjoy physical things so much more than I." Such an unselfish expression from my dear sister! I held her against me. "My shoulders can hold up this burden better than yours," I said. "Besides, I think there's a reason for all this." I still sometimes wonder why I accepted my lot as easily as I did.

I went through a period of extreme embarrassment and shame about being so helpless and dependent, but again I pulled out of it, somehow knowing it was dangerous to let myself wallow in such negativity; I must have had a maturity beyond my years. Besides, I was surrounded by so much love. Right after my accident I received three or four hundred cards, most of them from people I'd never met. People phoned Mom, me, the hospital. They sent flowers, came to visit. A Salisbury couple set up a trust fund to help with medical expenses. Because of all this kindness, I began seeing the world and the people in it through different eyes.

The biggest obstacle I faced during my year of rehabilitation was my bladder. My trousers had to be changed at least eight times a day because the violence of my spasm continually made me bypass my catheter. I'd be in a sweat, having just completed the long task of dressing myself, when I'd notice my pants were wet. I could have screamed! The doctors suggested an ileocystostomy, which would surgically redirect my urine through an opening in my abdomen, but I refused because nothing else had been tried, and I hoped for a nonsurgical alternative.

After I'd been in the rehabilitation center for seven and a half months, Jen Trow went to Conrade Hospital in Cape Town for a course on bladder training. When she came back, she removed my catheter and sat me on the commode, where I experimented with drinking different amounts of liquids and different time lapses between drinks. Jen said I should sit for only a couple of hours, but wanting to beat this thing, I spent the day there. And the next. I filled the time playing solitaire, doing jigsaws, reading, and recording when and how much I drank and when I heard a trickle below. We were trying to establish whether my bladder had a routine I could adapt to, but something amazing happened instead: on the eighth day I could actually *feel* my bladder emptying. Yahoo! "Now at least I know when I'm going to be wet," I joked.

Each day the feeling improved until the "I'm-wet" signal became an advance warning. First it was seconds, then it stretched to minutes and kept lengthening. After sixteen days on the commode I felt confident enough to get back into my wheelchair. Unfortunately, my spasm prevented me from getting onto the commode quickly or safely. As soon as I tried to maneuver my legs, out they'd shoot, usually just as I was transferring over, and if my hips decided to get in on the act by straightening, I'd wind up lying across the commode instead of sitting on it. Since the time span between bladder signal and bladder action was brief, rarely giving me time to deal with all this, Liz Charles, my occupational therapist, made a boxlike seat that held a bedpan and installed it on my wheelchair. At the signal I could zoom off somewhere private. As soon as I started moving about, my legs straightened with spasm and tried to stand, but because they were strapped to the chair, my bottom lifted enough for me to pull my pants down. When the spasm released and sat me down again, I could wee. Then I shifted around to get the spasm going again so I could get my pants back up. Afterward, I'd go empty the bedpan. I hated that box, but at least it kept me dry and independent most of the time.

The nurses had been continuing to catheterize me at night. I didn't think that was right, so while falling asleep I concentrated on the new urge-to-pee feeling, remembering exactly what it was like and telling myself over and over to wake up when I felt it. Within three or four nights I did. I didn't want to use a bedpan in bed because it didn't feel normal to wee while lying down (my bladder had been going for nearly eighteen years sitting up, and it must have remembered something), so eight or ten times during the night I'd call for the African night nurses. They were extraordinarily patient about trying to get me to the loo in time. Eventually I requested a lower bed so I could get there myself, without help.

Of all the problems women paraplegics go through, bladder control is the worst. Men can use a sheath, like a condom, that will contain a small accident. Women have to get out of a wheelchair, out of their pants, and onto a toilet. It takes forever. Bowel training was far easier; since most people go at the same time each day, it was just a matter of sitting there on a regular basis until my body established a habit.

Anyone who has an accident of this sort is visited by a multitude of preachers from every denomination. They might mean well, but they have their own ideas about what you should believe and in whom. The Reverend Frank Mussell was different from the rest, truly a man of God who had a logic about religion and healing that I admired. His coming around in the evening to pray with me gave me a tremendous feeling of peace. He also "laid hands" on me. Although I'd always considered that sort of thing nonsense, whenever he touched my lower abdomen I felt a tingling heat in my bladder, and after each prayer session my bladder sensation seemed to improve a little, which shouldn't have been possible with a total spinal cord severance. I also developed great faith in the power of positive thinking, reinforced by reading authors such as Norman Vincent Peale.

A year after my accident I went home. James had just built Mom a house in the Salisbury suburb of Waterfalls, one she'd designed herself before my accident. Almost as if she'd known she was going to need a special house, there were no hallways or narrow doors, and only one entrance had steps. Eerie wasn't the word for it.

Mom had always been unwavering in her love, which was so strong and deep it had kept me stable throughout a childhood marred by alcoholism and strife. During my year in the hospital and rehab she'd visited almost daily, no matter how tired she was from her long days at work. Now that I was home, she hovered about, desperate to help. I would not let her and hurt her deeply by accusing her of being the only person who treated me as an invalid. I wanted to do everything myself, block out the pity, push away the helping hands that actually held back my progress toward autonomy. My motto emerged: *if I need help I will ask for it.* I felt it best to make a real stand.

To my eternal gratitude, Mom moved beyond her wounded feelings, not only by stepping back but by giving me an occasional push. She presented me with the best gift ever, an old Ford Prefect already fitted with hand controls, which she'd bought from a disabled woman too old to drive it anymore. Mom recognized that the best way to hasten my recovery was to give me back some independence.

Pete

I WAS SUPPOSED to be looking for a job but kept putting it off. It was far easier to stay home. I was still uncomfortable going out among able-bodied people—embarrassed about my condition, about how I looked, about whether my bladder would behave. My self-confidence was pretty low. I had a couple of interviews, but it was always the same: I couldn't get up the stairs or into the bathroom, or the whole office would have to be rearranged in order for me to work there. They didn't call me back anyway, so what was the point? It was demoralizing as hell.

Mary and Wally Herbert generously offered me my old job back, but even though working with animals was all I'd ever wanted to do, I knew I'd continually have to make compensations for my handicap. I didn't want to be any less than I had been. Besides, things were different now, and I had to find a new path. That's what I told myself, anyway. On a deeper level, maybe I figured it would be less painful to cut that part of my life out altogether and to begin anew.

One day Liz Charles, my occupational therapist, phoned me. "There's an opening for a receptionist right here at Saint Giles," she said.

"I'm not interested."

"You have an interview tomorrow morning at nine o'clock." Knowing that a challenge had more effect on me than persuasion, she put the phone down without giving me time to respond. Consequently, I made my foray back into the real world in a setting where I felt comfortable.

During my year as a patient at Saint Giles the staff had often sent me to cheer up new arrivals. ("What am I supposed to cheer them up about?" I'd tease.) On one of my missions of good cheer and bull dust—my last, as I was soon to be off home—Sandy Brown pushed me into a room where a new patient lay in bed. "This is Pete Fordred," she said. "He knows you. You were in the same class in senior school." Embarrassed was not the word—I did not recognize him. The Pete Fordred in my memory was well-built and short-haired. This chap was painfully thin, with hair to his shoulders and a great, droopy mustache that partly obscured his mouth. My valiant attempt at conversation got little response, so I left. Perhaps Pete was depressed or embarrassed, I thought, as I had been early on. It never occurred to me he might just be shy.

I ran into Pete in physiotherapy a few times after that but never really got to know him. I did get to know his parents, though. With just six patients on the ward, they always stuck their heads in to say hello, and some evenings Mrs. Fordred came into my room if Pete's was filled with his friends. She wasn't much more talkative than her son, but her silences were comfortable. Besides, I did enough talking for both of us.

Not long after Pete's arrival I was released from Saint Giles, and when I first returned as receptionist, I ran into him only once or twice on the ten-acre campus. One evening Mr. Fordred came by the house. Pete was now doing physical therapy as an outpatient, he said, because his medical insurance as a government employee covered only the four weeks in the hospital and none of the rehab. By moving home early, Pete was saving his family a considerable amount of money, but each morning Mr. Fordred had to get his wife to work, Pete to Saint Giles, and then himself to his job. It was a lot of driving. Since they lived out my way and I was going to Saint Giles every day anyway, would I consider taking Pete in with me if Mr. Fordred brought him home?

For all of February I delivered Pete to his daily physiotherapy. Trapped in the car while I chattered away, he didn't have much chance to be shy (although if you ask him, he says he wasn't shy, just a very nervous passenger). Through him and through his parents, when I occasionally saw them, I began learning about this quiet man. For years, Mr. Fordred had dreaded calls from home about young Pete, because they often meant a trip to the emergency room. It wasn't that Pete was reckless, exactly; it was that he always wanted to know how things worked and what would happen if, for instance, he set off firecrackers in a glass bottle. His experiments with electricity had fried all the fuses in the house, and once he'd inadvertently set fire to the *kia*, the small, thatched-roof house out back where the African servants lived. Then, when Pete was nineteen, Mr. Fordred got the call every parent has nightmares about: his son had been in a serious car accident.

The irony of it was, Pete hadn't been driving recklessly, nor was he drunk. He and his friends Ian and Tony had eaten at a local steakhouse and were taking Tony home via a long, unlit road Pete wasn't familiar with. When Tony warned him about a notorious curve just ahead, Pete steered hard into it, found it less sharp than he'd anticipated, overcorrected, and lost control. The car hit an embankment, somersaulted onto its roof, and rolled down the bank, ending up on its wheels.

Pete found himself lying on his back in a ditch. Excruciating pain burned between his shoulder blades and he couldn't move his legs. "Ian! Tony!" he called out. "Are you all right?" Ian, unable to open the doors, crawled out a window. He had only a cut on his face. Tony was unconscious in the back seat; he had a concussion but would be all right. Pete, on the other hand, had been ejected through the windshield. Lying in the dark, bleeding profusely from cuts on his arms and face and unable to see anything through the blood pooling in his eyes, he was certain he'd die. Even during the ambulance ride he refused to close his eyes for fear he'd never wake up.

He passed out during the transfer to the X-ray table and awoke to the sharp pain of nurses stitching up cuts and picking shards of glass from his face and arms. He still couldn't move his legs. X-rays and a myelogram showed that vertebrae T3, T4, and T5 were crushed and the spinal cord blocked. A sample of spinal fluid contained no blood, and surgery to relieve the pressure revealed no obvious damage to the cord; the surgeon told him it was only bruised. Pete believed he'd be able to walk again, especially when he started to get sensation back in his legs. With the stiffness and achiness, however, came a tremendous amount of spasm, set off by just about anything: cold, pain, touch, even the light movement of the bedsheets. The physiotherapists worked hard to get him walking with braces on his legs, but his stomach and back muscles didn't function, and the spasm threw him off balance. Walking wouldn't be possible.

During our daily commute to Saint Giles all that February, Pete and I became friends. We usually had lunch together, too, outside in the sun. Then his therapy ended and he picked up where he'd left off with his five-year electrical apprenticeship. Before the accident he'd completed a year of technical college and two years in the field as an electrician. Now, knowing he could no longer participate in house construction, he concentrated on becoming an instrument technician. When he found a car with hand controls, he started showing up at Saint Giles for lunch and at our house for dinner. I was helping put together a regular wheelchair basketball game during this time and got Pete involved with that, and we also began training for the South African Championships for the

Disabled. This was a lot of togetherness, but I refused to consider it a "relationship." Whenever Pete and I began to get close, I pulled away. I'd always had trouble with intimacy—why, I have no idea. What I did know was that if you didn't let yourself feel, you couldn't get hurt. My accident had compounded the problem, because I didn't see how any man could want me now.

On the way home from basketball one night, Pete steered the conversation around to my hangup. "I suppose the trouble is that I am only half a man," he said.

"Don't be stupid. You're as much of a man as I've ever met. It's not your body that makes you a man; it's what you are inside and how you behave."

"Then why can't you apply that to yourself?" he asked gently. That really gave me something to mull over.

As any woman less bullheaded knows, if she is truly loved by her man, she feels all woman. Pete's ability to identify with my feelings, combined with his steady love and extreme patience, slowly melted my resistance. Besides, we had fun together and many a laugh at our disabilities. Although neither of us could point to a defining moment of acceptance, we had gradually developed similar philosophies about being paralyzed: no medical intervention could repair our spinal cords, so it was up to us to accept and adapt to the changes in our circumstances and make the best of them. "I have my eyes and my hands, which are all-important to me," said Pete, whose great love was making things. "We just have to get on with it, improve every day, and see what comes up." Neither of us dwelled on what had been or could have been. Acceptance of our disabilities meant we could get on with real living.

Shortly before the end of Pete's apprenticeship, we got engaged, but we kept it a secret until my twenty-first birthday. Mom invited about sixty people to the party. Pete waited until he saw her head for the kitchen, then followed her in. "Doll," he said (his nickname for her), "I need to talk to you." In his nervousness he rolled over her foot. "Could I marry Liz?" She said yes, of course, but later teased him: "What else did you think I could say when your wheel was on my foot?" During the party my uncle made a speech about how he'd known me since I was a kid and all that, and at the end he said, "By the way, Pete and Liz are getting married." Well, the crowd surged toward us. Everyone in the room was ecstatic, and once again the love and support overwhelmed me.

We got married in February 1975. Of course somebody wanted to bring in the press, make a big deal out of two people in wheelchairs getting married. "Mom," I said, "I'm just a normal person getting married to another normal person. I'm not an oddity. If I see any reporters I'll cancel the wedding." She knew me well enough to make sure none showed up.

Joan made me a beautiful dress, and I set a new fashion by going barefoot because shoes wouldn't stay on my feet. James escorted me down the aisle and gave me away in front of two hundred guests. The Reverend Frank Mussel, whose laying-on of hands had been such a comfort to me, performed the ceremony.

For our honeymoon we drove down to Durban, on South Africa's southeast coast, and rented an apartment there. One evening we had an experience that illustrates the laughs we got out of our handicaps. We'd nipped out to the grocery store, and when we returned, the door that we used because it had no steps was locked. "We can go in through the parking garage and take the elevator up from there," I announced. Without waiting for a response from Pete or thinking about the practicality of my plan, I set off down the steep ramp, yelling, "Whoopeeeeee!" At the bottom, my front wheels hit a small step that launched me a good fifteen feet through the air. Pete came down as fast as he could, though in a more controlled fashion, went down the step on his back wheels, and zoomed over to where I lay in a heap. When he saw that I was unhurt, he burst out laughing because my chair, to which I'd strapped myself, had come along for the ride and somehow twisted around underneath me so that it and my legs were all tangled up. Milk and orange juice ran in rivers around me. Pete nearly fell out of his own chair laughing, and of course the elevator doors chose that exact moment to open. The two passengers shot Pete a hard look for laughing at the poor "cripple" on the ground, then took me by the arms and started hauling me up, but since I was still connected to my chair, I just seemed to stretch. And where did they think they were going to put me? The wheelchair was upside down. They spoke no English, so it took a real effort in pantomime to persuade them to leave. I could sort myself out better than they could.

The following night we found the door locked again. "You wait here this time," Pete said. "I'll go down the ramp on my back wheels, get a key from the superintendent, and come back to open the door."

"No way. I'm coming with you."

"Then go on your back wheels." Tipping a wheelchair back when you go downhill allows the seat to remain level so you don't slide out, but it's a difficult skill to learn, and I hadn't yet perfected the technique. Halfway down I lost control and went barreling down toward Pete. When I hit the brakes, the chair swung around, tipped over backward, and dumped me onto the concrete on my head and elbows. That one hurt. I don't know how, but I climbed back into my chair right there on the ramp and slowly made my way down. After a lengthy discussion with Pete on how best to tackle the step at the bottom, I went over it backward. I wasn't keen on repeating the whole maneuver.

During the first two years of our marriage, Pete took charge of an instrument workshop while I worked my way up to assistant administrative director at Saint Giles. We competed in several sports, which meant a lot of training. Three times we represented Rhodesia in the South African Championships for the Disabled, where Pete played basketball, I played table tennis, and we both entered field events and swimming. Pete even set a new record in the fifty-meter freestyle. I was secretary of the Paraplegic Club, and we started a sports training program for young kids with disabilities.

We had fun, but what we really wanted was excitement. We craved a *real* challenge.

4

Let's Build a Boat

I HAD ALWAYS WANTED TO TRAVEL, but traveling as a paraplegic was a lesson in humility. Our airports didn't have those ramps that push up against the plane's door; passengers still walked across the tarmac and climbed a tall staircase to board. That meant we had to be carried up the steps and plopped into our seats, and once there, we couldn't get to the restroom. Trains and buses presented similar obstacles. And even if we could have overcome those, how would we have gotten around once we reached our destination if we couldn't rent a car with hand controls?

One day we were driving down a country road when out of the blue Pete said, "Why don't we build a boat?"

Being confined to a wheelchair made me want to burst at times. So did the thought of having an eight-to-five office job for the rest of my life. The more I thought about Pete's suggestion, the more I liked it. It was almost like being on Chaka again, galloping toward a difficult jump that others might think twice about but that I knew I could manage. Besides, it was a challenge, and challenges always got my blood going. This would be the ultimate challenge and, although we didn't realize it at the time, the ultimate in regaining our independence.

"Mad in the head" is what Pete's dad called us when we broke the news. The closest either of us had been to a sailboat was looking at pictures, but to us that was irrelevant. You couldn't go through life doing only the things you already knew how to do, could you? After all, the first time I'd mounted a horse I hadn't known how to do that either. Yet I suppose it's hard to believe that two paraplegics could dream not only of building a boat but of cruising in it. Why would we want to create more obstacles than we already had? If Pete and I had been sensible, we first would have tried dinghy sailing on nearby Lake McIlwaine, but we were young and impatient. We wanted a full-sized yacht now and a new lifestyle to go with it. Like others our age, we saw a world to conquer and endless possibilities somewhere "out there." It never occurred to us that being in wheelchairs and building a boat were an unheard-of combination.

In my normal fashion I went at the idea like a bull at a gate and found out as much as possible about buying or building a hull. By phoning around, I learned that right in the middle of the Rhodesian countryside, hundreds of miles from the sea, a company called Turner Yachts built oceangoing, ferrocement vessels. We drove out to meet Tony Turner and explained what we wanted to do. He, in turn, asked us a lot of questions that we answered as best we could, considering our lack of yachting knowledge and vocabulary. At first Tony was negative about our plan; (I'm sure he thought we were nuts). It took several visits to convince him of our genuine determination to succeed. Or maybe he sensed that trying to talk us out of our harebrained scheme was useless. At any rate, he became a valuable member of our initial planning team. We discussed how we'd control the sails, how we'd manage at sea, whether we'd sail on our bottoms or in our wheelchairs or in chairs on tracks. These questions and many more remained, for the time being, unanswerable.

The three of us threw around hundreds of ideas. First we had to decide what type of hull we needed. We looked at designs of 34-footers and 38-footers. Then Tony suggested a 43-foot Fijian with a 12-foot, 6-inch beam, flush deck, and a semi-fin keel. He already had the plans and the steel jigs (frames over which the hull is shaped) because he'd built one for himself; in fact, his boat, *Gwen*, had won the Cape Town to Rio race in her class. He offered to build us a hull at cost, around $3,000 Rhodesian (US $4,850) but emphasized that a hull represented only 10 or 15 percent of the work. Tony wanted us to understand what we were getting ourselves into.

Pete and I fantasized endlessly about the things all future yachtsmen dream of: exotic tropical islands, palm trees swaying in the trade winds, blue lagoons surrounded by sparkling white sand (sand and wheelchairs—we certainly didn't think that one through). It all sounded so romantic and exciting!

During the four months it took Tony to construct our hull, we saved every dollar we earned, read every sailing book we could lay our hands on, and mulled over what would have to be an unconventional interior. On Mom's verandah floor we taped the outline of the cabin floor space, then tried wheeling around on various layouts to see what would best accommodate our chairs. We knew there was nothing more frustrating than having a wheelchair jam and bash into something at every turn.

Tony made us a list of the basic materials we'd need, which brought us face to face with politics. Southern Rhodesia had always been virtually self-governing, with a long-standing British promise of eventual independence that would keep us in the Commonwealth but make us a protectorate, like New Zealand. Then the British government reneged on this agreement, with Prime Minister Harold Wilson insisting we move to majority rule. Our government wanted time to train those who would be coming into power and to educate black Rhodesians, half of whom were still illiterate, in the intricacies and responsibilities of democracy, which differed greatly from the tribal law to which they were accustomed. A gradual path to full democracy and a slow transition to majority rule—"evolution, not revolution" as Rhodesian Prime Minister Ian Smith put it—might prevent what was happening to some other African nations after they got independence. As European countries rapidly unloaded their African colonies, regardless of the cost to white Africans, Ghana, Nigeria, the Congo, Rwanda, and Uganda had gone through chaos, tribal violence, massacres, corruption, ruined economies, and in some cases civil war. All ended up one-party states or military dictatorships rather than democracies. Smith would do whatever it took to ensure a peaceful transition, even if that meant defying Great Britain. In 1965, on my twelfth birthday, he and his cabinet issued a Unilateral Declaration of Independence. More turnovers were on the horizon.

At first UDI meant little to me; all I noticed was that the grownups were excited and saying bad things about the British government. The first time it sank in was when I went to the cinema. Southern Rhodesians had always been more patriotic than the British and exceedingly loyal to the Crown; before a movie, the audience had stood to sing "God Save the Queen." But after independence, we stumbled through a new and unfamiliar national anthem.

In response to our UDI, the British imposed economic sanctions against us and urged the UN to do the same, claiming that Rhodesia (we had dropped "Southern" when Northern Rhodesia became Zambia) was racially biased and the African majority would have no say in running the country. This was not true. Our 1961 constitution approved by Britain spelled out a phased takeover that would give us a black majority government. But Harold Wilson presented Rhodesia as a danger to world peace and got the Security Council to apply mandatory worldwide embargoes on all trade with us. Wilson was convinced we'd capitulate within weeks. Instead we hung on for fifteen years.

In many ways, the sanctions were a farce. Our landlocked neighbors—Botswana to our southwest and Zambia to our northwest—had to ignore them: their imports and exports were transported through Rhodesia, many of their industries depended upon Rhodesian raw materials, and they needed our products because their countries were in economic ruin. South Africa, our most willing neighbor, facilitated shipments by road, rail, and air. The biggest joke was the oil embargo. Mozambique, to our east, had the nearest seaports. To prevent tankers from coming into the port of Beira, from which fuel could come by pipeline to our refinery in Umtali, Britain stationed warships off the coast. But Mozambique supplied us internally from its own refineries, and South Africa simply sent us bulk supplies by rail and road.

While our neighbors openly defied sanctions, the rest of the world played a two-faced game. With Rhodesia holding more than half the world's known chromium deposits, the Americans quietly made exceptions to sanctions in order to get what they needed. Eventually, under pressure from Union Carbide, they got the United Nations to remove chromium from the sanction list. As Rhodesia was one of the world's major tobacco producers, our government found a way to continue sales: an independent tobacco corporation successfully carried on trading for the duration of sanctions. In order to decrease our dependence upon other countries we learned to make products that formerly we had imported, and at the same time we stepped up our exports of food and mineral commodities. Unmarked cargo planes flew in and out of the airports. The Rhodesian government, so the story went, even took beef to England, the very country that was trying to strangle us.

As we became more self-sufficient, the outside world needed us more and we needed them less, which resulted in a low inflation rate, great expertise, and an abundance of manufactured goods. Wilson's sanctions backfired; during the years they were in effect Rhodesia's economy not only continued functioning but in some respects thrived. And sanctions ended up costing English tax-payers a fortune, which made Rhodesians rejoice. Sanction-busting became a national sport that everyone played, and it created incredible opportunities for entrepreneurs and trading houses. Each success story greatly lifted national morale—we'd show them! Rhodesians, pulling together, developed a fierce pride.

The greatest obstacle to trade, however, was not the embargo but a shortage of money. Since no other government recognized Rhodesia, our currency was worthless outside the country. Because the government needed foreign currency for essential imports, it imposed extremely tight controls on foreign exchange. For trips abroad, each person could take out only a small amount each year, a "holiday allowance" of $200 to $500 Rhodesian (US $300 to $750), depending on the current situation. Pete and I couldn't just order parts and materials from abroad. Nor could we make substantial buying trips to South Africa, because the cost of such a trip invariably ate most of the allowance. We did our best, though, to circumvent the restrictions. When South African friends came to Rhodesia, we exchanged their rand for our Rhodesian dollars. If they planned to buy a dinner service of Rhodesia's wonderful pottery, we bought it with our money and they reimbursed us in rand. If people we knew returned from a South African vacation with even 10 rand, and we could convince them to give it up, we'd buy it. All this was illegal, of course, but it was fun to dabble in the same black market where some entrepreneurs made a bundle. Anyway, why should we take the restrictions seriously when not even governments did?

Getting this foreign currency out of Rhodesia was a gamble, but if you succeeded, you could have a better holiday in South Africa and buy all the things you couldn't get at home. You just prayed you'd make it through customs on the way back, because the government had imposed strict import controls and high duty on nonessential goods and luxury items. People came up with some awfully creative descriptions for what they'd bought.

We never blamed our own government for this mess, only the British, and in particular, Harold Wilson. Ironically, the average Brit-in-the-street was rooting for Smith, who was enormously popular in England, whereas Harold Wilson was ridiculed by his own media —daily cartoons depicted our tiny proud nation cocking its nose at the mighty British Empire. We even had the support of the British armed forces, whose officers and men made it clear they would not act militarily against us. Why, I wondered, could the world not see what was really happening? What I didn't know was that Rhodesia had become a political pawn for more than one government.

Having grown up with sanctions, Pete and I were used to doing without, and some things we had never seen so couldn't really miss. But now that we were building a boat, our needs had changed, and we discovered that many basic items and raw materials were hard to find. For instance, we needed an abundance of brass or bronze screws and bolts (galvanized iron would rust near salt water), but brass was hard to come by and stainless steel nonexistent. We drove to Botswana to visit friends and buy brass screws and nuts; other friends brought the odd box back from South Africa; and I raided the local hardware stores until we had enough. Bolts were more difficult to find. During one of my many phoning sessions I located some brass rod, which Pete told me to buy. Now we spent our evenings on the verandah making bolts. We stuck one end of a five-foot rod into the chuck of an electric drill, which Mom held while Pete guided a die down the other end of the rod to cut the thread and I applied cutting paste as needed. Then we cut the rod into various lengths, screwed a nut on each one, and centerpunched two holes in the end to jam the soft brass into the nut's threads, permanently joining the two pieces.

Like eager prospective parents we regularly visited our hull, watching it develop from an iron-rod-and-chicken-wire frame to a smooth concrete boat. But where would we put it? Mom came to the rescue with an offer of her backyard. Then Pete, clever man, thought of putting the hull into a hole; that would bring the deck down to ground level and enable us to wheel across a boarding plank in our chairs. My brother James owned a civil engineering company and had just bought a backhoe, which he brought over one weekend. Like two little boys with new toys—James driving the tractor and Pete working the shovel—they excavated an enormous pit.

The day the hull arrived, Pete and I were keyed up with excitement. That morning we'd had the gates removed, the fence taken down, and the drainage ditches at the corner of the road and the driveway filled. When the truck arrived, it reversed diagonally across Mom's herbaceous border, lawn, and shrubs—mercifully missing the msasa trees—and backed down into the hole. We'd hired a twenty-ton crane, but it couldn't do the job, so another was brought in to help. As the two cranes lifted the hull, the truck drove out from under it, then the cranes lowered the hull into the hole and everyone scrambled down to prop it up with scaffold jacks. There was a lot of bungling! Tempers were short for the three hours it took to complete the whole maneuver. And poor Mom. She came home from work to find her beloved yard all churned up and flattened. "Not to worry," she said stoically. "It will recover." Sure enough, within a week she'd chatted up her plants and nursed them nearly back to normal.

Because the hull still sat a little high, James bulldozed dirt taken from the hole into an earthen ramp that ran up to deck level and then placed a couple of boards across the gap to form a rickety gangplank. I felt terribly unsafe crossing it—what if I rolled off and into the hole? Once on board I didn't feel much better, nor did Pete, so we got out of our chairs and lay on our stomachs to peer down into the hull. It looked so bare and cavernous! And so exciting!

I must be one of the most impatient people on this earth; had there been a way to get inside, I would have gotten to work right then and there. The following day was a Sunday, but we still couldn't start anything because we had no way to get below. Frustrated, I spent the day rolling to the windows or out onto the verandah to make sure the hull was still there. Pete laughed at me, while Mom was unusually quiet. Was it because she knew this intruder in her yard was going to take her daughter away? Whatever her thoughts, she always backed us. How lucky we were!

The first thing we needed was security on the deck. I don't recall whether we purposefully decided upon railings rather than the usual stanchions with wire lifelines or whether we simply didn't know any better, but thank goodness we did choose them because they were higher and more substantial. To make them, we borrowed a pipe bender, but at first we couldn't get the long steel pipes to bend gradually—at least not gradually enough to satisfy Pete. I started to realize what a fussy husband I had, although I have to admit our method was less than ideal: my wheelchair and I were supposed to sit on the pipe while Pete lifted, but we kept rolling off. Eventually we discovered that if we chocked up the pipe on either side with bricks and had Pete's fifteen-year-old brother John jump on it, we could get a perfect, gradual bend.

While Pete sat on his bottom drilling holes in the concrete deck for the stanchions we'd cut from lengths of pipe, I cut the base plates out of two-inch-wide plate, centerpunched them, and drilled holes in them. Then Pete tack-welded the stanchions in place. The final welding, which entailed balancing right on the edge of the boat, was too difficult for Pete, so he hired an African welder named Noah to do the job. Noah called the boat his ark.

I loved listening to Pete and Pop, Pete's dad, gleaning whatever knowledge I could from their conversation, though my endless questions drove them crazy. Their exploration of ways for us to get down into the boat, however, involved too much thinking, which taxed my patience. Whenever I saw Pete staring off into space, I spouted, "Come on, Pete, stop daydreaming! We have work to do!" One day he showed me an ingenious lift plan, worked out to the finest detail.

"When did you figure out all this?" I asked in amazement.

"While I was daydreaming." That put me in my place.

While Pete and Pop were making the lift parts, James's wife, Kath, their eldest daughter, Debbie, and I spread the floor bearers out on the ramp and painted them with black bitumen. This was a dreadful job, and once I got the tar on my hands, which for me wasn't difficult, I transferred it to the pushing rims of my chair and from there all over. Even after I was sure I'd cleaned everything, that tar reappeared for weeks.

Eventually Pop and Pete got the lift installed in the forward hatch. A steel frame supported an aluminum-grid platform that cantilevered out from a pair of two-inch-diameter poles. A 220-volt, half-horsepower motor drove two deck-mounted winch drums that wound up cables attached to either side of the platform. This system was only temporary until they could devise a lift that worked on 12-volt DC. For that one they decided that a hydraulic system would take up less space and also conserve battery power because we'd need power only to go up; to go down, we could open a valve and release the pressure in the cylinder. It would take time to make. Hydraulics weren't common, at least in Rhodesia, and everything would have to be fabricated by hand.

When James had installed the floor bearers and the first section of floorboards, Pete and I finally had access to the interior and a flat surface to roll on. Now the real work could begin. As our commitment to the project grew, we formulated a goal: helping other disabled people see that a damaged body doesn't have to signify the end of hopes and dreams. And because strangers often treated Pete and me as morons, incapable even of pushing elevator buttons, we could demonstrate to the able-bodied world that "physically disabled" doesn't mean "physically incapable," nor does it mean "mentally incompetent."

Creating a challenge and establishing a goal were the most important steps we'd taken since our accidents.

Progress and Red Tape

MOM WAS A GEM. She got home from work before we did and prepared dinner so Pete and I could be on the boat by 6:30 P.M. During the evening she brought us coffee, sometimes staying to chat or listen to our explanations and ideas. She was keen to see our progress and always admired our handiwork. If things were going well, she might hold something in place while we performed our balancing acrobatics with a screwdriver or drill, and she laughed along with us. Other times she saw our frustrations and knew to stay clear.

I felt unsteady on the temporary floorboards, which tipped up if I went near their edges. When I complained, Pete said dryly, "At least it isn't far to fall." To find out, I lifted a panel, slipped out of my chair and went exploring in the bilge. It was only about three feet deep and looked easy enough to get out of, but after a lot of cursing I was still at the bottom in a heap. Pete found this greatly entertaining, especially when he had to haul me out by my trousers.

The forward lift, because of its width and depth, didn't come all the way down to floor level, so we began sloping the floor up toward it. After several evenings I'd had enough of passing tools to Pete while he had the fun of doing the work. I wanted to do something constructive, even if what I knew about a square and tape measure was dangerous. "I want to build something," I insisted. Pete suggested that I begin with the clothes cupboards we'd decided to install on either side of the forward lift, and he explained how to get started. I began with great enthusiasm but soon got absolutely tangled up with angles and curves. Pete would hear what soon became a familiar cry for help. He'd explain once again. Sometimes I'd hurl the board and yell, "If *you're* so bloody smart, *you* can do it!"

"Oh?" His pretense of innocence was maddening. "I thought you wanted to learn." So I'd go and fetch the board, wheel back with it, and try again. And again.

Things continually fell off our laps, and as we leaned over to pick them up, something else would fall. Or we'd back up and find we couldn't move because something was in the way of a wheel or because an electrical wire from the drill or jigsaw had caught in the chair. It was worst at the beginning, when the floor was the only place to put anything. Rather than go into a rage each time, though, we used humor to cope with the endless parade of objects that misbehaved or got in the way or went in the wrong direction. We always put a "Mister" in front of the culprit's name: "Look here, Mister Chair, I'll just throw you in the ocean if you don't do as I tell you." Pete swore he'd get a box and put into it everything that gave him trouble; then, when we finally went sailing, he'd hurl it over the side. Humor definitely was the best approach.

When I finished the first cupboard and got it all screwed into place, Pete looked it over briefly, then said, "Right. Now take it apart and glue it." At that suggestion I did not like Pete *or* the cupboard, especially when it didn't fit as well the second time. Fortunately, he was patient, although the perfectionist in him must have had to swallow hard to accept my cupboard.

One day while Pete was finishing off the engine supports, he needed the welding machine, which was in the car. I offered to get it for him. "Give a yell if you need help," he said as I went up on the lift. I managed to heave the hulking machine out of the trunk without wrecking the car, then had to figure out a way to get it to the boat. What I needed was the wheelbarrow, but fat chance I had of pushing that around! The next best thing was my chair. I loaded the welding machine onto the footplates of my wheelchair, draped my legs over it, leaned back as far as possible to counteract its weight, and went slowly, slowly, up to the start of the earthen ramp, where I offloaded my cargo and turned my "crate" around. By wheeling up backward, setting my brakes, and then dragging the machine up to my level, I slowly inched my way up the ramp. An hour later I reached the gangplank, where I turned around again and bulldozed the welding machine across with my chair. At last I reached the boat, elated by my success.

"What kept you?" Pete called from below. I was tempted to take the machine back to the car.

I had to lie in wait for chances to get back at him. One evening the two of us wrestled with an enormous 6- by 4-foot bulkhead that went up, only to come back down for trimming, half a dozen times. Each time it went up, Pete, who was out of his chair, had to shove himself up the slanting hull, line up the holes in the bulkhead with the holes he'd previously drilled in the rib, and push the bolts through—all before he slipped down. I huffed and puffed, trying to keep the board up there and move it up or down as directed.

"Why don't we install a hook up there?" I finally suggested. "We can lash a line to your trousers and haul you up, and you'll stay put." Judging by the look he shot my way, my arrow hit the mark.

It was fascinating for each of us to see what the other could devise in order to perform a difficult task. I invented a way of getting up the sloping hull by stacking bricks against it. I'd lay a plank from my armrest across to the bricks, heave myself up onto the board, and drag myself across to tighten the Mister Screw that thought it had outwitted me. We always found a way of doing a job. Sure, it might take an hour to do what for the able-bodied would have taken five minutes, but it was best not to think like that; instead, we should feel satisfied by trying and succeeding. The enormous feelings of gratification we got from even the smallest physical achievements made us soar. Life as paraplegics had taken on new meaning.

We did a tremendous amount of work while on our bottoms. We could still move around, although this was far easier for Pete than for me. He sat with his legs in a lotus position, which gave him a stable base and kept his spasm at bay. To move, he'd use his arms like crutches, lifting his body and swinging it a "step" forward. His legs, in their lotus position, came along. My legs weren't flexible enough for a lotus position, so if I "crutched" like Pete, they stayed behind like sacks of potatoes. Instead I traveled by swiveling on my bottom, reaching back to retrieve my legs. It was pretty slow. And my ankles screamed whenever I dragged them across a surface, for even though my legs were paralyzed, the skin in places, particularly on my ankles, was hypersensitive.

Getting back into the wheelchair was another thing Pete did better than I. He sat on the footplates, put his hands behind him on the seat and lifted himself up in one swoop. I had to go through several steps. First, I sat in front of the chair and pulled my legs around until I could place my knees on the footplates. Grabbing hold of the chairback and seat, I heaved my body up and landed with my chest on the seat and my chin hanging over the backrest. Then, with my hands on the armrests, I did a violent push-up, at the top of which I twisted my shoulders so that my body followed and my buttocks ended up on the seat.

We used our chairs only to fetch tools or materials. Often after such a trip I would just have gotten out of my chair when I'd receive a message from my bladder. I'd have to climb back into the chair, ride up on the lift, and scream off to the house at ninety miles per hour to use the loo—a real pain. But all this physical activity greatly improved our fitness, agility, and balance, in dramatic contrast to the time when just getting dressed was exhausting. For the first time since our accidents we felt extraordinarily healthy.

One thing we hadn't taken into account was that planning would take up more than half our time because nothing was simple or straightforward. Some evenings we'd go down with a particular task in mind, then spend the whole evening talking about the way the permanent lift would work or how we'd support the engine or what sort of propeller shaft we needed. By bedtime we'd have accomplished nothing. Everyone turned to Pete for answers to these questions; he was expected to know what was going to happen and how to do everything. Since we are the same age, I wondered how he supposedly knew so much.

Time-consuming also was the fact that sanctions and our lack of money forced us (well, mostly Pete and Pop) to fabricate things we otherwise could have bought. Through an ad we found a reconditioned Mercedes 190D engine that had come from a pickup truck. This was a true stroke of luck because it was almost impossible to get any sort of engine in Rhodesia. Pete marinized it by making up a water-cooled exhaust manifold—a lengthy job of cutting, welding, and heaving heavy parts around—and then had it cadmium plated. We got a marine gearbox from a Rhodesian company that was able to import goods from South Africa. "At that price it must have gold bearings" was all I could say when I saw the bill. It was infuriating how much the marine dealers charged.

We hired four Africans to carry the engine to the lift and, once it was down, maneuver it into place. To give us more floor space for our wheelchairs, Pete had moved the engine mounts forward from the original plan. This seated the engine lower in the hull, which changed the angle of the propeller shaft, which in turn meant the gearbox mounting had to be changed. But the ever-helpful Pop made an adapter plate. He also made up the stuffing box for the prop shaft, and what a beautiful piece of machining it was! Whenever we joked that he should come sailing with us, he responded with an emphatic, "No ways!" But he had a real gift for using his mind and hands to a high degree of perfection. I was thankful Pete had inherited that.

The engine installation inspired us enormously because it was such a large, visible sign of progress. My woodwork was progressing too, even if my craftsmanship didn't equal Pete's and Pop's. I finished the clothes cupboards, installed the hand basin in the bathroom, and made another cupboard to go next to it. This enabled us to get our tools off the floor and onto shelves, so now we had only electrical cords and bits of wood to ride over.

The stove arrived but didn't fit between the bulkheads we'd sweated over; I had to move each one to the other side of the rib it was attached to, then dismantle the stove and put the gimbal bearings inside the casing rather than outside. When it was ready for mounting, I strained to hold the stove up, hold myself up, and line up the bearings. This entire project, which should have been straightforward, ended up taking me a whole week, but once it was done we had an oven, a broiler, and two burners, all gimbaled to swing with the boat's motion rather than slop hot food about. Next came the supporting frame for the galley sink and the cupboards below it. Because of our chairs, swing-open doors were out of the question, so sliding doors it was. Woodworking came easier to me now, but because the runners and track had to be perfectly square, I had problems with the doors. I tried blaming Pete, who'd made up the runners, but he wouldn't have it.

After considerable discussion about what sort of chart table was best, Pete suggested one that folded away to give us more room for our wheelchairs when we were in port. In theory this sounded brilliant, but when he explained how to go about building it, I started losing interest. "Too complicated," I said.

"Just do it slowly and you'll manage."

It was the hardest piece of woodwork I'd tackled so far. I worked on the verandah, where the table saw and planer were easily accessible, and I managed to plane off some of my thumb, which was dumb because I'd used the machine before. Pete's name was mud during this project, but I was proud of my finished work and secretly thankful he'd made me do it.

"You're almost done with your apprenticeship," was his only comment.

Pete had been working on the rudder stock. To get this long, heavy shaft into place, Albert the garden boy had dug a deep hole below the stern. With a couple of chaps manhandling the thing from below, and Pete guiding it from inside, they got it up and into place. Pete and Pop modified a rudder stuffing box we had bought from Tony and fitted it with the proper bearings. Then James lent us a worker from his firm, Pete took the day off from his job, and they cemented it into place.

After a phone search for small bits of scrap metal to use for ballast, I managed to get four tons of boiler punchings, which James, dear James, said he'd help cement in. The following Sunday we organized an assembly line. I was stationed on the earthen ramp, where I washed and weighed the punchings and oversaw the cement mixing. Whenever Pete called from the bilge for cement, boiler punchings, or water, James filled buckets, put them on the lift and sent them down to Pete, who poured everything into the keel. Mom and Kath kept us supplied with cold drinks and tea and at lunchtime set out a lovely picnic. Not only was the day fun in spite of the sweaty work, but it represented another huge step forward.

Our income dictated our work program. Every month we waited impatiently for payday, and when it came we bought for daily living just the absolute necessities; the rest went toward enough materials to keep us busy until the next payday. Before buying an expensive item like the engine, we stockpiled lumber so we could concentrate on finicky bits of carpentry while our bank balance recuperated. This system worked well, and I thoroughly enjoyed the buying and organizing of our weekly needs, I guess because it suited my stingy nature. Poor Pete had to battle to get even cigarette money out of me.

The legal procedure for taking a yacht out of Rhodesia was complicated and tedious. Having heeded Tony's advice to get an early start wading through the red tape, I'd already applied to the Rhodesian Reserve Bank, which controlled currency exchange, for permission to remove our boat. Shortly thereafter, the government clamped down on letting yachts out of the country because some people had been removing large amounts of capital from Rhodesia by building boats ostensibly for pleasure purposes, then taking them abroad and selling them for foreign currency. An acquaintance had even accused Pete and me of planning to do this. We were shocked because such a thing had never occurred to us. Yes, we were building a boat that would take us away, but we had no intention of permanently leaving the country we loved and were so proud of.

The logic behind the government edict eluded me; boatbuilders kept several industries busy, so why not encourage them? As a result of the action, some boatbuilders stopped production, others kicked up a stink, and in the midst of the furor came the reply from the Reserve Bank: permission for us to leave was refused.

I've always felt that if you want help getting something done, you should go straight to the top. In a huge country like the United States this wouldn't be possible, but in a small country like Rhodesia the white population was small, and high government officials didn't hide behind layers of underlings. So it was not a great feat for me to contact Prime Minister Ian Smith; I simply phoned his secretary, who told me to explain our situation in writing. Although he took his time, Smith did respond, advising me to reapply to the Reserve Bank. Pete was pessimistic, but by now I knew he usually was, whereas I seemed to go the other way—I was always convinced everything would work out.

By the time we got a response to our new application, the restriction on taking boats out of the country had been lifted, but owners had to leave behind an amount of money equal to their craft's value. The Reserve Bank wanted to know how much ours was worth.

What a daunting demand! After you'd put your life savings into a boat, what did you have left? And how would we value ours, anyway? For advice I called Tony Turner. As far as he was concerned, our boat, with its unconventional layout and large hatches, had no resale value. What wonderful news! Well, sort of. I asked him to put that in writing, then submitted his letter along with my own statement that we'd spent $12,000 Rhodesian (US $19,400). I held thumbs and waited.

I'd also written to South African customs to find out what was required for launching a Rhodesian boat. We could stay in their country for six months, they replied, and when we left, "the yacht had to be identified as the same yacht." That part was funny but the next wasn't: we had to deposit with customs a large percentage of the boat's worth—4,800 rand in our case (US $5,785)—as import duty. They'd refund it when we left. This really set me off. How could we come up with 4,800 rand when we weren't allowed to take more than our annual holiday allowance out of Rhodesia? And what if we didn't leave South Africa within the stipulated six-month period? Would we forfeit the money? Then the Rhodesian Reserve Bank sent us a letter requesting $12,000 Rhodesian as a guarantee we'd bring the boat back within two years—and upon our return we were to deposit enough foreign currency in

Rhodesia to pay for a Rhodesian company to transport the boat back from the coast.

So—in addition to what it would cost to ship the boat to South Africa, we were supposed to come up with a total of $12,000 Rhodesian and 4,800 rand *now* and, in two years, enough foreign cash to pay for return transport. The total amount would be around US $35,000. Utterly impossible.

After more than a decade of sanctions, however, Pete and I were accustomed to restrictive and ridiculous government logic and innovative ways of circumventing it. There had to be a way out. I applied to the Reserve Bank for an extra two-year period; they granted one year, so now we could take the boat out for a total of three. As for the money problem, we'd sort that out somehow, even if it meant staying and saving, however long it took.

Quitting was not an option. History had proved—and on a daily basis was continuing to prove—that as a people, colonial Rhodesians were hard to stop. Pete and I were Rhodesians through and through.

Usikusiku

THE RAINY SEASON was upon us, sometimes driving us into the house, where we ended up with the planer and jigsaw going in Mom's living room. This wasn't as messy as it sounds—the room was enormous, and the floor was slate— but not many mothers would have put up with it as mine did.

The boat's aft deck had a gaping hole where we'd intended to put a sunken cockpit until we realized how much headroom that would cost us below. Not that Pete and I needed headroom, but we always kept the comfort of able-bodied people in mind. For now we covered the back of the boat with white sheet plastic and draped another piece forward, over the lift; when we rode up at night we must have looked like ghosts rising from the deck. After wheeling off the lift, we'd cover the opening again and attempt a mad dash to the house, but anyone in a wheelchair knows that even to escape the rain, hurrying is nearly impossible. Your leg is bound to fall off the footplate, causing everything to slide off your lap, or something—in this case the plastic cover— catches on your chair and follows you. So you start again and resign yourself to getting soaked. Building a boat from a wheel-chair will either improve your patience or drive you mad. Sometimes I'm not sure which way I went, but I always tried to see the funny side.

We covered the hole in the deck with frames and plywood, then made a base for the eventual cockpit coaming. For this we cut four planks that were seventeen feet long and curved. To move them to the boat from the table saw on the verandah, I'd hold one end and Pete the other, and we'd move along in tandem with the plank on our shoulders or heads. We could also move 4- by 8-foot sheets of plywood on our laps, with one of us facing forward and the other backward. We fastened and sealed the planks by drilling holes through the cement or plywood, applying sealer, and quickly bolting down the wood. It was a messy job, requiring us to move quickly before the sealer set, and with it came the same old problem: once it was on my hands, it was everywhere. That seemed to be my specialty.

Pete and I took two weeks of vacation to build the wheelhouse. We'd read that a deck structure had to be immensely strong to withstand waves and that it shouldn't be high or large because of the windage, but ours had to be high enough to accommodate us in wheelchairs and broad enough to house the lift platform and the helm. We compromised by going for breadth over height. Because this made the side decks too narrow for us to negotiate easily, we built two sets of double doors, one forward and one aft, that enabled us to wheel right through from the aft deck to the foredeck. We went for minimum headroom in the wheelhouse, which meant we had to duck a little to get under the upper door frame. Construction was maddening as we held up awkward bits of timber and tried to measure between them so that everything would end up square. We didn't need legs, just more arms! But we eventually got the frame up and bolted through the cement deck. Manuel, a Portuguese carpenter who worked for James, offered to fit the plywood on the cabin. We were thrilled.

Because we were going to need a shipyard that was wheelchair accessible, had a crane that could launch a 20-ton boat, and was near a marina that was also wheelchair accessible, a tour of South African ports seemed in order. We borrowed a trailer, loaded it up with camping gear, and hitched it up to our car. Always up for an excursion, Pop and Pete's brother John came along.

Durban, 1,200 miles south of Salisbury, was the nearest large South African port, but we gave it a miss; too many people had warned us about its formidable red tape, as well as unfriendliness toward inland yachtsmen. Instead, we headed for Port Elizabeth, 600 miles farther down the coast. Unfortunately, Port Elizabeth's shipyard turned out to be totally inaccessible, with steps everywhere. Since I'd already learned from my marathon phoning sessions that none of South Africa's smaller ports had a crane big enough, we continued another 475 miles west to Cape Town, just around Africa's southwest corner and on the Atlantic Ocean. The shipyard was fine, but we found the Royal Cape Yacht Club imposing and formal, with steps leading down to the trots, or floating docks. Up the coast another hour or so, though, was Saldanha Bay, the best natural harbor in South Africa. As soon as we got there, we knew this was where we wanted to be. The marina was small, homey, and down to earth. The few accessibility problems weren't insurmountable. We decided to launch in Cape Town, then as quickly as possible move to Saldanha to finish the boat.

In all these places we got odd looks and reactions. People in wheelchairs apparently didn't go out in public in South Africa, so I expect seeing two of us at once was a shock. And when we asked about mooring a sailboat, everyone was dumbfounded. They definitely thought we were off our blocks.

Having spent nearly all our annual holiday allowance, $280 Rhodesian (US $450) each, on a sextant and radio direction finder, we headed back, arriving just before what would be our last Christmas at home. (Mind you, I don't think many in our families believed that.) The new year, 1978, seemed a good time to learn something about navigation, so we set aside Monday nights for arguing about where we might be and how we had gotten there. At this juncture we mastered only coastal navigation, if you can call it that when you do it on land. During my lunch breaks I tried to learn the theory of celestial navigation, but to this day I'm convinced you should learn the practice first, then the theory; otherwise it makes no sense.

Pete started on the exhaust system. First he bent a wire into the shape he needed, then he tried to coerce a 10-foot-long, 2-inch-diameter pipe to match it. He manhandled this pythonlike beast into the bilge while letting loose a stream of descriptions on its vital statistics. I offered to help, but only when he was thoroughly fed up did he relent. What a stubborn chap! Which was just as well, as it was a stubborn pipe. You shoved it and it shoved you back, making you overbalance and fall backward with the pipe on top of you. After banging and grazing our fingers we eventually got it into place. Then we spent another three evenings wrapping it with asbestos lagging and securing it.

Our portholes arrived. We'd had them cast in bronze by a company that Tony recommended, but they still had to be finished off and chromed. The studs had to be silver-soldered onto the face plates, a job Pete decided I could do. He showed me how to use an oxyacetylene torch, and with a bit of practice I mastered it, but there were ten studs to each porthole and fourteen portholes in all. Tedious. Worse still, I had to clean the portholes afterward so they could be chromed. This meant removing all the bronze residue with a grinder, then using sandpaper and steel wool to make the surface sufficiently smooth to hold the chrome. I'd seen enough portholes by the time I finished. James helped with the installation, standing on a drum down in the hole while Pete and I worked from the inside, bolting the frames in and putting in quarter-inch-thick tempered glass. We were fortunate to have James help with the part of this job we couldn't do on our own. He and Kath were always unselfish with what little free time they had.

Next on my agenda came the wiring and plumbing, which Pete, again, had decided I could do. First I ran all the wires for the lights and engine. I'm not very good at dealing with tiny things, so there was a lot of cursing while I soldered the ends of the wires (to my fingers much of the time) and fitted them into the switches. Sometimes hot solder dropped on my feet and made my legs go crazy with spasm. Well, at least I could feel it, so that was good!

We had custom-ordered two diesel tanks, three water tanks, and a shower sump tank, all made of a low-grade stainless steel. When Pete and I installed them, not only were they heavy and cumbersome to move around, but they took up all the available space in the bilge, which complicated the plumbing. I am not suited to that occupation at all, where everything has to bend around, under, and over. I never thought it possible to contort my body into so many angles.

Pete had moved on to the rudder. He cut the steel plate with oxyacetylene and the inside gussets by hand, then welded everything together. Even though hollow, the thing was colossal and extraordinarily heavy. To protect the inside from rust he left a small hole, poured in epoxy sealer, then had Albert the garden boy and Langton the house boy tip it this way and that way to spread the coating. When Pete started to weld the hole he'd left—BOOM!—the rudder blew itself off the trestles. The other welding held, though, so he tried again to seal the hole. BOOM! The rudder went flying off the trestles. At this point, Albert—who had only recently left his *kraal* (village), in the bush and showed up on our doorstep looking for work—took off around the house and hid, unable to understand why this thing kept going BOOM! and jumping on its own. I went after him, and when I explained that it wasn't witchcraft or magic, just the epoxy fumes igniting, he bent double with laughter. Anyway, to end the story, the finished rudder had bulges, but the hole, at least, did get sealed.

After Pete and I had spent months fretting about the $12,000 deposit required by the Reserve Bank, James came to the rescue. He'd learned that instead of handing over the entire deposit in cash, it was possible to have someone guarantee payment if we didn't bring the boat back, and the insurance company that covered his business had agreed to act as middleman. I wrote the bank and asked if they'd accept the offer. How fantastic to have that off our minds and for someone to have so much faith in us! I didn't worry that we mightn't make it back in time, leaving James liable for that much money, because I'm such an eternal optimist that I knew I'd make it happen, whatever was required. I'd never let him down.

Sometimes I was convinced the government switched things around on a daily basis just to keep everyone in limbo, so once our documents were drawn up and submitted, prudence suggested we leave as soon as possible. The lowest quotes we got for transport were $6,500 Rhodesian to Cape Town or $4,500 to Durban (US $10,500 or $7,275). Durban it would have to be, and we cursed ourselves for not having gone there to check it out because now we had no idea how accessible the place was for our wheelchairs. In addition, this change of plans meant we'd be starting off in the Indian Ocean rather than the Atlantic and would have to negotiate 1,000 miles of some of the world's most notorious waters and round the Cape of Good Hope to reach Saldanha Bay, if we decided to go there. Still, the $2,000 difference was substantial—not that we had the money even for the less expensive transport.

Again James came to the rescue. He found someone whose low-bed truck was going empty to Pretoria in July to pick up some equipment. By leaving early, it could first take us to Durban, and since the travel costs to Pretoria and back were already covered, all we had to pay was the fuel cost for the extra mileage from Pretoria to Durban and back. What a breakthrough! I informed the Reserve Bank of the offer and asked them to let us know as soon as possible whether they'd accept James's insurance company's guarantee for the $12,000 deposit.

I also wrote to the South African Provincial Road Department for permission to haul our boat through South Africa. The qualified engineer we hired to provide the required official measurements of the boat's length, width, and height cleared us up to the railings but said the wheelhouse wouldn't fit under bridges. It was fixed solid; we could never remove it in one piece. So after all the effort we'd put into its construction, using two whole weeks of vacation time, it had to come off. James again lent us Manuel, who made braces for each upright and then sawed off the top two feet. It was too painful to watch.

When Pete's grandmother offered us a small inheritance of hers that was frozen in a South African bank because of exchange restrictions, I wrote the South African customs to ask whether they'd accept this account as a guarantee we'd remove the boat from the country within the required six months. I could have done without all the letter writing. It ate up my time when we had hundreds of better things yet to do.

Now that a deadline loomed, tension mounted. In addition to our regular jobs, Pete and I were working six hours each night and thirty-six hours over weekends. We certainly didn't suffer from insomnia!

I took a day off work to finish a project on the boat. While riding the lift up at lunchtime, I left my finger on the button too long. The platform hit the deck-mounted drums, which in turn snapped the cables, and I dropped so fast I was practically in free fall—it was the greatest speed I'd attained since being in a wheelchair. The ensuing bone-jarring crash flattened one of my rims. I shouted and whistled until Langton's worried face peered down at me. I assured him I was OK, but that my *jinga* (bicycle), was broken. I needed our "Model T," a dilapidated extra wheelchair we used for showering. Getting to the house in that *jinga*, which had no bearings left to talk about, was a slow process. I phoned Pete and told him I'd broken the lift. He sighed. "How did you manage to do that?"

"The cables broke. And could you bring me home another rim? One of mine has a flat edge."

"Are you OK?" he asked, suddenly concerned.

"Oh sure, I feel great. It's two o'clock and I can't finish my project. I'm sitting in this piece-of-junk *jinga*, and a new wheel is going to set us back another $25." My grouchiness let him know I was all right. I didn't tell him my legs were trying to break loose from their straps and my ankles had started to swell.

Upon investigating the lift, we found that bits of cement had been chipping from the edge of the hatch, finally allowing the platform to rise above deck level and hit the drums, which snapped the cables. Since this was just a temporary lift, we needed only to get it going again and keep it functioning until the permanent lift was built. That design had continued to be a dilemma. As there was little knowhow in Rhodesia on hydraulics, Pete and Pop had spent countless hours discussing not only how to build a hydraulic lift but how to make it small enough that it wouldn't take up half the boat. One evening Pop showed up with a funny-looking gadget. "It's the hydraulic ram," Pete said to me. "Get moving and paint it, seeing as you've been moaning about it never arriving." I laid the ram on trestles and hung its support brackets from a line. Someone should have known better than to let me loose with a spray gun because I got everything white—me, the lawn, and parts of my chair. I really enjoyed using that spray gun, even if Pete was disgusted.

Pete had made a tank that would act as a reservoir for the oil, and brackets for a large starter motor that would run a pump and valve. Once my paint had dried, Pete, Pop, and John bolted on all the parts, some to the deckhead under the wheelhouse and the rest under what would be our bunk. Late that night Pete connected the motor to an old car battery, then sat on the platform and pushed the button for the lift's trial run. Up he went at a great rate. He pushed the "down" button and descended so fast he actually bounced when the platform hit bottom. Sporting a huge grin, he went up and down a few more times. "It's too fast," I said and left him to it. Taking the old lift up and leaving the control on deck, because Pete had said he'd use the new lift, I headed for the house and bed. In the morning my normally good-natured husband was a grouch. "Didn't either of you hear me shouting my lungs out last night?" he crabbed at Mom and me. After playing with his invention until the battery went flat, he apparently had yelled and yelled for someone to come and put the old lift down. He'd finally given up and exited through the lazarette hatch, which was about four and a half feet off the floor and really difficult to reach, let alone climb up to. His arms were strong enough to get his chin onto the deck, but how he'd heaved his torso and legs up was beyond me. He'd then moved along on his bottom almost forty feet to the forward end of the boat and gone down on the old lift to collect his chair.

Mom asked Langton in ChaLapalapa, a universal pidgin used by the Africans, since they spoke so many different dialects, if he'd heard Pete calling *usiku*, "in the night." Pete and I had been searching for a name for our boat and liked the sound of *usiku*. Our Shona dictionary informed us that the correct word was *usikusiku* (pronounced *you-SEEK-oo-SEEK-oo*), which means the hour between day and night, at either dusk or dawn. *Usikusiku.* Our boat had a name.

On weekends, two Africans we'd hired had been troweling epoxy on the hull to fair it out. Next they rubbed it down to give it a smooth finish. And then came a Saturday when Silus, one of James's foremen, began brushing on paint. The result was startling: in a matter of hours, *Usikusiku* metamorphosed into a yacht.

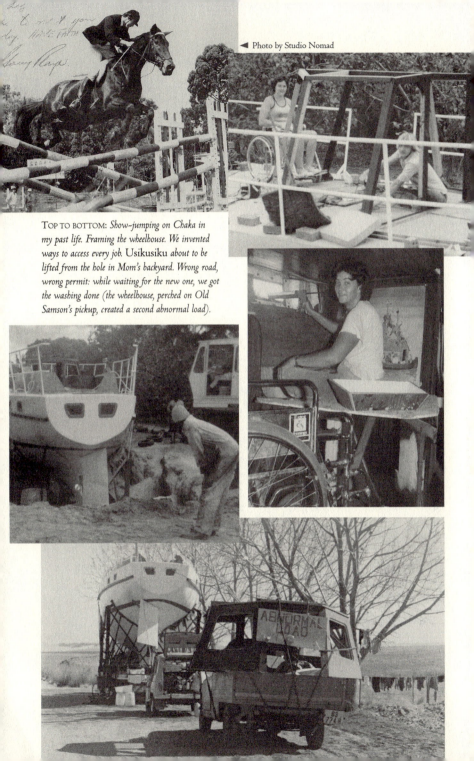

◀ Photo by Studio Nomad

TOP TO BOTTOM: *Show-jumping on Chaka in my past life. Framing the wheelhouse. We invented ways to access every job. Usikusiku about to be lifted from the hole in Mom's backyard. Wrong road, wrong permit: while waiting for the new one, we got the washing done (the wheelhouse, perched on Old Samson's pickup, created a second abnormal load).*

The Move

JULY ARRIVED. We weren't ready, but the truck was going and so were we. Leaving meant being on our own to finish construction. If we stayed in Rhodesia, though, we'd most likely make mistakes that would be expensive and time-consuming to undo. We had to get to South Africa and the sea so we could be around other yachtsmen and learn from them.

Two weeks before the truck's scheduled arrival, Pete and I quit our jobs and worked on the boat full time. Because we needed the cash, we sold our remaining hand-controlled car even though with it went some of our independence. Mom took me shopping for stores, and we began packing the boat. Not knowing exactly what Pete and I would need, I loaded up all our tools, leftover building materials, clothes, books, and everything we conceivably might use, so we ended up with little space in which to move.

Pete was managing on three hours of sleep a night. Pop was practically living down in the hole, where he was constructing, right around the boat, the cradle that had to withstand the four-day, 1,200-mile journey ahead. I alternated between packing and phoning my cousin Val at the local bank to ask if she'd heard from the Reserve Bank, which hadn't yet told us whether they'd accept

James's insurance company's guarantee for the deposit. What was their problem? Did they think we weren't serious or were they all just slack? I had Val inform them that the truck was in our yard and they had better come up with something. I hadn't heard from the South African customs, either, though they'd had our documents for three months and knew about our offer of transport. Were they being stubborn or just plain inefficient? As a generally well-organized person, I couldn't stand the chaos.

We had the fence taken down and the drainage ditch along the street, where the driveway met it, filled in for the low-loader truck, whose arrival generated much excitement on our part. It was enormous! The drivers—Tiny, who was six-foot-four, and Shorty, who was built like an American fire hydrant—parked it with one end near the hole and the other end near the kitchen door. The following morning a bulldozer and a 30-ton-capacity mobile crane rumbled up the road. Since the hole was too steep for the low-loader to back down into, our plan was for the crane to lift the cradle with *Usikusiku* in it and wait while the bulldozer pushed the soil back into the hole and leveled it off. Then everyone would manually rotate the boat 180 degrees so her bow faced forward, the low-loader would back underneath, and the crane would lower *Usikusiku* onto the truck bed. Friends and family showed up to watch the big event, which was going as planned until the crane could no longer hold the boat and abruptly put her down. The uneven ground caused the cradle to twist and tilt, whereupon it crushed the hull like an eggshell in three places.

Pete—already in a foul mood from pushing his chair through deep sand, which was all but impossible—went ballistic. I was on the phone (to my cousin Val at the local bank, as usual) so didn't find out about the mishap until half an hour later. I went and had a look. Mom kept glancing in my direction, expecting me to erupt too, but I took one look at Pete and left it as it was. What was done was done, and there was nothing anyone could do about it now, the mending would have to come later. What should have been a joyous occasion, however, was marred by the accident and by the idiots at the Reserve Bank.

We'd gotten our mast and boom from the same aluminum manufacturer that had made Tony Turner's. Once *Usikusiku* was on the truck and fastened down, we asked for ten volunteers from the crowd of family and friends to get the spars up onto the deck. With half the team lifting and pushing from below and the rest pulling from above, they got the 50-foot mast up and laid it lengthwise along the deck, then did the same with the boom. Anyone not involved in that was making trips up a ladder with boxes that I hoped were being stowed as efficiently as possible, now that I no longer had access to the boat. Noah was welding extra reinforcing bits onto the cradle for the ark that would leave him behind.

We'd made stern davits for our future dinghy but hadn't yet attached them. Since Pete and I would need a way of getting on and off the boat during the trip to Durban, James hurried to affix one davit. At 1:00 A.M. he finished, and Noah stopped his welding. At 2:00, Pete and I fell into bed exhausted. At 4:00 we dragged ourselves to consciousness to prepare for our 6:00 A.M. departure.

Even though we'd been saying good-bye for the past two weeks, friends and family members turned up for a final farewell. My mind, though, didn't have time to let emotions intrude because it was crammed with a million details, not the least of which was the Reserve Bank. Was leaving before we heard from them a huge mistake? This nagged at me until I could no longer negotiate that negative path. They'd better damn well clear us by the time we reach the South African border, I told myself. Then I shut it off.

Telephone company employees were disconnecting and moving phone lines. Municipal workers stood by to lift live electrical wires. John, Pop, Pete, and I climbed into Pop's little Renault, while Old Samson, who worked for James, brought up the rear in one of

James's trucks that we'd piled high with leftover lumber. John had fitted the cars with flashing lights and ABNORMAL LOAD signs and had fastened a large flashing light on *Usikusiku*'s stern. We were ready to go! After lots of hugs and kisses, Mom and I tore ourselves apart, resorting to teary eye contact as the Renault pulled out of the drive. Then I shut that off as well. Instead, I looked back at two years of work and an unknown future, all riding on the low-loader. Everything looked so ungainly! We'd heard about a Rhodesian yacht that fell off its trailer and had to be bulldozed off the highway. I hoped that wouldn't happen to us!

Usikusiku rocked gently as she inched across Mom's garden and front lawn, then down the driveway and onto the asphalt street. The main road south was a mile away. That mile took us an hour. Watching the truck negotiate the turn onto the highway—a sharp turn with steep drops on either side—was agonizing. Once on the main road we could achieve the thrilling speed of thirty-five miles per hour, but never for long before overhead telephone wires brought our little caravan to a halt. The local municipal workers stayed with us for several hours to lift them, and after that we took over for the rest of the trip to Umvuma, 120 miles away, John climbing into the boat to lift each wire. Houses gave way to farmlands and then we were on the veld—Rhodesia's broad, grassy savannah. The timeless African beauty and the rare opportunity to simply sit and look at it put me into a trance; four days of this should be a vacation in comparison with the past few weeks. But I was always knocked out of my reverie when we stopped to lift another line.

I was knocked out of it permanently when a blue-uniformed policewoman appeared, waving us down. She informed us we were not allowed to leave Rhodesia and must offload in Fort Victoria. Although it wasn't clear who had issued these instructions, I assumed our friends at the Reserve Bank were involved. We drove the Renault to a nearby farmstead where we phoned Val, who confirmed the order. I had no intention of following it! Off we all set again, minus our spirit; even *Usikusiku* looked depressed.

From Umvuma on, another concern jacked up our stress level. In the early 1960s, even before Rhodesia's Unilateral Declaration of Independence from Britain, militant African nationalists had begun organizing acts of terrorism. The conflict that followed had as much to do with the age-old tribal rivalry between Bantu and Zulu, whose Rhodesian offshoots were the Matabele and Mashona, as with opposition to the white government. Extremist leaders were jostling for the power to rule when white rule finally collapsed. Although acts of sabotage targeted manufacturing, transportation, farming, and even education in an effort to destabilize the country, their main target was the average rural African, who had little knowledge of or interest in politics. Massive intimidation campaigns toward women and children as well as men ultimately displaced hundreds of thousands of rural families, who fled to neighboring countries.

In 1972, guerrilla incursions had escalated to the point of civil war, with Mashona against Matabele, radical offshoots of both groups against the white government, and Rhodesian troops— black and white together—trying to eliminate the terrorists. This bush war was similar to the Vietnam war in that it was without battle lines. The two main terrorist groups used neighboring countries—particularly Mozambique after it fell to a Communist regime and openly declared war against Rhodesia—as springboards from which to launch offensives. The guerrillas making these cross-border raids for the most part avoided the cities, although after they blew up a fuel dump and a store on the outskirts of Salisbury, we no longer went fishing, camping, or picnicking. Land Rovers converted by the army into strange-looking anti-mine vehicles we called "Rhinos" roamed around town, prepared to contain any trouble. By then, 1978, every healthy, adult, white Rhodesian male had enlisted in the military or been drafted, usually doing six weeks of duty followed by a week or two off.

In order to safeguard its citizens and keep trade with South
Africa flowing, the Rhodesian government encouraged anyone
traveling by road to join convoys, for which it provided armed
escorts. These convoys of a few to as many as a hundred vehicles
left two or three times a day for the trip from Umvuma south to
Fort Victoria and then on to Beitbridge, at the South African border. Knowing we'd never keep up, I'd asked the army and police
for a special escort, so at Umvuma we rendezvoused with soldiers
driving two pickup trucks that had machine guns mounted in back.
Now all of our eyes scanned for terrorists, a threat ridiculously
contrary to the splendor of the countryside. Five hours later our
escort delivered us safely to Fort Victoria, seventy-five miles from
Umvuma. So far so good. The only thing I dreaded more than
Usikusiku falling off the truck was some idiot shooting holes in her.
Or in us.

Urgent messages awaited us in Fort Victoria, telling me to contact the police and my brother. First I phoned the police, who
wanted to know our plans. We were leaving first thing in the morning, I told them, and set a time for meeting the escort. Next I
phoned James, who said under no circumstances should we follow the order to offload; he would sort out the problem from Salisbury. We spent the night with friends and at the crack of dawn
were back at the boat.

Although we left Fort Victoria directly behind the main convoy, the veld soon absorbed it, and our own little convoy rumbled
on alone. Our route gradually descended from Rhodesia's mile-
high Mashonaland plateau to the midveld, where the countryside
was less lush. At least it no longer was flat: the road wound through
rolling hills and around *kopjes*, outcrops of granite boulders piled
atop one another in amazing balancing acts. Now that we were in
tribal trust lands, every so often we passed a *kraal*, a small village
of huts made with poles, *daga* (mud), and cow dung and thatched
with the long grass that grew on the veld. The midveld, already dry

because of the climate, was stripped of vegetation as a result of the ongoing drought and overgrazing.

From overhead we would have presented a curious picture: two wheelchair-dependent sailors in a car that led a yacht across a dusty, goat-eaten, inland plain, with a truck full of lumber trundling along behind, and with military vehicles fore and aft, like armed bookends holding the strange parade together. The farther we drove, the hotter and more arid it became. I wish I could say we saw herds of wild animals, but during this time of drought they'd moved elsewhere. By the time we reached the lowveld, the horizon was broken only by the stark silhouettes of baobabs, called "upside-down trees" by the Shona and "cream-of-tartar trees" by us. Their gargantuan trunks (those over sixty feet in circumference are thought to predate the Christian era) sprouted ghoulish, gnarly branches that clawed at the cloudless sky. When we spotted a couple of African children selling green, fuzzy baobab seedpods on the roadside, we stopped and bought some, splitting them with a hammer to get at the powder-covered seeds that give a tang at the back of your mouth. Out of boredom we sucked on too many, so by the end of the afternoon everyone's teeth were on edge.

When the border town of Beitbridge appeared in the distance, our escort melted away and we rolled up to the customs house on our own. Our passports and papers went in. We waited and waited, but they didn't come out; apparently the Rhodesia Reserve Bank had not yet released us. Without a clue as to what or how James was doing on his end, Pete and I parked our wheelchairs at the bottom of the front steps and pestered anyone entering or leaving the building about how we were progressing. "It should come through in the next hour," we were told time after time.

That "next hour" stretched into four days in a "town" that held nothing save the customs building, a hotel, and a couple of pubs. Tiny, Shorty, and Old Samson found accomodations at the nearest *kraal*. The rest of us slept in the boat, which was still so full of boxes we couldn't move around at all. Since our cash reserves were small, we cooked and ate on board, washing dishes and ourselves with water from a jerrican. We did use the hotel bathroom—not a problem for the others, but for Pete and me it was a real strain. So was getting on and off the boat. We rode up and down in a tire strung up to the single stern davit, but because we hadn't set up a proper block and tackle, John or Old Samson had to do the heavy pulling for us. And since the tire hung a couple of feet out from the deck, climbing in and out was tricky. I hate heights and didn't like maneuvering my clumsy body while suspended fifteen feet off the ground. Once Pete and I got off the boat in the morning, we stayed down until it was time for bed.

How James did it I'll never know; the Reserve Bank hadn't even looked at the insurance issue yet, but he pushed until it was sorted out. The government asked for a $600 Rhodesian (US $970) annual premium, which James's insurance company would pay. James would reimburse the insurance company, and Pete and I would reimburse James from the money we had to leave behind in our Salisbury bank account. James also got his insurance company to guarantee the 4,800 rand to South African customs, which had refused to accept the money in Pete's grandmother's frozen bank account. Guilt gnawed at me, because I knew James had enough problems running his own business without sorting out our mess.

Late on our fourth day at Beitbridge the Reserve Bank at last granted us permission to leave the country. But could we? No, customs closed in ten minutes, so no one would deal with us. We were first off the mark in the morning, though, and they quickly sorted out the paperwork, but then they wanted to weigh the truck to see whether we'd been overweight traveling from Salisbury. Why hadn't they done that during the four days we were parked in front of their building? My patience stretched dangerously thin, especially when they spent an hour and a half weighing each axle. And then, although we were 120 kilos over the limit, they let us through with no fine. What the hell had been the point?

We lumbered toward the bridge. It looked so narrow! Would we fit? Soldiers on both sides stopped the traffic. With mere inches either side of *Usikusiku* and the truck, we crossed Kipling's "great grey-green, greasy Limpopo," now reduced by drought to a stream, and entered South Africa. The officials on that side, who'd been following our four-day saga, quickly cleared us.

Messina, our first South African town, was just ten miles ahead, but we couldn't get there because the tram lines were too low. The police officer who came to help was furious. "You didn't call in advance," he sputtered. "Your permit expressly states that you must contact the police from outside each town so we can escort you through."

"Well, we *are* outside the town!" was all I could think to say to such nonsense. We managed to calm him down, and eventually the power was turned off and the tram lines lifted. After that, the day improved not at all. The going remained slow because all the telephone wires were lower than the regulation height; we couldn't go ten minutes without stopping for one.

Fifty miles later that particular problem was replaced by another that would plague us for the rest of our journey: the Great Escarpment, a series of mountain ranges that sweeps all the way around southern Africa, dividing the Great African Plateau from the coastal lowlands. The geological forces that formed it 300 million years ago were so violent that the granite faces sometimes drop more than a mile, straight down. Because we were an "Abnormal Load," the authorities planned our route through South Africa, and they had us sparring with the Great Escarpment five separate times on the way to Durban. On secondary roads.

The first range we encountered was the Soutpansberg, in the northern Transvaal. Just before the town of Louis Trichardt, where the other traffic burrowed beneath the mountains via the Verwoerd

Tunnels, we had to turn off and take the hard way over. The truck crawled painfully up each incline before barreling down the other side, nearly out of control. Because the road was cambered for speeds higher than ours, *Usikusiku* leaned markedly on the curves, and if the truck had to move onto the dirt shoulder to negotiate a turn, the whole lot looked as if it would topple over. Pete refused to watch, just read his book and smoked one cigarette after another. The rest of us kept an eye on Old Samson, who had to stop periodically to pick up pieces of lumber that had rattled off the truck.

On our second night in South Africa, the seventh since leaving home, we stopped at Loskop Dam in the western foothills of the Drakensberg Mountains. Darkness descended before we found a place large enough for all three vehicles to pull over. Howling wind rocked the boat, which was parked at such an angle I was sure she'd fall over. No sleep that night! The following morning no one breathed while we crossed a bridge so small I was convinced it would collapse. A short time later a railway bridge appeared in the distance. It looked pretty low. Pop suggested that those of us in the Renault go ahead to measure it, and his instincts were right: it was four inches lower than indicated on our maps; the road must have been continually resurfaced without taking bridge height into account. Considering we'd had to pay an engineer to measure *Usikusiku* and arrange to get permits through these back roads, you'd think the South African side could have gotten its own measurements straight.

How would we turn around? Pete had one idea, Pop another, Tiny and Shorty a third. Tempers heated up. In the end, Tiny and Shorty, being the drivers, won the battle. Off to one side, just before the bridge, was a two-track farm lane. They turned down it, reversed into a gateway used to move cattle from one paddock to another, and successfully pulled out again.

Which way now? John and I went off in the Renault to find an alternate route. We drove around for an hour and a half before we found a twelve-mile-long dirt road that crossed the railway track rather than going under it. We went back and fetched the others. John and I felt smug about our discovery until our detour approached the town of Hendrina where, lo and behold, another low bridge awaited. There were no other roads through.

Pete sighed in resignation. "Okay, let's cut off the railings."

We bought hacksaw blades and elected John to do the cutting. Aware of how much work we'd put into those railings, everyone was deathly quiet while he sawed. The davit that James had put on at the last minute so that Pete and I could get on and off the boat was the same height as the railings, so that had to be removed as well, meaning that John would have to bolt it on each night so we could get aboard and take it off in the morning after we got down. The cut-off wheelhouse, which had been riding on the fore-deck, had to come down as well. The farmer in whose gateway we were parked lent us some of his workers to help lift it off and perch it upon Old Samson's woodpile, where it stuck out so far on either side we had a second "Abnormal Load." At least that gave us a good laugh, the first in days.

Now *Usikusiku* could pass under most of the wires as well, which sped up our progress, although it meant fewer bathroom stops while waiting for the truck. A couple of times I had to use the bedpan in the back seat while Pop and John kept their eyes forward. Also, because of our detour we'd missed the pickup point for our next permit. Each South African province issued its own paperwork for abnormal loads, and we'd left the Transvaal and entered the Orange Free State at a place other than where the government had routed us. But we couldn't face going miles out of our way, not after cutting off our railings and not just to pick up a piece of paper. Accepting the risk of getting caught, we plowed ahead.

Usikusiku must have looked guilty, because just a few miles from safety, a policeman pulled us over and asked for our permit. I explained why we didn't have one. "You can't move any farther without it," he said.

"Please, sir, we're way behind schedule and it's just ten miles to the next province. Couldn't we go on? Please?"

"You and the drivers should be put in jail for traveling without a permit," he said. I wondered if the local jail had wheelchair-accessible restrooms. Since government office hours were over, we ate dinner and went to bed. Early the following morning I went into Vrede, the nearest town, and phoned Pretoria to explain our situation. A new permit would be put on the 9:00 P.M. train, I was told, and would arrive at Villiers, sixty miles from Vrede, at midnight. At sunset the temperature plummeted. We huddled around a fire, discussing the future of our country. Tiny and Shorty expressed the deepest concern. On trips to Zambia and Mozambique they'd seen how the breakdown of the infrastructure had disabled everything. As eager as they were for majority rule, they didn't want to see that happen in our land. Pete and I worried, too, for the families we were leaving behind.

At 10:30, John and Pete and I set off for Villiers, whose "station" turned out to be a junction of railway tracks, what we call a "hoot-and-whistle stop." We shivered in the bitterly cold wind until 12:45 A.M., when the train came through. No permit was on it. We got back to the boat at 3:00 A.M., tired, cold to the core, and utterly despondent.

A bit of sleep and the light of morning gave me the initiative to begin again. John and I took another drive to Vrede, made another phone call to Pretoria, and were told: Oh dear, we forgot to put the permit on the train. So sorry. We'll send it by car.

The car took six hours to reach us. That small-town policeman, puffed up with self-importance, never knew what misery and inconvenience he had caused. He probably didn't even know that we did finally get the permit, because we never had to show it to anyone—and we were out of his jurisdiction in less than ten minutes.

Two hundred miles later, another policeman stopped us. South Africa is a huge country with many villages so small that you never knew you'd gone through them, which apparently we'd done. "You were supposed to contact us before entering Greytown," the policeman said after looking at our permit.

"I'm sorry. I didn't know we'd reached the town," I replied, which somehow offended him.

"Look here, lady," he said, "this is normally a 50-rand fine. This time, though, I'll only charge you 10 rand."

"What did he mean by 'this time'?" I asked Pete as we drove off. "If that twit thinks we're going to do all this again, he's crazier than we are. And I swear he put that ten rand in his pocket."

Someone must have thought we'd enjoy taking the scenic route into Durban, because next we found ourselves on an up-and-down ribbon of a road, forty miles of it unpaved, that meandered through the Valley of a Thousand Hills. On several inclines the truck actually had to tack one way and then the other, its enormous wheels spinning at the edge of the road, mere inches from the drop beyond. If *Usikusiku* slipped over, it would be the end. Tiny and Shorty were sweating buckets and afterward said it was the most difficult driving they'd ever tackled. During the final miles they let her rip on the declines, so that from ahead in the Renault it looked like the dirty great truck was going to run right over us. I wasn't sure whether they hoped the speed would get them up the next hill or whether they'd simply had enough of the whole ordeal and wanted to get it over with.

Although the Valley of a Thousand Hills brought us toward Durban from the north, our official route had us skirt the city and approach from the southwest. From the coastal town of Amanzimtoti we contacted the Durban police for an escort. Once again our cumbersome load had to negotiate tight turns, narrow roads, and heavy traffic, and at one stage the police had to move a traffic light. They were well organized, though, and we ultimately reached the

Port of Durban's dry dock. So much for the four-day trip. We had tried, but somebody didn't want us to get there when we wanted to and stretched it to fourteen.

One final hitch awaited us. The wind was blowing too hard for *Usikusiku* to be unloaded, and because it was late Friday afternoon, we'd have to wait until Monday to offload unless we were willing to pay double the rates. Well, that was out of the question. With the Rhodesian government supporting a growing war machine that required arms, ammunition, helicopters, military vehicles, fuel, and other materials, foreign exchange restrictions had become even tighter than usual. Although the government had given us permission to take the boat out for three years, they'd allowed Pete and me to take out the usual annual allotment of $280 (US $450) each in foreign currency, nearly all of which we'd already spent on fuel for three vehicles. We'd have been allowed more if we were emigrating rather than leaving on tourist visas, but then the boat wouldn't have been allowed out—and anyway, we didn't want to emigrate; we were, and planned to remain, Rhodesians. But staying over the weekend meant that the truck would leave Durban, with a load still to pick up in Pretoria, on the very day its twelve-day South African permit expired. What a mess!

Tiny and Shorty kindly offered to sort out the permit dilemma themselves, to my great relief. I couldn't cope with that problem when Pete and I had enough of our own: a damaged boat, little money, and the sudden realization that we'd just spent two weeks in hell to get to the filthiest, most dismal place we'd ever seen.

Durban Demons

FIRST THING MONDAY MORNING we offloaded *Usikusiku* onto the hard. Then Tiny and Shorty rolled out in the low-loader and Old Samson rattled off behind them in the truck. Pop and John stuck around for a week, and then they too drove away. Pete and I were on our own.

Homesickness flattened me like a bad virus. How could this be? We'd finished the initial phase of our venture and plunged into the next, so I should have been eager to move ahead, but instead I was drowning in the emotional impact of separation from friends and family. Pete and I were twenty-four years old and had been married for three years, but neither of us had been away from home on a long-term basis. Sure, I'd moved out at sixteen, but my family had been a phone call or short drive away, and we'd gotten together frequently. Now I was 1,200 miles away and overcome by a tremendous sense of loss. During the past month I'd been consumed with departure preparations, government authorities, *Usikusiku*'s safety, and the complications on the road of cooking, washing dishes, doing laundry, and finding accessible bathrooms. I hadn't had time for feelings other than anger and frustration about all the holdups along the way. A heap of delayed emotions had accumulated: grief over leaving loved ones for an unspecified amount of time; worry about money for sails, winches, and all the other equipment we had yet to buy; guilt about deserting poor Mom.

This last was a killer. Pete and I had filled Mom's home with activity, laughter, and a goal that drew in both our extended families. Suddenly she was alone in a house that must have seemed deathly quiet, and she'd have to give up even that, just because I wanted to go off adventuring. Joan had married and moved out near James, about a forty-minute drive away. James didn't want Mom on her own, so she had decided to sell the house she so loved and move to an apartment. She was a strong, resilient woman who would survive, yet I swore I'd make up for it somehow, even if only by succeeding.

Compounding my depression was the dump we were living in. Not *Usikusiku*—although admittedly she was crammed, cluttered, and unfinished—but the dry dock, where enormous ships came for repairs and painting. The whole place was a trash heap that swarmed with so many millions of flies you could hardly see the light covers for them. It stood in a grimy industrial area where prostitution was rife and the nearby beer halls produced a steady stream of drunken men and women. Our only entertainment, if you could call it that, was to watch the women go out all spruced up and come back drunk as lords to the field we were on the edge of, where they could hide their booze and get picked up. Or to watch a hooker being chased by a man who was being chased by another man because she was his favorite. It was enlightening, to say the least. My mother would have had a fit.

One night we were awakened by a loud, jarring banging, like someone whacking on the hull with an iron bar. Pete did one of his single-leap-into-the-wheelchair maneuvers and zoomed up on the lift. By then we were hearing slurred, drunken shouts of "You steal my woman, man! I'll get you!" Pete peered down from the deck to see a furious man swaying on the pavement below. The anger slowly turned to embarrassment. "Ach—sorry, man, I have the wrong boat, man." He dropped the bar and staggered off. Pete came back down to bed. "Do I have the right woman, man?" he inquired, leaning over me. Of course he did!

Oh well, we'd be launching in two weeks, we thought. For that amount of time I could cope. We'd had a stroke of luck, if you can call anything connected with a damaged boat "luck." Not only had *Usikusiku*'s hull been crunched when the crane dropped her, but two portholes had cracked during the trip. If we'd bought our freight insurance in Rhodesia, we'd now have been compensated in worth-less Rhodesian currency, but we'd bought it in South Africa and so were paid in rand. The insurance company even contracted with a company to do the repairs, which took that task off our hands, and covered the cost of one crane lift and one month on the hard. Another boon came in the form of some wonderful workers that the shipyard office sent over to help us get the wheelhouse back on deck. Not only did they hoist it up and settle it in place, but after we'd reinforced it, they put in the windows and hung the doors.

Without anyone to help us get on and off the boat, the tire system Pete and I had been using became a suicide mission. We'd noticed a portable, scissors-type lift platform that the workers used while cleaning and painting the hulls of cargo ships, so I called Ivor DeBeyer, the owner of the ship-painting company, and asked him about the contraption. He immediately offered the use of his spare, which he brought the following day. He asked only that we "lend" it back whenever he needed it. What a godsend!

In the lowest position, though, the platform was about six feet off the ground, so we had to figure a way to get up to it. Working in tandem, we used our chairs as bulldozers to shove some old railway ties to the stern of the boat, where we piled them into steps of a sort, starting about a foot above our seats. At first I looked at this pyramid and wondered how I'd ever get up because I wasn't nearly as adept as Pete at lifting myself. But once I'd done it, I was really chuffed to have conquered another challenge. Before pulling ourselves up the "stairs," we'd tie our chairs to block and tackle so that once on deck we could haul them up. We timed each other whenever we went up or down, goading and teasing to speed up and not let the team down. When we began this game, it took around twenty minutes from wheelchairs to *Usikusiku*'s deck or vice versa, but we eventually pared the time down to seven minutes. Little things like this kept up our morale while we dealt with the countless frustrating situations our paralyzed bodies created.

Pete began the arduous job of reattaching the railings. He cut lengths of steel rod that fit inside the stanchions and, with a borrowed welder, joined everything together. In spite of the fifteen-foot drop to the pavement below, he sat on his bottom at the edge of the deck to do the welding. That he could now balance this way, which he hadn't been able to do the first time we'd put on the railings, demonstrated how much his physical fitness had improved. I was constantly amazed by how we still were progressing, five and six years after our accidents.

I busied myself stowing the contents of all our boxes so we could move around and live more comfortably on board. When Pete was done welding, I painted the railings. No spray gun this time; I had to brush the paint on, which wasn't nearly so much fun. When that was done I attacked the deck leaks and made one of many futile attempts to seal the forward hatch. When I'd completed all of my jobs necessary for launching, I began building cupboards above the galley sink. Meanwhile, Pete had been installing all the through-hull fittings: seacocks for the engine-cooling system, toilet, wastewater tank pump, and bilge pump, plus transponders for the SumLog (the device that measured speed and distance) and the depth-finder. He moved on to the mast, making a masthead fitting and running cables for lights and the VHF radio antenna.

We began our day at 6:00 A.M., finished at midnight, then began the daily routine of showers and laundry in the shipyard's bathroom. I washed clothes, towels, or sheets in the tiny sink there, then brought them back to the boat and hung them on the railing to dry. I also tried to get a couple of letters off home before we tumbled into bed. Our "To Do" list was unending. It seemed we added two items for each one we crossed off, so our stay soon exceeded the two weeks we'd planned on. Neither of us had ever worked so hard. ("Working on two women every day doesn't leave time to do anything else," Pete scrawled on a letter I was writing to Mom.) To reduce shopping and cooking time, we ate canned goods, peanut butter sandwiches, and such. And since going up and down was time-consuming, even at top speed, we tried to stay on board all day, going down to the bathroom only for emergencies. I used the bedpan for piddling, and when the shipyard workers had left for the day, I tipped it over the side into the field. I didn't feel too bad about doing this; after all, Pete went over the side all the time, and the field already served as a bathroom for the wild night crowd—one reason we had so many flies.

In spite of the incredible din of cranes, motors, trains, and more, life in the dry dock was fascinating. While working on deck we could watch huge ships, even tankers, come into a slip that would then be closed off and pumped dry. Ivor DeBeyer's many workers swarmed like ants over the huge hulls they cleaned and painted. They could complete a full-sized ship in twenty-four hours.

The daily rains began. To our great disgust, after all we'd gone through to seal it, the wooden part of the deck, particularly where we'd made the base for the cockpit seats and coaming, leaked in about a dozen places. The pots I set out created not only a melody of drips but an obstacle course for our wheelchairs. We had to lift each one, roll through the dribble, then lean over to put the pot back. "Is this supposed to be a boat or a sieve?" I asked Pete. "I just hope, come launching time, that the hull does better than the deck."

One rainy night Pete slipped and injured his arm. During the four days before he could go down again, it came home to us that we absolutely mustn't hurt ourselves, especially our arms, which were all we could count on. The same would be true when we went sailing; we'd have to be extremely cautious. And we had to design the boat and the sail plan so that if either of us did have an accident, the other could sail her single-handed. I didn't like to think about that.

Another night after our showers, we waited for the rain to let up and then raced each other down the road until we reached our trash can, which we'd emptied as usual on the way to the bathroom and left for retrieval on the return trip. "Please, God," I prayed out loud, "just once, let us get to bed dry." We were halfway up the lift when the heavens opened; God and I must have had a communications gap somewhere. "Dear Mom, wish you were here," Pete deadpanned, which sent us into hysterics at the thought of either of our mothers in this filthy place, soaking wet and penniless. What a contrast to our dreamed-of beaches and palm trees!

Pete's sense of humor became more alive than I'd ever seen it. Whenever I began to wallow, he went out of his way to buck me up, and for the first time I became aware of how solid he was; he was the anchor that grounded me. Without our former support network, we had only each other to confide in or talk things through with, so from now on the success of this venture depended upon how strong a team we could form. We grew closer than I'd imagined possible. Each of us automatically stepped in when the other needed it, often without being aware of it, and this was just one aspect of what made our marriage so good. It *was* good, too. The stresses we were under would have destroyed many relationships, but ours grew in depth and understanding during this grim period.

We lived in an incredible mess. I was sure we wouldn't need half the odds and ends we'd accumulated, but I had to be tactful about throwing anything out. I patiently waited until Pete was in the right mood, and then I suggested we have a clear-up. After getting rid of a mass of junk we still had a ton left, but at least it was more organized. We never stayed tidy for long, though. Either we had to put up with living in a workshop or we had to spend a couple hours every night putting everything away. That was out of the question. Every hour counted because if we stayed more than three months at the dry dock, the price would skyrocket from 22 rand per month to something like 160. I couldn't even relate to a price that steep when our financial situation was so bleak we could hardly buy food—and what we did buy we had to fight the flies for. We didn't even have the money to phone home.

During a week's break from the rain, we asked the shipyard's chief engineer whether there was someplace closer than the yacht chandleries in town where we could get some sealer for the wheelhouse and deck. He referred us to a middle-aged Greek who had a boat at the far end of the yard. Instead of telling us where to go, though, the Greek chap handed us a nearly empty can of sealer. Not exactly what we had in mind! Still, we offered to pay him for it. His expression left me feeling like a bum out begging for scraps and castoffs.

That afternoon he stopped by *Usikusiku*, introduced himself as Tassos, and peppered us with questions. The following Sunday we awoke to thumping and crashing on deck. By the time we got up there, the whole of our back deck was covered with food. For once I was speechless. Tassos waved aside Pete's attempts to thank him and explained that he owned a ship-provisioning company, as if that would make his charity more palatable. A few days later a sheet of marine plywood arrived, and the following Sunday he again loaded our back deck with goodies. By so willingly giving when we were struggling, and by having faith in us when we were low, Tassos gave us another incentive to succeed. And his generosity taught us much, not just about receiving but about giving, because only by becoming humble enough to accept his continuing gifts did we begin learning how, in turn, to give of ourselves.

About this time a minor disaster threatened to derail me. The reinforcing of my front wheel had weakened so much that the tire kept coming off, leaving me riding on the rim. It was infuriating! Twenty rand left and I wasn't about to spend it on my chair. Since I was working on the back deck, sitting on my bottom, I tried to ignore the problem.

"Liz, I've fixed your chair!" Pete shouted up from his workbench one afternoon. I found him actually cackling over his ingenious invention—a solid wooden wheel. It had no bearings but worked well enough. "I was tempted to put the hole off center," he smirked, and I could just picture myself lumping along.

That night after showers, when we had our usual race down the road to the pickup point for our trash can, I would have given anything for my camera, because a howling wind snatched the can off Pete's lap and sent it skittering along the pavement. He tore off in pursuit, trying to cut in just ahead of it like a cowboy cutting out a steer. The effort triggered his spasm, so his legs began shaking like crazy. I was fifty feet behind, killing myself laughing. He finally caught the thing and put it back on his lap, whereupon it sailed off on another gust and clattered through the shipyard with Pete and his shuddering legs in mad pursuit. They passed our boat at a great rate, with me shouting encouragements as Pete flew another hundred feet, still hot on the trash can's trail. It might not have equaled the Grand National, but it was a whole lot funnier. Or perhaps my sense of humor was becoming a bit distorted. At least I still had one.

We often wondered what people thought when they saw something that reinforced their belief that mental handicaps always accompanied physical ones. "Shame! Look at that terrible woman laughing at that poor man!" or "That handicapped couple must be crazy." Once, during a vacation at Victoria Falls years before, Pete and I were racing down the paved pathways when we hit an arched bridge. In an imitation of the Wright brothers' first flight, my chair and I went airborne, soared a respectable distance and miraculously landed upright on the other side. My sister Joan and her husband Ian nearly choked laughing, while two old ladies nearby glared and tut-tutted. I suppose they would have preferred to see Pete and me sitting demurely in our chairs with blankets over our knees while Joan and Ian pushed us sedately about.

Never! If you have to be in a wheelchair, you might as well have fun.

Soon after our arrival in Durban, the local press asked us for a story. Would they be willing to pay for it? I asked. They offered us 50 rand for rights to the whole saga. We said we'd think about it. That same night a bright and bouncy photojournalist named Peter Duffy asked to be our agent. We said we'd think about that, too. The following morning the local press printed a story using odd snippets of information from our brief conversation with the first reporters. Wanting to head off the competition, Duffy quickly drew up a contract whereby he'd pay us 100 rand up front plus 10 percent of the income from future articles. When he assured me that all agents dealt on the same percentages, a little warning bell rang in my brain, but when you're flat broke, 100 rand seems like a fortune. We signed.

Before leaving Salisbury we had signed a contract with the American tabloid *National Enquirer*, which had deposited US $200 into a South African bank account in our name and promised US $1,000 for each article they published but they alone had the power to decide when and what to write about, and they committed to just two articles. Now, in our desperate need for foreign currency, we asked them to print their first article just after our launching, covering our story up until that point, but they declined. Only much later did we learn the sensationalist nature of the *National Enquirer* and that we'd likely have to sink the boat, spend a month in a life raft, and cannibalize each other before they'd print a story about us. Meanwhile, that contract blocked the North American market for Duffy, who bubbled with ideas. He'd have to restrict himself to the South African and European markets.

Duffy introduced us to the idea of sponsorship, of getting a company or companies to pay some of our costs in return for exposure and publicity. For that, however, we needed positive press coverage and lots of it. Instead, we continually got slammed: Duffy wouldn't let reporters talk to us unless they first paid him, which they refused to do, so they pestered the port authorities and yacht club officials for information or they simply made things up. One story said we'd been forbidden to launch the boat. That really got my dander up—we needed the papers to print facts, not gossip. We discussed this with Duffy, but he wouldn't change his approach. "It's such a great story!" he said. "Why wouldn't people pay for it?" By now we suspected we'd made another mistake by signing Duffy's contract, but we couldn't undo it. And we did look forward to his lively, energizing visits. He sometimes turned up with fresh bread or a home-cooked meal, and he organized several *braais*, or barbecues, on board *Usikusiku*. His kindness and consideration always lifted our spirits.

A new twist cropped up: nearly every member of every committee from the Point Yacht Club came to "inspect" us. They all made it clear we were attempting the impossible and were barmy to boot. The harbor authorities weren't happy about us either. "Sailing is a very strenuous sport which requires a lot of physical stamina," said the acting port captain to the press. Strength and stamina Pete and I had in abundance. Why couldn't anyone see that? Still, we accepted these opinions as only to be expected. We knew we were ignorant about sailing, but we also knew we weren't stupid and could learn.

Looking back, I see what a lot of confidence we had in ourselves. Perhaps too much, although without that oomph, that zeal, that we-can-do-it attitude we surely would have failed. We weren't altogether foolish, though; we agreed that if our sailing trials were disastrous, we'd stop. We weren't going to go out and die just to prove a point. We weren't that stubborn.

Captain Hub Rountree, the port liaison officer, who oversaw all sailing activities in Durban, came round to see us nearly every week. Sometimes he'd describe all the horrors we were going to face, or kick the wheelhouse and say, "This thing will come off with the first wave that hits it." Other times he'd ask, "Are you still carrying on with this crazy venture?" "Of course we are," we'd answer. "Hmmph!" he'd grunt, then come down below for a cup of coffee and an amicable chat. Whenever I saw him coming our way, I said to Pete, "Hey, guess who's here? I wonder if we're in for it today."

After a while we figured out that Captain Rountree's gruffness was a mask for his concern. He'd begun to like us and, I think, to respect our determination, but he was the person ultimately responsible for determining whether or not we'd be allowed to sail. *Usikusiku*, being a new boat, had to be registered and deemed seaworthy by the Port Authority before she could be launched. The Offshore Sailing Committee of the Point Yacht Club worked hand in hand with the Port Authority; they would inspect us and report to Captain Rountree, who would pass final judgment.

When members of the committee visited us, one of their main criticisms was that our lift was battery powered. Whatever would happen if it broke down? Half these men were office workers who didn't know the first thing about electricity. Did Pete get no credit for being a certified electrician? Did they think we couldn't read? We were forever reading about electrical things breaking on boats. We told them we planned to install a manual backup system, and in a pinch we could climb out the lazarette hatch. At this they gaped in disbelief. Did they think our arms were paralyzed too? Why couldn't they grasp the fact that Pete and I, with our own hands, had built virtually the whole interior of our boat?

The lift must have heard something about its being able to break down because it promptly did so, burning out the armature in the starter motor. That night Pete and I decided to be difficult by going to the showers anyway, I suppose to prove we *could* get out. Since we already knew we could go through the lazarette (he could, anyway, so I assumed he could haul me up after him, if need be), we tackled the main hatch. We strained and grunted like weight lifters, raising the heavy lift platform an inch at a time and shoving things underneath until we got it as high as possible while still allowing us access from our chairs. Pete, monkey that he is, had no trouble negotiating the remaining three feet to the deck, but his fat old wife couldn't do that. At least I'd had the foresight to provision myself with a twenty-five-liter water bottle to use as an extra step. After much huffing and puffing I got onto that, but launching myself up the rest of the way required a fit of temper. "We'd better not use this method if there's ever a fire down below," Pete commented to the sprawled heap of arms and legs on the deck. Not wanting to repeat this exercise, he had the broken armature repaired and bought a spare starter motor at a junkyard.

When Pete had reconnected the steering and engine control cables, he reckoned we were ready to launch. Captain Rountree sent down a naval architect named Brian Gowans to check *Usikusiku's* seaworthiness. First Brian went tapping around on the hull, listening for voids in the cement, I suppose. Then came the inquisition. "How do you propose getting out of the boat when the lift breaks down?" he began.

"We'll install a manual hand system before leaving, but until then we'll go through the lazarette," we explained for the umpteenth time.

After casting a doubtful look our way, Brian removed his jacket, crawled through the opening from the aft cabin into the lazarette, climbed out onto the deck and closed the hatch after him. "How will you get in from the outside if the hatch is closed from the inside?" came his muffled voice from above. And then, "How will you get out from the inside if the hatch is closed from the outside?"

Pete and his pipe fumed equally hard. I practically chewed off my tongue to prevent myself from telling Brian to go take a flying leap, because any escape from Durban depended on our staying on his good side.

We flunked the inspection anyway. I swear there was a conspiracy between Brian and the Offshore Sailing Committee because the rules thrown at Pete and me seemed to multiply beyond what was required for other boats. Even though we'd completed the items on the original list given us, now Brian announced that we wouldn't be allowed to launch until *Usikusiku* was fully rigged for sailing. That was ridiculous—we didn't even have our sails! In addition, he said, in case of engine failure on the way across the harbor to the Point Yacht Club, the windlass had to be functional and the anchor ready. We had neither. After anticipating the excitement of launching, we now looked forward to more weeks in this Durban dump. Our spirits sagged.

Tassos came to the rescue by delivering an anchor, chain, and rope. Unbelievably, the harbormaster drove Pete to a chandlery owned by a man named Del, who had offered to help if we ever needed anything. We needed a windlass, Pete explained, and then outlined our financial position: down to scratch but with a *National Enquirer* story on the horizon either here or in Cape Town. Del, bless him, blessed us with credit. Even more astonishing, he later trusted us to leave Durban when we still owed him for everything.

Pete cut a block of wood for a base and bolted down the windlass. He made a roller to guide the chain over the bow. He cut a hole in the deck for the hawse pipe, which fed the chain into a large plastic trash can he'd fastened down in the forepeak. In order to run as many lines as possible aft to the cockpit, I constructed channels under the wheelhouse floor. To direct the lines into the channels, Pete and Tassos made stainless steel brackets for the turning blocks and mounted them on deck.

We had done everything required of us. We had no sails to attach the running rigging to, nor did we have sheets and halyards, but *Usikusiku* was ready, in an emergency, to "sail" to safety. Come launching, Brian and that damn committee had better show up with bedsheets to hoist.

We scheduled the launching for October 27. When I called Ivor DeBeyer to thank him again for the scissors lift and tell him we'd be done with it as soon as we painted *Usikusiku*'s bottom, he sent over a huge crew that slapped on the antifouling in less than fifteen minutes. I suppose *Usikusiku* seemed like a toy in comparison with the freighters and tankers they usually worked on. When Tassos presented us with fenders and mooring lines, I summoned the courage to ask him for a 150-rand loan to pay for the crane, whereupon his driver delivered an envelope containing 300 rand. Grateful as I was for the money, I was even more grateful that Tassos hadn't brought it himself. If he had, I would have cried.

Launching day dawned upon a dirty, messy deck, but without running water we couldn't do much to clean up. Brian Gowans showed up and made Pete fire up the engine even though *Usikusiku* was still high and dry. After about a minute Pete switched it off. He wasn't prepared to run it any longer without salt water going through the heat exchanger to cool it, he said. Brian left, looking rather put out.

The next arrivals were those well-known Rhodesian racing yachtsmen Pete and Tom Addison, who had sailed with Tony Turner on *Gwen* (*Usikusiku*'s sister ship) in the Cape Town to Rio race. They'd first come to meet us when the boat was in the hole in Mom's yard and they'd willingly shared their knowledge in spite of their skepticism about our plan. Now they were in Durban looking for sponsors for *Spar*, a racing boat they'd built themselves back home in Umtali, and they offered to help with our mast and then take us to the international jetty at the Point Yacht Club, a mile away across the Bay of Natal. Duffy and his girlfriend showed up with a bottle of champagne. Shipyard workers ran the slings under *Usikusiku*. They paused while I proclaimed, "God bless this boat and all who sail in her!" and smashed the bottle of champagne on her hull. Then the crane lowered her into the water. Miracle of miracles, she floated! For the time being, anyway. The crane lifted her back up until her deck was level with the dock so that Pete and I could be "hopped" over in our chairs, then down she went again, into the sea. Pete headed straight for the lift. I sat in suspense until the lift hummed him back up. "No leaks," he announced tersely. "She floats."

"Of course she floats!" I laughed. "That's what she's supposed to do!" A born worrier who dwells on things mechanical, Pete the Pessimist had been missing sleep for worry the boat would settle in the water and keep on going down. Now he managed a smile, and I think *Usikusiku* would have smiled as well, had she been able. Pete fired up the engine, and that worked properly too—a real relief because we'd seen more than one fancy yacht towed away with engine problems right after launching. The slings came off, Tom Addison took the wheel, and we motored out of the dry dock and around the corner to tie up alongside the wall. Short as it was, our first cruise was awesome.

A smaller crane lifted our 50-foot mast and gently placed it on its support, at which time we discovered that the stays we'd had made in Rhodesia were too long. Out came the mast and off went the rigger to his workshop to shorten the stays. Back he came, up went the mast again—and now the stays were too short! We added bits of chain, a rather ugly solution, but with so much else on our minds that's how we left it.

The rigging problem had eaten up most of the daylight so we

postponed our move until morning. Duffy and his girlfriend went off for food and more champagne. The Addisons and a few others joined us on board for a launching celebration so festive that at one stage I wasn't sure which was moving; the boat or the crane next to it or me.

Usikusiku was alive at last, as if her baptism had triggered a heartbeat. She was becoming so much a part of us, it seemed that together we three formed one being. That night, while Pete and I lay in bed listening to water lapping against the hull and barnacles crackling on the jetty walls, I had a chance to reflect on the day's happenings and what they meant. Words can't describe how I felt, although maybe "apprehensive" covers it best. We were starting a new chapter and with it would come a new set of problems. We'd have to prove ourselves again, too, this time in sailing. But heck, we'd already shown everyone we could build a boat, so maybe now they'd start to take us seriously, I thought. Then I closed my eyes and let *Usikusiku* gently rock me to sleep. Already we were in a different world.

Poor Neighbors

Y OUR ANTIFOULING is out of the water" was the first thing Pete Addison said when he showed up to take us to the international jetty at the Point Yacht Club. "She also seems tender."

I knew that if the bottom paint showed, *Usikusiku* was sitting too high in the water. That meant that Pete's careful calculations about weight and water displacement, and consequently where the water-line should be painted, were wrong. But what did "tender" mean? I'd never heard that term. Pete Addison saw my perplexity. "She rocks too easily from side to side," he explained. "I noticed it when I jumped down onto the deck. If she rocks that much just from my weight, she'll be pretty uncomfortable at sea. We can correct both problems by adding ballast." Horrors! I didn't even want to think about that! Although putting in the original ballast had been a fulfilling day of family teamwork, the job had been huge, even with all the volunteer labor we'd had back home. I shoved the thought of ballast out of my mind.

Also added to our work list was battery rewiring. No longer on shore power, we'd run both batteries down using the lift the day before, so we didn't have enough juice to start the engine. Once we got to the international jetty we'd have to isolate the batteries, using one for the lift, lights, and so on, and reserving the other solely for the engine. This was a mere hint of the modifications necessary to make *Usikusiku* a self-contained, independent entity now that she was afloat.

Pete Addison borrowed a battery from a car and jump-started the engine. Finally, after three months of living in garbage and filth, we cast off our mooring lines and motored away from Durban's disgusting dry dock. "The Offshore Sailing Committee actually told me to make sure you two wore life belts today," Pete Addison chuckled. Had he known the effect his words had on us, he would have kept them to himself. Those chicken-brained committee people were deaf and blind when it came to recognizing our accomplishments as paraplegics. We'd swum for Rhodesia and physically built our boat. Did they really think we'd fall overboard and drown? Again someone had spoiled the mood of a special day. Damn them!

Pete and I survived the mile across the harbor—a harrowing voyage for paraplegics, the committee seemed to think! The night before, Pete Addison had asked the yachties on a group of boats rafted up together at the international jetty if we could go on the inside, and they'd considerately agreed, so we nosed our way in between the jetty and the sloop *Dabulamanzi*. After we were settled and had a chance to look around, however, we felt like slinking back to the dry dock, because in contrast to her gleaming neighbors, *Usikusiku* looked like a street urchin. Three months on the hard, without running water, had left her caked in grime. Her deck screamed for fresh paint. Gear was heaped and scattered about in a most unseamanlike fashion. Talk about poor neighbors!

While Pete tinkered with the engine, I strove to make *Usikusiku* more presentable. I balanced stuff on my lap (of course it dropped off a couple of times), then either took it below on the lift or piled it up so I could access the deck. Then I dug the hose out of the lazarette, heaved it onto the dock, and asked someone there to hook it up for me, since the tide was not yet high enough for us to put out a board and wheel across. What a treat—shore water on tap for the first time since leaving home! I went to work with the sponge and deck brush, trying not to notice the eyes aimed in our direction or the buzz of conversation all around us. You can imagine what they thought. When people first got to know us, it took time for our wheelchairs to "disappear," and under these conditions that might never happen. But there was no point worrying about it. I just got on with my work to the best of my ability.

I was scrubbing away when Brian Gowans, the naval architect Captain Rountree had appointed to torment us, turned up. "I hear your engine broke down on the way," he said.

"First we've heard of it," I snapped. What was his problem, anyway? I knew he didn't approve of what we were doing, but if he'd kept his mouth shut and been less aggressive, he could have helped us make logical decisions. Instead, all he did was put our backs up, not to mention dampen our spirits, every time he came around.

Pete and I settled into our new roles as full-fledged members of the liveaboard, floating, yachting community. We liked this new lifestyle, where you did what you liked, when you liked, how you liked. Though we still missed small conveniences we'd previously taken for granted, we reckoned time would put that right. We almost never went into town; in fact, we hardly got off the boat because for that the tide had to be high enough that we could slide a board over and wheel across. If the plank's angle was steep, we went on our bottoms. If it was really steep, we stayed on board.

Bathing on board saved tons of time, even though our revolutionary sunken shower design turned out to be a dud. In the bilge we'd installed a large stainless steel sink that we accessed by lifting the floorboards. Getting in was okay, as was washing with a shower head on a flexible hose. But when you got out, you had to drag your clean, naked bottom across the dirty floor to your wheelchair, and by the time you got back into it, you were dirty and sweaty again. Still, it was preferable to showering ashore; the one time Pete and I had gone to the Point Yacht Club to shower, some women in the bathroom had made snide comments about people using the facilities without paying dues. On the whole, we just didn't feel welcome there. It wasn't so much what people said as what they didn't say. I'm particularly sensitive to the vibes people put out: there's "friendly" and there's "not friendly," and the members of the Point Yacht Club were in the second category.

Duffy's girlfriend managed to track down the sails we'd ordered from a Cape Town sailmaker long before leaving home and that for the past two months had been lost in transit. Their arrival meant sailing! That is, if we could complete the hundreds of odd jobs on our list. We attacked them feverishly, determined to make *Usikusiku* not only seaworthy but presentable for James and Kath's approaching visit. They didn't need to come all this way to spend two and a half weeks on a grungy boat tied to the dock.

Being with family again was wonderful, especially with family so eager to help out. James loves lists even more than I, so upon his arrival he began enumerating our many undone chores. Kath went off shopping. In Rhodesia you couldn't find anything that wasn't made there and few varieties of what you could find; even something as mundane as toilet paper came in just one brand. South African stores, by contrast, were filled with an enormous variety of products. Kath came back loaded with goods to take home and goodies for us, including fresh meat and veggies, a real treat after months of eating ship's stores. That first night I tidied the saloon and whipped up an enormous meal. Because sweeping and cooking had never been major interests of mine when there were more important things to do, James got an enormous charge out of watching how domesticated I'd become.

He and Kath went off on a fishing launch for a day, returning with dinner to cook and seasickness stories to share. Kath had wanted to die, she said. James hadn't felt well either, and for the first time ever they expressed concern for us. My stomach was like a rock, I assured them; Pete might be affected, but not I! Anyway, Pete had always thought he could find a way of counteracting the boat's motion, perhaps by gimbaling our chairs or putting a trolley on a track so we could swing like the stove.

James roamed the jetty, meeting our neighbors and picking up useful bits of information that he passed along to us. Maybe these folks weren't so unfriendly after all. Pete and I had been a bit stand-offish, I had to admit. Pete was shy, while I wanted to get on with my work and not waste time socializing. That's what I told myself, but maybe some of the "old me" was still around, embarrassed about the anomaly of being in a wheelchair on a yacht. People who weren't used to the proximity of a wheelchair could feel uncomfortable at first, and compounding that was what we were doing. Did they think we were naive? Foolish? Ignorant of what we'd face at sea? Most likely they just assumed we were crazy. Well, that was a certainty, although our neighbors suffered from the same malady: a restlessness that made us all uproot ourselves from conventional life and go wherever the winds blew us. That was the idea, anyway.

James, even though he wasn't a sailor, performed a valuable service by helping ease Pete and me into the yachting community. We learned that conversation wasn't a time-waster if you were brain-storming, and that everyone was eager to share hard-earned knowledge and to pitch in whenever someone needed a hand. Our new friends gave us ideas on self-steering gear, which would free us from continuous helming. They patiently answered Pete's incessant inquiries about rigging and equipment. Brian and Marian, an Australian couple, alerted us to potential problems and how to deal with them, and Brian began teaching us celestial navigation. When they left, Neville, an American on *Southern Cross*, took over, driving us to the beach to take sun sights and then ferrying us back to *Usikusiku* to work them out. Our first position put us five miles inland, but we were getting the idea.

Pete's favorite example of helpful neighbors occurred one evening when he dropped his pipe overboard and I then lost the broom and bucket trying to retrieve it (thank goodness everything floated, even the pipe). Ruth, from the boat next door, stripped naked and dove to the rescue, a show Pete enjoyed so much that I knew his pipe was bound to go overboard again.

Pete and James had been mulling over ways of rigging the mainsheet so it wouldn't cross the cockpit and create a wheelchair hazard. One day James disappeared, returning hours later with a massive pipe bent into a wide U. He and Kath turned it upside down and bolted it through the deck, outboard of the cockpit coaming. The sheet blocks would clip onto it, he explained, eliminating the need for a mainsheet traveler in the cockpit. In the old days the piece of equipment designed to keep the mainsheet from chafing on the guardrails was called a "high horse." Ours was an extremely high horse! Then someone remarked that it looked like a roll bar, so that's what we called it.

I'd been arguing with myself about the ballast. I just couldn't face calling all around to locate scrap metal; arranging for it, plus cement and sand, to be delivered; and then braving the wrath of yacht club members who would jump on us from a dizzying height for unloading tons of material onto their jetty. It all seemed too much. I suppose we belonged in a boatyard rather than at the largest yacht club in South Africa, but the international jetty had the irresistible attraction of being free. It also gave us daily contact with people who were already doing what we planned to do and from whom we could learn.

We needed the additional ballast, however, and James, bless him, found sand, cement, and two tons of scrap steel and rented a truck to bring it back. As he prepared to reverse the heavily laden truck down the jetty, a ten-year-old who lived on one of the boats came out to "direct" him. "Let's get one thing straight," said the lad. "If I say 'port' it means this way and if I say 'starboard' it means that way!" James, who is used to driving all sorts of heavy equipment, managed to keep a straight face until he was back on board.

The following morning we set up our assembly line. Kath and I filled buckets with one-kilo pieces of steel and, to save the lift's battery power, Kath lowered them with a rope to Pete and James, who spread them into the bilge. Kath and I then mixed cement in buckets and transferred it below to be poured over the ballast. The effort was exhausting, but the result was worth it. *Usikusiku* felt stiffer and more comfortable, even while tied up. And the waterline was where it was supposed to be.

To meet the Offshore Sailing Committee's requirement that vessels have an alternate means of steering, James made an iron tiller, which Kath took off to be galvanized. The two of them pushed themselves so hard at home that they deserved to relax on their vacation, but as usual they worked like Trojans. Having them around was inspiring, not only because of their physical efforts but because we could discuss problems and options with them and get positive feedback. That was a real improvement over the scorn and discouragement we'd had from officials and committee members.

Eventually we hammered *Usikusiku* together well enough to convince Brian Gowans that we were ready for our maiden sail. Stowing everything took us a full day. The following morning we jostled our way out from the jetty, which meant a lot of untying and retying for the six yachts rafted up outside us. Once we were clear and out in the bay, the two lads we'd conscripted to help out hoisted the mainsail and jib. Brian took the wheel, which was pretty awkward for him since the wheelhouse didn't have standing room and the seat wasn't yet built; he had to sort of hunker down. He soon moved to the cockpit to test the emergency tiller. After jibing a few times, he asked the crew to harden sail and pointed *Usikusiku* upwind until she heeled over from the wind in her sails.

I sat in my wheelchair on the foredeck, hanging onto the railings to keep from tipping over or rolling about. To feel *Usikusiku* moving under me, harnessing for the first time the power of the wind, was awesome. Her cumbersome body, which out of the water was as awkward as mine when I was out of my chair, in the water moved as spiritedly and playfully as a dolphin. I felt the same whenever I was in the water, where my body was no longer heavy and unmanageable but light and maneuverable. I gained new respect for *Usikusiku* that day. I'd watched her emerge from a hole in the ground, have pieces of her hacked off, be lugged on a truck across two countries, and then covered in filth in the dry dock. During this maiden sail she shrugged off her construction persona and began a new life of freedom in her natural element. Witnessing it was like being present at the miracle of birth. I gave silent thanks that I was alone on the foredeck.

Brian appeared content with the day's sail. He'd relaxed considerably since my brother arrived; James wasn't building a yacht from a wheelchair so had to be saner than we, it seemed. For my part, I sometimes questioned Brian's sanity—I'd never before, and haven't since, seen someone wear a suit to go sailing.

The day after that first sea trial, James and Kath left. Their absence utterly depressed us. To make matters worse, Christmas loomed, our first away from family. I fantasized about flying Mom down; Pete ruminated about hitchhiking the 1,200 miles home, if only for a day or two. But just before the holidays, life perked up. Some of Pop's friends showed up and delivered goodies from home: cookies, chocolate, sweaters, and a chess set. Pop had sent along the backup hand system for the lift, a complicated-looking thing that must have taken a lot of work. Good old Pop! On Christmas Eve, Tassos dropped by and insisted we come to his house the next day for Christmas lunch and a different slant on the holidays: countless bottles of retsina, a table piled high with Greek food, and Tassos's friends and relatives chattering away in Greek. We didn't understand a word, but the atmosphere was happy, warm and welcoming.

As a new year, 1979, dawned, there was nothing new about our cash situation. Financial woes continued to plague us; in fact, I think money problems created more stress than anything else we encountered during what became a six-year venture. A 5-rand bill that blew over the side one day was a catastrophe, and more than once we were down to nothing. But time after time, just when we reached a state of despair, riches dropped into our hands. A great deal came from Tassos, our guardian angel—whatever would we have done without him? I hope that in my lifetime I'll be able to help somebody as he helped us, not only materially but from deep within.

A Rhodesian who was farming in South Africa gave us 100 rand and wished us well; half an hour later he returned with a case of beer to cheer us up. Wow! A beer for Pete—that would do him good. A farmer in Marendellas, near Salisbury, sent a check. How incredible! James and Kath had left us 200 rand, which we lived on for weeks. I spent the last 20 rand on paint for the foredeck, a frivolous purchase, but to hell with it. With that nagging job finished at last, *Usikusiku* looked so much better that the morale boost alone was worth the expense. With our last 50 cents I bought Pete some tobacco. I knew he'd prefer cigarettes, but pipe tobacco was cheaper and I must have been feeling good-hearted to have bought even that. Mind you, he was a grouch without it.

The most touching contribution came from an elderly woman in Salisbury who sent us $2 Rhodesian attached to a note: "Peter and Liz Fordred—bon voyage, you brave young people. This old-age pensioner won't need vitamin tablets this month. Your pictures on my mirror will be tonic enough, so the $2 normally spent on vitamins can go toward your trip." It was signed "Senior Citizen."

Everyone who supported us—family, friends, and strangers—strengthened our resolve to get the show on the road. We wanted to inspire others to release their spirits from their disabilities and reach for the stars.

Sea Trials, Skipper Trials

ITH *USIKUSIKU* TIED TO THE JETTY, Pete and I hoisted the mainsail on our own for the first time. What a hassle! We ended up with tangles of rope all over the place, but at least we refrained from arguing about how to do it. Our second attempt was smoother—until the wind came up and we had to drop the sail so fast it draped itself all over the wheelhouse and deck. Someone suggested we rig up lazy-jacks—lines running from the masthead to the end of the boom—to keep the mainsail in check while we reefed or furled it. Alf, from *Dawn Treader of Lune,* helped us with that and with setting up sheaves and eyes for slab reefing, which would spare us from having to climb onto the wheelhouse to shorten sail. Pete and I experimented with it and found that reefing was now easier, at least in port, but we didn't think we'd be able to manage at sea. Still, little by little we were adapting *Usikusiku* to our needs. The biggest decision, however, remained: would we be sailing in or out of our wheelchairs?

One night we awoke to rustling and scraping in the wheelhouse.

Pete dove from bed to wheelchair and rocketed up the lift, shouting and swearing. Although the intruder hadn't had time to steal anything, he jumped up onto the jetty and simply sauntered off, obviously knowing we couldn't give chase. If I'd had a gun I'd have filled him with buckshot, just for his attitude. Out of naïveté and overconfidence, no doubt, I never felt unsafe, although most likely we were safer when we took on our first crew member. Allen was a South African about our age who claimed to be an experienced sailor and offered to take us to Cape Town. We prepared for another trial sail, letting him serve as skipper. Four lads from other boats offered to come along.

"Shouldn't we sort out the mainsail before we leave?" I asked Allen. It was still reefed from Pete's and my experiments.

"No. We can do that once we're out in the harbor."

That seemed strange, especially since the crew had plenty of time while Pete and I were getting out the headsail. For this we went below and Pete went up on the forward lift until he could roll into the forepeak, an 18-inch step up from the rest of the flooring because of the curved shape of the hull. he opened the locker door wide, then climbed from his chair onto the workbench. Reaching around the trash can that held the anchor chain, he pulled out sail-bags until he found the genoa, which he rolled into his chair. A shove on the chair rolled it onto the lift, from where I could retrieve the sail before pushing the chair back to Pete. While he put everything back together, I carried the sail on my footplates up the main lift and to the foredeck, where I dumped it out of its bag and prepared to hank it on, as I'd seen other crew do before setting out.

"Don't worry about that," Allen said. "We can do it once we're out." Having everything ready before we cast off seemed to me the logical way to go, but I know I'm bossy and will argue that black is white, so I let my logic slide and redirected my mental energy into controlling myself. A skipper is the boss, so Pete always told me.

While the boats tied up outside of *Usikusiku* did their shuffle, I reversed out—rather nicely, I thought, and was still congratulating myself when I noticed that we were barreling straight for another yacht because I hadn't shifted all the way into neutral. Allen successfully fended us off, but still—how embarrassing! Red-faced, I pointed *Usikusiku* toward the narrow channel that led from the yacht club into the harbor. Just as we entered it, wisps of smoke curled up the lift shaft and a horrendous smell assaulted me. "Smoke!" I shouted. "Something's burning!" Pete, who was still in his chair on the foredeck, shot into the wheelhouse and down the lift with one of the crew hot on his heels, or rather hot on his wheels. Pete actually beat him down because the ladder we'd installed vertically down the aft side of the lift shaft was difficult to negotiate. Besides, you'd be amazed how fast Pete could move.

"The exhaust lagging is burning!" he yelled. "Switch off the engine, Liz!"

I shut it down in a hurry.

"Get that mainsail up!" shouted Allen from the cockpit.

Up went the mainsail, still carrying a double reef. In the light winds it didn't even fill, and as we slowly lost boat speed, we lost steerage as well. We squeaked through the narrow channel but began drifting down on a freighter being maneuvered by two tugs. The tugs reversed engines, and all three vessels furiously sounded their horns.

"Raise the genoa!" Allen bellowed above the din, but it still wasn't hanked on. We were really in the soup.

Skipper or not, I assumed command. "Pete!" I called below. "I have to start the engine, just for a couple of minutes!" I fired it up and steered *Usikusiku* out of harm's way, while two of our rent-a-crew shook the reef out of the mainsail and the other two hanked on and raised the genoa. The freighter and tugs continued blasting at us until we were well clear.

Apart from the mast falling down or the boat sinking, not much more could have gone wrong, and no one within a mile could have missed the show. We slunk back to the jetty in disgrace. "I wonder when Captain Rountree will arrive to jack us up," Pete muttered during the tying-up shuffle. What a mess! Getting out of the way wouldn't have been a problem if we'd had our sails organized, a lesson Pete and I wouldn't forget. As for Allen, seeds of doubt had been sown, but we shoved them aside. What choice did we have? People weren't exactly lining up for the privilege of skippering us.

When the exhaust pipe had cooled, Pete cut off the lagging and found that the inner layers were charred black. How could that be, when the purpose of asbestos was to insulate the hot exhaust pipe? Someone said the exhaust should be water-cooled. Pete accepted that and added it to the work list, but he wasn't convinced it was the whole answer. As with all mechanical mysteries, he mulled it over and over, going through the engineering, the physics, the circumstances. His Sherlock Holmes deductive reasoning eventually zeroed in on the propeller. It must have been overloaded, he decided, and appointed Allen to go over the side to check. Sure enough, the blades were overgrown with barnacles, after just two months in the water.

Shortly after our little fiasco in the bay, Colin from *Dawn Treader* appeared—whether delegated by the other yachties or acting on his own, we never knew. No one thought Pete and I would be able to sail on our own, he said, because of unexpected events such as the one we'd just experienced. He was concerned we might be pushing ourselves irrationally, mainly because I was such a bloody stubborn woman that I didn't stop and think, nor was I capable of quitting once I'd committed to something. "It would take just as much courage to pack it in as it would to carry on," Colin concluded, trying to offer us a face-saving way out.

"Go and stuff it," I wanted to say, but I held my tongue because Colin was a nice guy whose opinion we valued. Once he'd gone,

Pete and I discussed his comments as objectively as possible. I conceded that I didn't always stop and think—Pete says I'd enthusiastically start building a roof without giving thought to first erecting walls—but his levelheadedness kept me in check. We didn't have a pretty boat, a finished boat, or lots of money, but those weren't reasons to give up. Unless we had conclusive evidence that we couldn't sail a boat on our own, we would give it our best shot. If we failed, at least we'd have tried. And as far as I was concerned, we hadn't even gotten to the trial stage. We were still organizing the boat to fit our physical capabilities. So Colin didn't put a dent in our resolve; he may actually have spurred us on because, as he said, I'm a bloody stubborn woman. Everyone notices that right off, but few people realize that Pete is just as bad. In fact, he may even be worse. He's just quieter about it.

Captain Rountree, as unimpressed as Colin was with our performance, delivered an official missive that stated new conditions for leaving:

1. *You must have on board a minimum of two experienced crew members.* Well, Allen had already moved on board. He rounded up John, a young Greek who had sailed from Australia on one of the other yachts. John recruited Stan, a Durban lad who hadn't sailed before but was willing to give it a try.

2. *Someone on board must have a local Pilot's Exemption ticket or the equivalent.* Allen began studying for the test, which was scheduled to be given soon.

3. *You must sail out in the Bay of Natal a minimum of three more times.* For the first of these, we went out to swing the compass, taking the compass adjuster along as our skipper. Pete stayed below to keep an eye on the exhaust pipe, which he'd relagged with the grade of asbestos cloth used by commercial vessels. Allen seemed nervous and was giggling like a young girl, so I helmed, turning *Usikusiku* to "300 degrees" or "180 degrees" or whatever the adjuster shouted out. Since metal near a compass distorts the reading, we made

two deviation cards, one with a wheelchair at the helm and one without.

When the compass adjuster had finished, the lads hoisted sail and I killed the engine. Pete, looking a tad green after three hours of smelling the last shreds of old asbestos burning off, joined us in the cockpit. For the remainder of the day we had no major problems. *Usikusiku* wasn't easy to sail the way she was set up, so we'd have to find ways to improve things, but apart from that we had a lovely afternoon sail in conditions gentle enough for Pete and me to concentrate on what we needed to learn.

Early in January, Allen took his Pilot's Exemption test. While we were all waiting for the results, he learned that his brother had been killed in a hit-and-run accident. He hurried home to Johannesburg to be with his mother and would go on to Cape Town for the funeral. He'd be gone for a week or so.

We took the extra time to start a major job. Someone had told Pete that some huge pieces of lumber had been discarded outside the shipyard. They were roughly sawn, about 10 feet long, 10 inches wide, and 6 inches thick, and weathered almost silver, but beneath the surface was a hardwood that, if not mahogany, was a close match. We checked around and were told they were rubbish and we could have them. Pete had them cut into boards 5 inches wide and 1 inch thick, and John and I busied ourselves making toe rails for the deck. With the leftovers, John and Stan made a helmsman's seat for the wheelhouse, with 10-inch-high sides to support Pete and me. After I'd sanded and oiled everything, it looked fantastic.

Ian, a friend of Duffy's who'd done yacht deliveries, took us out for our second required sail. He signed out at the harbormaster's office, as required, but we'd barely cleared the channel when our VHF, the universally monitored short-range radio, crackled to life, and we heard Port Control asking another yacht to chase us down and send us back. Now what? Did they think we were sneaking off? In broad daylight? When their office building was on a bluff overlooking the harbor?

Ian went below and said into the VHF handset, "Port Control, Port Control, *Usikusiku*."

"*Usikusiku*, Port Control," said a thickly accented Afrikaans voice. "Be good boys and come back into the harbor."

"Excuse me, Port Control, but we have clearance."

A pause.

"Ahem. That's confirmed, *Usikusiku*. Ahem. Have a nice sail. Port Control out." Ever since leaving Rhodesia we'd been on the receiving end of marine officialdom's insults, forced to jump at their every capricious command. It had been like a constant obstacle course. Now for a change *they* had screwed up, and we thoroughly enjoyed the turnabout. Also the sail. The breeze was gentle, and we had a good day.

A yacht-racing Dutchman named Arp took us out for our third required sail. As soon as we had the sails up, he put me on the helm. Off the wind I was terrified of jibing because from inside the wheelhouse I couldn't see the sails or feel which direction the wind came from. On the wind I slid across the floor every time the boat heeled, and with only the wheel to hang onto, my course went to hell. Arp, in disgust, dismissed me from the wheel and took over with the tiller.

"Harden up!" he barked to the crew. "Do you think you're on holiday?" What I wanted to know was, did he think we were in the Fastnet or was he just trying to demonstrate how inadequate we were? Cranking in the sails made us heel over even more. In the strongest winds we'd yet experienced, *Usikusiku* sliced through the water as never before, her gunwales swallowed by the water roaring down the sidedeck. The sensation of speed was exhilarating but got me worrying—I couldn't imagine keeping up this kind of sailing for days on end. Even more disturbing, Pete really labored when he took the helm. He needed one hand to hang onto the boat, which left only one hand for the tiller, and that wasn't enough. If it was tough for him, I'd be useless.

"We didn't sail like that across the Indian Ocean," John whispered to me on the way back. Well, that was a relief! Later, other people told us that pushing a boat that hard was unnecessary, that putting the gunwales under water actually cut the speed. My worry dissipated, at least about that.

Other concerns had emerged, though. Pete and I had still been arguing the chairs-versus-bottoms issue. Because he was unable to work well from his chair, Pete thought we should be out of our chairs at sea. I, being less mobile than he, had fought the idea. Until this sail with Arp. Realizing, for the first time, how precarious a wheelchair could be on deck, the idea of installing tracks and a clamp-type system to secure the chairs to them went right out the window. Only by sitting on our bottoms would we be safe. But how would we get around on deck and how would we reach things down below?

An even greater concern was that *Usikusiku* was a dog to steer. The wheel was too small and had too much reduction, so you kept turning it until the boat began to respond, and by then you'd already oversteered. Moreover, helming from the wheelhouse wasn't practical because you were isolated from the sails and wind. Nor was the tiller going to work for us. Add to all that the awkwardness of humping sails around with wheelchairs, and the fact that no matter how we trimmed the sails we couldn't balance the helm, and major changes appeared to be in order. One was roller furling. It was relatively new, at least in this part of the world, and we'd seen it only once, on the American yacht *Tabaitha*, but Pete knew it was for us. He scrutinized the system and got drawings from Jim and Carol, *Tabaitha*'s owners, but because of the time and labor involved he wouldn't be able to tackle the project until we got to Cape Town. We had other ideas, too, but wanted to confirm them with more sailing before we spent any money. Oh, for a rich sugar daddy so we could buy and try until all was sorted out! Still, if everything had been served up on a platter all our lives, we wouldn't have developed the backbone to persevere.

Our next goal was getting *Usikusiku*'s clearance from the Offshore Sailing Committee. I was confident we'd pass; Pete the Pessimist was not. Lo and behold, when the inspector came round, he not only passed us but refrained from lecturing—a welcome change. Later he even presented us with a gift from his company: a dan buoy to mark the position of anyone who goes overboard.

Two weeks had passed without word from Allen; it seemed he wasn't coming back. Admittedly, we were relieved, but now we faced the task of finding someone else to get us to Cape Town. We tried hard to persuade Ian, but he had too many business commitments. Then I met another Stan, an older man who seemed experienced enough, and my hopes soared that he'd take us. Instead, "Old Stan" (as we called him to differentiate him from our Young Stan) went to see Val Howells.

We already knew Val, who at the moment was tied up about five boats outside us. Hale and fit at fifty-three, he spoke with an Anthony Hopkins–like Welsh accent and looked like Sean Connery sporting a Hemingway beard. Val knew more about sailing than anyone else we'd come across. In 1963 he'd competed against Sir Francis Chichester in the OSTAR, the Observer Single-handed Transatlantic Race, and now he was sailing single-handed around the world.

Val dropped in and asked how things were going. Upon hearing how the Offshore Sailing Committee kept trying to hold us back, he said, "Forget what everyone else says. You have to prove to yourselves whether or not you can go it alone." Suddenly, with that one sentence, the path ahead of us was clear, straight, and well-marked. And then came the stunner: Val offered to sail with us to Cape Town. "By the time we get there," he said, "you'll know where you stand."

Had Pete and I been able-bodied and upright, our knees would have buckled from the shock. No one except Allen—who, I'm convinced, was using us to score his first captain's job so he could bluff his way into another—had been interested in taking us to Cape Town. Why would someone like Val, who'd gone down in the annals of sailing history, want to take time out from his circumnavigation to help us? At the time I had no idea, but in retrospect I think it was because, having been on the frontiers of solo long-distance sailing, Val knew the joy of accomplishing something no one else had done. And he was so self-assured, so secure about who he was, that he didn't need to protect his status. He sincerely wanted us to succeed and to break a barrier of our own; first, however, he wanted us to know exactly what we were in for. "Durban is one of the worst ports in the world from which to start a sailing venture," he said. "It can be a tremendous challenge even for experienced yachtsmen."

Pete and I hadn't even been offshore yet. We'd gone to a talk about sailing from Durban to Cape Town and learned that these waters are some of the most dangerous in the world. The winds of the Roaring Forties—between latitudes 40 and 50 degrees south—encircle the globe unimpeded by land, generating tremendous swells that make their way north to Africa. Cape Agulhas, the southernmost tip of the continent, is where the Indian Ocean and the South Atlantic, with their attendant weather systems, collide. So do two main ocean currents: the tropical Agulhas, coming from the Indian Ocean, and the frigid Benguela, coming up from the Antarctic. The African land mass interferes by adding its own weather systems to the mix, and the resulting collision of air and water can create unholy winds, freak waves, and unpredictable currents. This is why no yacht can leave the Bay of Natal, even for a day's sail, without permission.

All of this was driven home when we heard, after *Dawn Treader* and *Endymion* had left, that both blew out their mainsails in the first gale they encountered. The news forced Pete and me to confront something that, despite our extensive planning, we hadn't previously thought about: we could easily damage or break gear we couldn't afford to replace. We'd have to sail conservatively.

Val wanted to leave as soon as possible. It was already January 21, and after the 1,000-mile trip with *Usikusiku*, he still had to return to Durban and bring his own boat, *Unibrass Brython of Milford*, to Cape Town. Then he'd be off to Wales to complete his circumnavigation. Ideally, he'd ride out of the Southern Hemisphere as summer waned and enter the Northern Hemisphere as summer was beginning there. So with his trademark efficiency, Val looked over *Usikusiku*, drew up a list of things to buy and do, and packed us all off in various directions.

About the same time we'd met Old Stan, we'd met Alan Foster, a gentle, cheerful fellow who was a definite improvement over our first Allen. This Alan would have given us the world, but being as broke as we, he instead offered to look after Val's boat. Then he borrowed a car and took me around town to solicit provisions. Tassos had already sent masses of food, mostly staples. A supermarket donated R50 worth of perishables. Tassos had given us a 44-gallon drum of diesel, so *Usikusiku*'s tanks were full, but Alan and I talked a fuel company into giving us 50 liters to store on deck. A small shop donated a kerosene lantern and some flashlights. My list was complete.

Val paid our accumulated mooring fees out of his own pocket and got clearance to leave. (Captain Rountree, needless to say, was greatly relieved: not only were we getting out of his hair, we were being skippered by one of the world's best.) En masse we headed to the immigration office in town to fill in the crew forms required for departure.

As long as I was there I thought I'd inquire at customs about the formalities involved in getting a second extension on the time limit for keeping *Usikusiku* in South Africa. I'd gotten her original six-month visa extended to nine months, but I was concerned about how long everything seemed to take. Not to worry, said the agent, the R4,800 bond would be canceled upon our departure from Durban. No, I explained, we weren't leaving the country now, just going to Cape Town. He still insisted the bond would be cleared. We'd originally been told that James's insurance company (meaning, ultimately, Pete and I) would have to pay the import duty if we didn't leave South Africa within the stipulated time. But I wasn't about to argue—it was less debt to worry about.

That night Val took us out for dinner, and when we got to the restaurant we found tables filled with our friends. What a wonderful surprise! Then, when he went to pay the tab, Jim and Carol from *Tabaitha* had already covered it. Another great lift! Late that night Pete and I tumbled into bed, physically exhausted yet buoyed up by the incredible generosity and support of the many friends we'd made during our six months in Durban. Our high spirits temporarily eased the money worry: we had a whopping 3 rand to our name, which wouldn't pay a day's mooring fee anywhere. But it was best not to dwell on that. Miracles had happened before and perhaps they'd happen again. Meanwhile, we'd take one day at a time.

The Cape of Good Hope

JANUARY AND FEBRUARY are the best times to cross the South Atlantic. The southeast trade winds come farther south, so can be picked up sooner after leaving South Africa, and the weather in general is at its most favorable. "The Golden Highway" is what sailors call the route to South America that time of year. Most of the boats on the international jetty had already taken off for Cape Town. From there they'd sail across the Atlantic, then go on to the Caribbean, the United States, or Europe. Although *Usikusiku* wouldn't be ready to make the crossing this season, at least we were part of the parade to Cape Town. Pete and I were in high spirits about our first ocean passage.

While we were making our final preparations for departure, I heard Port Control calling *Southern Cross*, which now was tied up next to us. I told Neville, who was hanking on his sails, to turn on his VHF, then heard the harbor authorities informing him that if he didn't leave within thirty minutes, he'd owe mooring fees for another day. Muttering about how petty and ridiculous they were, Neville cast off his mooring lines and motored away to shouts of

"Happy sailing!" and "Good luck!" A couple of hours later the few remaining international yachties gave us a similar sendoff. We were really on our way!

The VHF emitted bursts of crackling and unintelligible noise as we motored out, so Val went down and fiddled with it, but he gave up as we neared the port entrance. Just as he reappeared in the cockpit, a police motor launch zoomed up alongside us.

"*Usikusiku*, turn around!"

"What's the problem?" Val asked.

"Ach, man, just do as you are told! Follow us back in!"

We did a 180 and headed back, angry and deflated. Again someone had punctured our balloon of exuberance.

We tied up alongside a tugboat, whose radio Val used to call the port authorities. He returned red-faced and steaming mad. "They say we owe sixty-five cents because we stayed past noon," he fumed. On Friday, when he'd paid the mooring fees, he'd asked for Monday to be included. Apparently it hadn't been, and now some office peon was ruffling his feathers at us. Even more infuriating, *Southern Cross* had been warned about this, so why hadn't we? Val hitched a ride to the port captain's office, where he sounded off at Captain Rountree about the error. Rountree was most apologetic, but that didn't restore our excitement or the three hours we'd lost. Or lessen our embarassment when we learned how many newspapers had turned the incident into a major story. Again we departed Durban, this time without fanfare but, we hoped, for good, because Pete and I never wanted to return.

Val split us into two watches: he, Young Stan, and I made up one; Old Stan, John, and Pete the other. Val delegated the cooking to John and Young Stan. "You won't even have to peel a potato, Liz," he said. "I want you and Pete to just watch and learn, so you can make the right decision about whether or not you can do this." I wasn't about to argue, particularly when, as soon as we got out of the harbor, large swells attacked us. They rose on our port quarter and built into eight-foot green walls that I was convinced each time would break over the boat. At the last second, though, *Usikusiku's* stern would gently lift, and they would slip beneath her. If we survive this next one, I kept telling myself, then logically we'll survive the rest. Looking at it now, I don't see any logic at all in that.

Once I trusted the water to go under and not over us, I actually enjoyed the sensation. It was tiring, though, so four hours later, when the next watch arrived on deck, I didn't hang about. I swiveled myself toward the lift. My stomach was unsettled, but I wasn't prepared to think I might be getting seasick. Not me! I was healthy as a horse and never got sick. But dear heaven, I felt rough.

I worked myself over to the lift platform, picked up the control unit and pressed the "down" button. *Usikusiku's* pitch and yaw made the descent trickier than in port. With one hand I held the control unit, kept a finger on the "down" button and clutched the edge of the lift platform. With the other hand I held onto the rim of the hatch and when it passed out of reach I grabbed successive rungs of the ladder that served, along with the engine cover lower down, as the aft wall of the lift shaft.

Down below, I didn't have far to go because Pete's and my double bed was right around the corner. But could I get up onto it? I'd been able to shift myself over easily enough from my wheelchair, but that had been stowed for the trip. First I tried to get onto my knees and from there work myself onto the bed, but with the boat swaying all over the show, I didn't have much control over my body. Next I tried using the motion to help heave me up, but I just crashed down onto the floor again. This was not going to work—that bed might as well have been Everest. I swallowed my pride and called to Old Stan, who was in the galley making coffee for his watch. I hated this kind of helplessness!

The motion that had been so exciting on deck was no longer fun. The bunk, although firmly attached to the hull, was moving wildly, at least in its relationship to a fixed point in space. Back and forth, up and down, side to side it went—I felt like a baby in a manic cradle. I slid open one door of the cupboard that ran the length of the bunk and stuck my hand in to keep from rolling off the bed. If I dozed off, though, my hand would relax and let go, which meant I couldn't doze off. Not that I could have slept anyway. To minimize travel time we were motorsailing, and the noise down below was deafening.

The smell, as well, was terrible. Either shreds of old exhaust lagging were frying or the new lagging was heating up. I have a strong stomach for smells, but this one I couldn't handle. Even breathing through the blanket didn't filter out the noxious odors that assaulted my nose before heading straight to my stomach. Many people say being seasick makes them wish for death, but I didn't want to die; I just wanted to feel better. Besides, I was certain I'd get over it.

The noise and motion, coupled with the anxiety of my first night at sea, made relaxing impossible. A couple of hours passed before I began to feel even slightly sleepy, and at that point my bladder started sending signals. Typical! I sat up, shoved my legs off the bed, grabbed onto a convenient piece of the hand lift system, and with the help of the boat's motion lowered myself to the floor. I yanked closed the curtain to block this part of the boat from the aft part and worked my way over to the loo.

Pete and I were wearing socks and Bata tackies—high-topped sneakers—to protect our feet and ankles, and thick jeans to protect our rears from bruises and sores, so I worked up a sweat getting my pants down. Then I couldn't get up onto the seat! No way was I going to call for help again, this time while lying bare-bottom on the floor. Instead, I got the bedpan out of the cupboard. By the time I'd used it, emptied it, pumped out the toilet, and worked my pants back up, nausea assailed me. I retched into the toilet and pumped it some more. This bathroom routine was the pits! The worst part was knowing I'd have to repeat it in two hours or so, and taking half an hour each time wasn't going to work. I'd have to come up with a new system.

What did our first sunrise at sea illuminate? Good old Durban—in all that crashing around and holding on, we'd covered just five miles. How demoralizing! We should have had a boost from the fast-moving Agulhas Current, which usually hugs the coast all the way around to Africa's south coast, but it had decided to move offshore for a while. In its place ran a strong countercurrent that apparently thought we should stay in the Indian Ocean rather than head for the Atlantic.

It's amazing how things have a knack of breaking down as soon as they know you're going to sea. Not only had our fancy new VHF, which a friend coming from England had smuggled into Rhodesia for us, squawked its last, but the new radio direction finder (RDF) also was on the blink. Well, at least until Pete could check them out, although, by the look of his green pallor, not for a while yet. I was beginning to suspect gremlins and wondered what else they'd been into. *Usikusiku*, at least, seemed to be staying in one piece, which was more than I could say for myself. I felt truly lousy. Pete, too, was disgruntled with this sailing lark. When Val later brought the VHF up to the cockpit and placed it in Pete's lap, my poor husband turned an even deeper shade of green while trying to focus on the circuitry. He gave up on that but did manage to fix a loose connection in the RDF.

The second day brought east-northeast Force 5 winds, making our bearing almost dead downwind. On another point of sail that 20-knot wind could have made for a great ride, but when coming from behind it didn't provide enough oomph to move a 20-ton sloop that didn't have running poles and could fly only one headsail. We continued motorsailing, which meant the tail wind blew the exhaust into the cockpit and increased my nausea. Val suggested I try what he called the "natural method" of overcoming seasickness, which was to go about your business and ignore how awful you felt until eventually you got your sea legs. My sea legs must have been as paralyzed as my real legs because I never did build up any of that so-called natural immunity. Even medication didn't help much, and anyway, I couldn't stand how dopey it made me. Time drags when you're seasick. Had I been able to take my turn at the helm, it might have gone faster, but I couldn't manage the tiller. Val disconnected the steering cables to the wheel, which eased the strain a little, but in any swell it was still heavy going. Even Pete could barely manage. Unable to brace himself with his legs as the boat rolled about, he had to hang on with one arm, leaving only one for the tiller, which required massive force in these seas. In addition, he had to sit on the deck, which put the tiller at head level and his eyes too low to see the headsail through the wheel-house windows or to spot approaching ships.

Even discounting this idiotic emergency tiller, which plugged into a fitting just forward of the lazarette, the entire cockpit configuration was unworkable. The design was unorthodox to begin with. *Usikusiku*'s flush deck allowed a wheelchair to roll from bow to stern without impediments, but this meant we had no cockpit well, just 18-inch-high bench seats that Pete and I couldn't get onto. Even if someone had helped us up, we still couldn't have sat there because they had no backrests. So we were relegated to the cockpit floor, which by now felt like concrete. My legs ached from keeping them crossed to give me a more stable sitting base, and my back ached from not having anything to lean against comfortably. This two-thirds-paralyzed body shouldn't have been able to feel anything, but I hurt all over from trying to brace myself and hold on and counteract the constant motion. And my stomach muscles were so sore from retching that every movement was excruciating. The only positive thing about being seasick is that you might lose some weight, but knowing me, I wouldn't. I still had this mania about eating to stay alive.

The Natal coastline, although fairly straight, has green rolling hills that lend it a gentle beauty. I have no memory of it though; the only green rolling hills I saw were the wet kind. Just as well—if I'd seen solid land, I probably would have rolled over the side and swum ashore.

Below, raw diesel fumes now mingled with the exhaust smoke and the smoldering asbestos; the fuel line had become clogged with pieces of the cork used for gaskets on the tank inspection covers. Poor Pete had the horrible job of clearing it. Sucking diesel is vomit-producing at the best of times, so I can't begin to imagine what it's like when you're seasick. Pete would suck on the fuel line, scurry to the loo to throw up, then go back to the engine for another suck before scurrying back to the loo. I felt awful for him.

The following day he was feeling better and had another go at the VHF. He found a tiny hair lodged in a microswitch; it was merely a matter of removing it, and voilà, the radio worked. But if Pete was feeling well enough to accomplish something, I wasn't. At this point, if he'd so much as hinted that he wanted to sell the boat and forget this so-called adventure, I would willingly have agreed. "If this is sailing, you can have it," I told Old Stan. "Sell this rolling bitch and get me onto something steady."

We'd gone so far offshore to pick up the Agulhas Current that Africa was nothing more than a suggestion on the horizon. As we headed into East London, however, those tantalizing, hazy shapes solidified into stable, solid, get-in-my-wonderful-fast-moving-wheelchair land! The chair I'd refused to acknowledge when it first appeared in my life now represented the independence to care for myself, to do simple things like make a cup of tea. Asking people for every little thing was not my scene at all.

East London is South Africa's only river port of significant size. Once we'd tied up, Pete and I, in turn, hung from the boom in the bosun's chair I'd made out of parachute webbing and heavy-duty awning material, while Young Stan cranked us up with a halyard. John, pulling on a lateral line, hauled us over to the dock and lowered us into our waiting chairs. I felt like a bale of cargo being offloaded from a ship. That humiliation was offset by the 10-

rand note I found in my purse—it must have come from Alan, which meant it was his last bit of cash. Small as this contribution was, it more than quadrupled Pete's and my net worth, bringing it to a whopping 13 rand.

The younger lads went off for a well-deserved bash, while Val and Old Stan headed for the yacht club for a pint. Pete and I just pushed around town, not wanting to spend anything and not in the mood to socialize, just relieved to be on land. We hardly spoke. My head swirled with questions about what the hell we were doing, and I assumed his did the same, but neither of us dared voice our doubts this early in the game. Eventually Pete began to talk about how he could improve the steering, the cockpit seating, and other things that made sailing difficult for the two of us. His positive attitude lessened my aches and pains. I acknowledged to myself that the trip had been awful so far but figured that things would improve with time. The main problem was that Pete and I hadn't been able to do anything ourselves.

A couple of guys at the yacht club overheard Val and Old Stan talking about how the tiller required so much muscle that you could actually see the heavy iron pipe flex, and the next day they showed up with wood and tools and beefed it up by bracing both sides. Pete and I were painfully aware that the entire steering system was impractical, but redoing it had to wait for Cape Town. As did dozens of other jobs. The exponentially increasing list included changing the steering system, moving the compass from the wheelhouse to the cockpit; making lee boards for the bunks; lowering the cockpit seats; making Pete's and my bunk lower or somehow easier to get onto; and inventing a way for us to reach the toilet, sink, and galley equipment when we were out of our chairs. The amount of work ahead was almost too staggering to contemplate.

Val was frustrated by *Usikusiku*'s slowness compared to his sleek *Unibrass Brython*; I could feel his agitation building during the three days that a front kept us in East London. The delay paid off, though, because the next leg, from East London to Port Elizabeth, was gentler. That, plus our now knowing what to expect, decreased Pete's and my anxiety. Pete even managed a cigarette or two.

Since we weren't totally incapacitated by nausea this time, Val cut some small lengths of rope and showed us how to backsplice, making a loop at the end and threading the strands back in. He also taught us how to make whippings that kept cut rope ends from unraveling and looking ugly. Once we mastered the technique, if not the aesthetics (there definitely was an art to it), he brought us sheets and mooring lines to work on. Making things look professional suited my tidy mind, and doing something useful was satisfying. My enthusiasm waned whenever I had to focus on anything close up, but I forced myself to carry on. The sea gods must have approved because they rewarded us with our first sight of a seal, an awesome experience for total inlanders.

Val, who had been trailing a heavy-duty fishing line from *Usikusiku*'s stern, was really pleased when he caught three tuna—well, two and a quarter tuna; something had eaten most of one. He got right down to cleaning and gutting the catch on the lazarette hatch, from which the blood ran all over the place, including into the cockpit where I was sprawled. I retreated to the wheelhouse and added another item to the work list: invent a way to make the aft deck drain overboard.

We reached Port Elizabeth in just twenty-six hours. I didn't feel so desperate to go ashore this time, but Pete and I had promised to phone a reporter friend of Duffy's who would relay our story to him. The jetty was high, with a rickety perpendicular ladder. No way we could get up that! So the lads borrowed a dinghy and lowered Pete and me and our wheelchairs into it; then John rowed us to a slipway and pulled the dinghy as far as he could up the ramp. He opened our chairs and held them next to the dinghy. Our legs got wet, but at least the chairs were dinghy height, so we could easily climb over onto them. Then, bless him, John pulled us up the steep ramp.

When we got back to *Usikusiku*, a photographer and a reporter were waiting to interview us. As usual, we couldn't talk to them, thanks to our contract with Duffy. We were fed up with this arrangement by now; nobody in South Africa was going to pay to write a story about us. I'd moaned to Duffy about it, but he was such a funny, lighthearted person that I couldn't stay mad at him for long. Besides, he believed in us, which was worth plenty. Shunning reporters, however, garnered only adverse press, whereas Val felt we needed positive publicity, and lots of it, if we wanted to get sponsorship. He heard more of the gossip than we did, and apparently it wasn't good, although he considerately spared us the details.

The usual procedure in a new port is to find the local yacht club or pub where sailors gather to have a drink and swap yarns. Even though I'd gone ashore to make phone calls, I didn't want to go for an extended period. Of course Val wanted to know why. "I'd just as soon stay on board and tidy things up," I told him.

He pressed harder.

"Well," I said, "it could be embarrassing."

"What do you mean?"

"You know, the loos. Most have steps or tight corners to negotiate, and I might not be able to get into them without help." I strongly felt that if I couldn't manage on my own, I shouldn't go.

"Nonsense. You need breaks from the boat. And do you plan on sailing around the world without seeing any of it?"

Certainly not; the whole point of sailing was to go places. The idea, though, wasn't to have help each step of the way. I knew Val and Old Stan harbored no resentment about what they had to do for Pete and me, and I never heard a whimper of complaint from John or Young Stan about their work load of four hours on, four off, plus galley duty. But I'm simply not a person who enjoys sitting and watching everyone else do things (even though seasickness made it easier to stomach, so to speak). Pete and I needed to maintain our independence, and we could see that going ashore was going to be a major problem. For now though, giving in was easier than bucking Val's insistence. At the yacht club I was able to take a proper shower, and to my surprise, that alone was well worth the hassle of getting there.

South Africa doesn't have many conveniences for yachts because few sailboats have big engines, so fuel docks are scarce except in commercial ports. Old Stan, though, hobnobbed around until he scored us some free diesel. I paid little attention to how he worked his magic, just felt relieved that someone else had taken the initiative to solve a problem.

Two days later we left for Mossel Bay. I'd hoped I might shake the seasickness by this third leg of our trip, but no such luck. The latest nausea-producing odors came from under the floor next to my bunk: wastewater from the sink had somehow bypassed the waste tank and wound up in the shower pan, which then overflowed and dribbled into the bilge. The toilet valves leaked too, adding to the olfactory stew. Delightful! Nothing like disgusting smells to trigger even worse motion sickness.

I always felt a little better on deck, out in the fresh air and with a horizon to look at. Pete and I got out the sextant to practice taking sun sights. Easy enough in theory: just look through the scope, move the index bar to bring the sun's image down, then fine-tune with the micrometer head till the sun "kisses" the horizon. Well, it had been easy enough on land. At sea, sitting on the cockpit floor, I couldn't see properly, but even if I could get to a higher position, how would I hang on? I couldn't use my legs to brace myself, and I needed both hands for the sextant. And honestly, when the boat was rolling heavily from side to side, how could you be expected to hold the sextant exactly vertical? How did you adjust everything quickly enough to capture the sun's angle only from a wave top? How did you make the sun kiss the horizon when the horizon was all lumpy? What if, when you finally put the sun where you wanted it and called out "Mark!" your assistant was puking over the side from having looked at the stopwatch for so long? "Don't worry," said Val. "Using the sextant is an art that comes with experience." Lots of experience, I imagined. Understanding the principle would have to do for now, because no way could I look up figures in the nautical almanac, calculate a position line, and draw it on the chart. All I could see was the bottom of a bucket. I didn't give a damn where I was.

Now that we were in major shipping lanes, the amount of traffic frightened me. At night I'd see lights all around but couldn't figure out which way they were going because the red and green port and starboard lights weren't always clear. Val said that would come with experience too. I just hoped I'd get enough on this trip, because Pete and I would be alone on the next.

The days were still warm, but at night the temperature dropped into the forties, with wind and dampness taking the wind-chill factor considerably lower. Since leaving Durban we'd gone nearly five degrees, or 300 miles, farther south, and I swore I could feel Antarctica's icy breath. Shortly after my accident my internal thermostat had gone wonky, and now I suddenly and permanently lost my tolerance for cold—cold meaning anything below 60° Fahrenheit. I shivered continuously, even in bed.

There were nights when I tumbled off the bunk, mattress and all; I must have fallen asleep and let go of the cupboard. Leaving the mattress on the floor would have helped, but not with all that toilet leaking going on. Thank goodness the guys were understanding and always gave me a hand back onto the bunk, although sometimes I had to doze against it until someone came along. Why had we wasted time and wood on a wheelhouse seat that served no purpose since we didn't helm from there? Instead, we should have made leeboards to keep us in our bunks, but because we'd never sailed overnight, we'd overlooked these simple yet vital items. I saw little of Pete and wondered how he was managing.

Mossel Bay's appearance in the distance was a relief. Mossel Bay is one of South Africa's few natural harbors, although its small size has kept industry at bay and allowed it to remain a quaint fishing village protected by a ring of hills. Because Pete and I were a novelty and because Val was famous in yachting circles, the Mossel Bay Yacht Club invited us to a fish *braai*. Getting there was an adventure. The guys lifted us, chairs and all, onto the tug we were tied next to. Then, even though neither of us is particularly small, Val hoisted each of us on his back and carried us up two flights of stairs. At fifty-three (which seems ancient when you're twenty-four), he was amazingly strong and fit. I enjoyed watching him hold forth at the yacht club, where his sailing reputation, coupled with his good looks and charm, made him the center of attention.

We got some welcome attention too: over the following days a German who wished to remain anonymous donated 100 rand to our cause. The local Rotary Club matched it, and a local yachtsman sent over some canned food. We truly felt adopted by the people of Mossel Bay.

We had plenty to keep us busy for the six days that the weather kept us there. Pete cleaned out the fuel lines and filters in an effort to get rid of all the bits of cork. Val checked all the rigging, then went over the side and scraped the barnacles off the prop. Jim from *Tabaitha* had given us his spare toilet in Durban, so now we installed it in place of our dysfunctional one. We also disconnected the shower outlet to stop the contents of the wastewater tank from bubbling up through the drain and out into the bilge when we heeled over. So much for my plumbing. Pete and I decided to clean *Usikusiku*'s topsides so she'd look smart when we arrived in Cape Town. We rigged block and tackle up to the boom, attached the bosun's chair, and lowered ourselves into the dinghy we'd borrowed from *Southern Cross*, which had arrived in Mossel Bay ahead of us. By hanging onto the rub rail with one hand and reaching up with the other, we could scrub all the way up to the toe rails except at the bow, where we used the boathook to push the sponge around. The exercise felt good.

One morning we pushed up a hill with Val to see a famous tree that had served as a post office for the galleons that had once plied these waters. The sailors would put their outgoing mail in an old boot that used to hang from a branch and pick up any letters that were going their way. A brass boot commemorates the spot.

On February 1, Pete's and my fourth wedding anniversary, Neville and Louise from *Southern Cross* turned up with champagne. The following morning Val announced we were going on an "anniversary cruise." We motored around Seal Island, a rocky cay where seals gather to mate and raise their young. Then someone suggested we anchor and go for a swim.

Getting in the water was one feat I was sure I could manage on my own. Sitting on deck by the railing's open gate, I worked the bosun's chair underneath me. It was attached to the middle of the boom with the mainsail sheet's block and tackle, and the boom was already out over the side with a rope going forward to keep it from swinging back amidships. As soon as I'd pulled myself up enough to clear the toe rail, I swung out over the water. Had I stopped to think—not my forte—I would have eased myself down, but instead I gave a whoop and let go of the rope.

The 70-degree water strangled my vocal cords in mid-whoop and sent my legs into spasm. I was still gasping when I caught sight of Pete. The cold water that made my legs go rigid caused his to shake so violently that his entire body was shuddering. I nearly drowned laughing—not that I looked much smoother than he. We thrashed about until a wind shift brought Seal Island's stench our way. It was time to get out anyway, before our hands got too numb to haul ourselves up.

This was the first time in ages that Pete and I just relaxed and had fun, away from the anxiety about what lay ahead. I think Val wanted us to see the positive side of cruising life. He described how much better it would be in the Caribbean, where the water was clear and warm and the weather less violent. Sign me up! Enjoying myself was easy when I wasn't seasick.

After a week in Mossel Bay, waiting for a front to go through, we awoke to a morning of fine weather, so we took final showers at the yacht club and set sail. Old Stan had returned to Durban, which put an extra load on Val, but he remained as thoughtful and considerate as ever. We were blessed to have him, especially considering we'd been so desperate for a skipper that we would have taken just about anyone. I can't begin to imagine what a disaster this first sailing experience could have been with the wrong person. Val's knowledge and personality made him the ideal person to initiate Pete and me into the ways of the sea. He took on the role of teacher, did whatever was necessary to keep us comfortable, insisted we go ashore, and helped us compile what turned out to be a forty-seven-item list of changes we needed to make before we could sail *Usikusiku* on our own.

He exuded confidence that we could do it. Being paraplegics was in and of itself not a valid reason for giving up, he said; he'd met a man without hands who'd sailed across the Atlantic using his teeth. How incredible! He also thought we'd get the sponsorship we so badly needed. Thanks to him, I felt more positive and Pete began to lead the way with new ideas. Perhaps our mission was not impossible.

From Port Elizabeth to Cape Town the coast undulates with rocky promontories that flank huge, unprotected bays. The weather undulates as well, with fronts moving through every three or four days. Neville had organized a radio schedule with us whereby we'd call each other at two o'clock each afternoon. During one of our chats he warned us about a low-pressure system moving toward Cape Agulhas. Val was visibly concerned, which of course concerned me. "I'm not worried about our safety; I just don't want you to experience bad weather," he explained. "Let's hope we get to the cape ahead of the low."

His hoping must not have reached the weather gods because within hours the wind began to build. We were beating into it, making good only about 1 knot of forward progress even though our boat speed on our long tacks out to sea and back was four or five times that. Sloppy seas tossed *Usikusiku* about like a toy and ushered in the return of seasickness. The 30-knot Antarctic wind pushed its way through my clothes and into the very core of my body. I layered on sweaters and a jacket but couldn't manage a second pair of jeans because getting them on was nearly impossible, which meant I wouldn't be able to get them off quickly enough when I had to go to the loo. I stuck with the one pair and froze. Even so, the wildness of the wind and sea, and the element of danger, made for exhilarating sailing.

Val disappeared down the hatch. Seconds later he poked his head up and informed Young Stan and me that one of the diesel tanks must have ruptured because a lovely, oily cocktail was swilling over the floorboards. I heard him tell Pete to man the bilge pump and I pictured my poor, tired husband rolling out of our warm bunk onto the slippery floor and propping up the bed board and mattress with a rod to get at the bilge pump, which lived underneath. Better him than me, though; I couldn't have sat down there heaving that handle back and forth without heaving into a bucket at the same time. I didn't even want to see the mess. What I wanted was to get hold of the guy who'd made the tanks. It seemed that if you didn't do something yourself, you never knew if it was done properly. Not that I should talk, looking at my plumbing history.

Pete was close to exhaustion from having to suck out the fuel line whenever the engine stopped, which happened frequently because *Usikusiku*'s motion had again stirred up the bits of cork. Eventually he camped out among the sail bags in the saloon so that he didn't have far to go when the engine stopped.

By morning the storm had passed, and so had most of our first voyage. I dragged myself to the foredeck to watch the sun rise behind a group of knobby mountains called the Twelve Apostles. Seals, probably mistaking *Usikusiku* for a giant version of themselves, frolicked around us in the soft glow of morning. Pete joined me to watch the show. He still looked haggard but said he'd had the best sleep in ages. I'd missed him because, being on different watches, we'd seen each other only in passing.

During the night we had rounded the Cape of Good Hope— "the fairest cape in all the circumference of the earth," according to Sir Francis Drake—and looming ahead of us was Table Mountain, a spectacular reward for our having made it to Cape Town. When we poked our bow into the yacht basin, a barrage of horns greeted us. Neville and Louise from *Southern Cross*, Jim and Carol from *Tabaitha*, and all the other boat people streamed to meet us. I forgot I'd ever been seasick.

When Are You Leaving?

THE IDEA OF SALDANHA BAY as a destination had faded away. Now that Pete and I were part of the yachting scene rather than back home dreaming about it, we knew we needed to be in a large city that had whatever resources we'd need to finish the boat. At any rate, Cape Town was the jumping-off point for ports abroad. We'd remain there until we were ready for our run down the Golden Highway.

Our renewed enthusiasm replaced my worries about future sea-sickness. It hadn't been all that bad, I decided, and could be overcome. Most cruising people told us they got their sea legs after three or four days, and we hadn't been out for more than two and a half at a stretch so never had a chance to get acclimated. Besides, we'd enjoyed many parts of the trip. Any other concerns I had were dissipated by Pete, who was brimming with ideas for modifying *Usikusiku* now that we knew exactly what did and didn't work for us. We could do this thing we'd planned.

We'd been tied up at the fuel jetty directly in front of the Royal Cape Yacht Club for a week now, and were being pressured to leave.

I guess we'd outworn our welcome. The trouble was finding a place where getting on and off the boat would be easy. Some club official suggested we go to what was known as "Globe wall," because it ran parallel to the long building belonging to the Globe Company ship repair business. It seemed to be the place for people who wanted to work on their boats or who couldn't afford the club's mooring rates or who didn't fit the formal yacht club image. Pete and I set off for a look, but halfway there we turned back. The route along the seawall was strewn with obstacles, and after it rounded the narrow corner of the harbor, a series of concrete drainage gutters and what looked like giant chains formed wheel-chair roadblocks. Back at the boat, the commodore of the yacht club awaited us. "I assume you've organized going to Globe wall," he said. "It's time to move on." Granted, Pete and I didn't look like we might spend money at the restaurant and bar, but an attempt at subtlety would have been nice.

You couldn't get much farther away than Globe wall; we were practically banished from the kingdom. Still, although the yacht club's members might have been snooty, its employees weren't. The club launch towed us over (Pete had removed the tiller and was working on the engine). The club handyman kindly scrounged up a boarding ramp, which Pete outfitted with wheels so that it wouldn't scrape on the deck when *Usikusiku* moved around.

At high tide we pushed across—a bit nerve-racking, as the ramp was barely wider than our chairs—to reconnoiter. Turning left was out of the question because the wall dropped to a lower level, with five concrete steps leading down. That meant we had no choice but to run the obstacle course to the right. The drainage gutters were just over a foot across and about four inches deep, and the soil along the edges had eroded away from the concrete, leaving ruts on either side. We had to take them at an angle, in slow motion. Alternating with the gutters were those enormous chains, anchored in the ground and draped over the wall for boats to tie onto. As usual, Pete and I challenged each other until we became expert at negotiating the course. In places, going over the chains put our chairs at a horrific angle and in danger of going off the wall, which had a nine-foot drop. If anyone was with us, we had them walk ahead because they generally had heart failure if they watched from behind.

Staying on Globe wall did have some advantages, like getting water and power from the workshop in the Globe building. Plugging in meant we could use our power tools and keep our batteries on a trickle charge without running the engine every day. Getting water wasn't so easy, at least at first. One of the workers pulled our hose through a window and connected it, but by the time I got back on board, someone had chucked it out the window. I went over again, and it was thrown out again.

All this getting on and off the boat eventually made me mad. I wheeled across the gangplank, did the dance over the chains and gullies, rounded the far end of the Globe building, and went up the road to the workshop's front entrance. I burst inside. The place ground to a halt because a woman, particularly one in a wheelchair, didn't fit into the surroundings. But I was a woman on a mission. I found the manager who said previous yachties had spoiled it for everyone else by filling up their tanks and tossing the hose back ashore without turning off the water. I explained that if we couldn't get water here, we'd have to transport it on our laps, in heavy containers, all the way from the yacht club. I promised that it would always be turned off when we weren't using it. The manager apologized, spoke with the workmen, and after that all I had to do was whistle for the water to come on.

For my first large project I tackled the wheelhouse, which was going to become a plain old deckhouse. On the port side I made a bunk, with a leeboard, about six inches off the deck. On the starboard side I removed the wheel, compass, and engine controls to make room for a dry gear locker for books, charts, sweaters, and so on; this would reduce trips below while we were at sea. I built a second chart table and a wet locker for foul-weather clothing and installed a second bilge pump that was larger than the one under our bunk. Then I moved the VHF, SumLog, and depth-finder up from down below.

While I got on with all that, Pete went into thinking mode. All during our trip from Durban he'd been formulating a way to make not only *Usikusiku*'s headsail roller-furling, but her mainsail as well. This concept was so new that he hadn't seen any boat with such a system. He knew it existed, but those masts had a built-in slot that held the rolled-up sail. Pete decided to make ours externally roller-furled, with drums on the bottom and swivels at the top.

When are you leaving? is a question frequently asked of yachties. It was a question Pete and I began to dread. Initially, we thought we'd need six to eight weeks to make our changes, but we came to realize what an unrealistic time frame that was. Even though we worked like demons so that Val would see real progress when he sailed in on *Unibrass Brython of Milford*, our long job list hadn't shortened much when he arrived.

Val helped us sort through it because we'd added to it so many times that it badly needed organizing. The three of us brainstormed, aiming for ideas that would solve two or three problems at once, and formulated a master plan for the cockpit, since so many aspects of it needed changing. We also spent countless hours chewing through various options for the sails and rigging. We ultimately ended up with a formal game plan that we submitted to the Royal Cape Yacht Club's Safety Committee for approval.

Our biggest stumbling block was a lack of money for materials. Val had put the word out that we were seeking sponsors, so when he got a message to phone someone, I got excited. Maybe this was it. The "someone" wasn't exactly a sponsor, however. And it turned out to be two someones. Max Leigh was one of the top journalists for the *Argus*, a Cape Town newspaper. Peter Willis was some sort of businessman (he never gave us details). They suggested starting up a fund. Peter would organize it and see that everything was legal; Max would write articles to publicize our cause. Pete and I shuddered at the idea of a fund—it seemed too much like charity—but couldn't afford to turn down any offer. Besides, Peter and Max so enthusiastically wanted to help.

Back in Durban, Val had taken steps to get us unhooked from Duffy. He'd spoken with a friend who had a friend who was a lawyer, and that wonderful man, whom we never met, took our case without charging us. When Duffy ignored all his correspondence, that apparently nullified the contract. We regretted separating from Duffy on a bad note, when he'd been such a morale booster our first few months in Durban, but were relieved to get on with publicity that would benefit our cause.

Max treated us kindly in his column called "Talk at the Tavern of the Seas," using as his byline "The Wanderer." He wrote, "Although I have seen what the sea can do, I am convinced that Peter and Liz should be allowed to do their thing." "That's why I have no hesitation in appealing for support for the trust fund which is being created for them." That initial publicity garnered 280 rand.

We also, from the day we arrived in Cape Town until the day we left, received a 10-rand check every month from a Durban woman we had never met. Another person, who asked to remain anonymous, donated a gold Krugerrand, worth 260 rand at the time and a lot more when the price of gold later skyrocketed. Pete and I decided to keep it as a talisman, however, and vowed not to sell it unless we reached the verge of starvation.

Although every little bit helped, the donations soon stopped. We reckoned we needed 8,000 rand to finish the boat, 2,000 to finish paying off the sails and other gear, and 200 for Del, the chandler owner in Durban. The sail company was allowing us to pay as we could, but we felt we really must settle with Del. Unbelievably, Peter

Willis sent him a check. Now we were short only 10,000 rand (more than US $10,000).

Ultimately, Pete and I had to admit that the sponsorship idea was a dead loss. Through the newspapers and the yacht club, all of Cape Town must have known how badly we needed financial backing, but every lead petered out. It was understandable, I guess, because the consensus was that we'd go out and sink—which wouldn't exactly be good for a company's public image. OK, we'd do it on our own, even if that meant putting off our departure for a year. In a way we were relieved to reach that conclusion, because now we'd have the time to plan carefully, build properly, and organize ourselves thoroughly. Our lives depended on it.

Usikusiku was still an untidy mess, more workshop than home. In such a small space it didn't take long to cover every surface with tools and pieces of various projects. Not only was the boat cluttered, but we were moored just 100 yards from the corner of the harbor where all the filth and oil collected. At low tide the smell was revolting. Whenever we had visitors I felt slightly ashamed of our unglamorous existence and wished we could afford carpet and cushions to smarten up the interior. Pete's mom chose this messiest of times to spend a couple of days with us to reassure herself we were all right. She loved having an excuse to visit Cape Town, where she'd grown up, but she certainly couldn't have been impressed by my housekeeping.

In March, Mom and my cousin Val came to visit. During the weeks leading up to their arrival I could hardly bear the excitement. Mom was making her first-ever visit to Pete's and my home! I cleaned and cleaned, working myself into a frenzy to make everything right. If we couldn't offer islands or palm trees, just a smelly, dirty harbor, she wouldn't mind; she knew we'd get there someday. All she wanted for now was to make sure her kids were OK.

At last she arrived, and I couldn't get enough of her. I could hug her whenever I wanted! Best of all, I could be mothered a bit. Mom and Val had always been a dynamic duo, and they now lightened up our too-serious lives, filling our home with fun and laughter. As a bonus, since this was a new calendar year, they had managed to get Pete's and my annual holiday allowance from our Salisbury bank account. That gave us some badly needed cash.

Pete and I felt empty after they left. *Usikusiku*, without their jokes and nonsense, wallowed in silence. Then it was Val Howells's time to go, too, another sad parting. Pete and I needed supporters, and Val was one of our biggest. At yacht clubs and at pubs frequented by yachties he'd acted as a buffer by going in our stead and replacing gossip with facts, offering frank opinions about what we could and couldn't do but always standing up for us. People listened to him because he wasn't an armchair sailor, like many of those who seemingly had nothing better to do than talk about how foolish we were.

I was especially grateful for what he said when he was quoted in Max Leigh's column: "One cannot write these people off. Even after 36 years at sea, I am not qualified to say they cannot do what they want to do merely because nobody else has done it before. I don't believe anybody else is qualified to say so either. And when they have done what they set out to do—not if—the motivation, encouragement and inspiration they will have given others who have to overcome disabilities will be beyond price."

As usual, Pete and I dealt with our homesickness by burying ourselves in work. The cockpit was a big job that wouldn't cost much, so I got stuck with that. I lowered the existing seats and added another one athwartships for the helmsperson. When Pete had finished turning all six drums for the roller-furling, he decided that the engine gauges, as well as the switches for the deck and running lights, should be near the helm, so he rewired everything to come up through the deck and to a Plexiglas-covered panel he built into the cockpit coaming.

This massive project entailed removing the aft cabin deckhead to get at the wiring, so upon its completion he rewarded himself with something he'd really looked forward to making: the steering pedestal/compass binnacle. Someone had given him a large gun shell casing which he bolted to the deck and topped with the compass. He was so chuffed with his creation that he got out the sewing machine and stitched up a waterproof cover for it.

Next came the wheel, but how could he make it? When the Globe worker who had caused the trouble about the water came by one day for a chat, I casually asked him where we could get some stainless steel tubing rolled into a wheel. He offered to get the Globe tube shop to make it up. Pete gave him a drawing and the measurements, and the chap later returned with a perfect hoop. Pete welded spokes from that to a center hub and had his steering wheel, which he mounted to the shell casing. He also made the gears, quadrant, and other parts for the new steering system. I'd certainly married a clever chap.

The rigging was his most complicated task. The idea was to control everything from the cockpit, with all possible lines leading aft. In addition to roller-furling, he wanted to change *Usikusiku* from a sloop to a cutter. This meant the headsails could be smaller and thus easier to manage and also would give us a staysail we could use as a storm sail. Such a change wasn't simple: he had to reinforce the mast by adding an inner forestay, and make a boom and the fittings to put everything together.

He always seemed to be at his lathe these days or cutting stainless steel plate by hand with a hacksaw. He managed the long-term loan of a welding machine, a godsend because he could weld as he went along. When he ran out of plate he'd push for miles and miles on all-day excursions through the city and on to industrial areas such as Woodstock or even Paarden Eiland to scrounge around the scrapyards for more. It was worth the time and effort because for only 20 or 30 rand he could get as much stainless steel as he could carry, usually 50 or 60 pounds. Long pieces he balanced on his lap; smaller bits he packed into a huge bag that hung on the back of his chair—it's a wonder it didn't tip him over. I carried groceries the same way. We usually didn't feel the extra weight, but if we did, there wasn't much we could do about it.

When Pete was involved with a project he liked to be undisturbed, but with a wife like me he hadn't a chance. I was always wanting to know what he was making and how it was going to work. This drove him crazy, but I loved learning and putting in my two cents' worth. I sometimes disagreed with his theory, which stunned him at first because no one had ever questioned him before. We got into some pretty fiery discussions on the how-tos of everything. Eventually he got used to me and ended up giving extremely detailed explanations so that I understood what was happening. As time went on, this worked to our mutual advantage: for me because I gained an understanding of what could be done and how, and for Pete because he had someone to toss ideas around with.

On most nights we packed up around 9:00 P.M. and bumped along to the Royal Cape Yacht Club, where Val had pulled strings to get us temporary memberships. If the tide was out, the ramp could have as much as a 65-degree incline, in which case Pete would get out of his chair and go up backward on his bottom, taking one end of a rope with him. I'd tie my end onto the footplates of his wheelchair and he'd pull it up, then toss the rope down for mine (he had made raised edges on the ramp to keep the chairs from rolling off). Then it was my turn. But with the ramp this steep, I'd soon be in a temper of frustration because Pete could get up and I couldn't; I just seemed to slide down.

We came up with a system whereby I tied the rope around my waist so Pete could keep enough tension on me to stop the backsliding, and we generally ended up laughing our heads off at the absurdity of it all. Low tide did have one advantage: the tougher it was getting up, the more fun it was going back down—we were like kids at a playground trying to outdo each other on the slide.

Pete would have kittens at how fast I slid, then he'd shoot down even faster. Amazingly, we didn't get splinters, at least I never looked for any.

As much as we needed that boarding ramp, Pete hated that its wheels squeaked from the constant rain. Oiling them seemed to bring on more rain, so we let the squeak go until we couldn't stand it any longer. Sometimes a wheel popped off in the middle of the night, and then the ramp would scrape across the deck, sounding as if it was tearing the boat apart, until one of us got up and put the wheel back on.

Another thing that kept Pete awake—I could sleep through anything except the scraping ramp—was that floating bottles or bits of wood often squeezed their way in between *Usikusiku* and the trot (the floating dock between us and the wall) and bumped incessantly against our hull. An able-bodied person could have hopped down and lifted the offender out, but for us it was a major effort. Getting dressed was a pain, too, so if it was late enough that no one was around, Pete would sit on deck in his birthday suit to fish a "whatever" out of the water with a pole.

One morning I spotted a 44-gallon drum on the trot and asked Pete if he knew how it got there. It was banging on the hull, he said, and while I "slept my head off," he put it there. The fact that I could sleep through just about anything worried me because Pete was something of an acrobat, and I was afraid he might fall over the side while I slept. Mind you, he probably would have found a way up. I still can't figure how he lifted that drum out.

Winter arrived, bringing gale after gale. I hated the cold, and most of all I hated the swell that worked its way into the harbor when the wind came from the northwest and blew unimpeded across Table Bay. In May we had a record storm that closed the harbor and sank a cargo ship off Muizenberg, on the other side of the Cape peninsula. Waves worked their way into the inner harbor and broke right over our obstacle course. *Usikusiku* bucked and yanked against her warps—seasick in the harbor, now that was a new experience!

A neglected steel boat behind us broke three of her warps and threatened to bash down upon us. Pete went over there—a long process that meant getting out extra ropes, crossing our wildly weaving boarding ramp, getting out of his chair at the five concrete steps, lowering his chair over the side of the steps and then climbing down into it, lassoing cleats and bollards on the wayward boat and tying her up, then getting back up the steps and boarding *Usikusiku* again. Whew!

As soon as that storm ended, we had one from the other direction. All it did these days was rain and blow like hell. How did people live here all their lives? It drove me insane after the calm weather of Rhodesia. One evening when we went off to the yacht club to shower, a typical Cape Town gale was blowing. Why we were going was a good question. It was bloody cold, and pushing against the wind was going to be a pain, so why not just stay on board, even if we were filthy from the day's work? That was my idea. Pete's was to go anyway because it was Friday, movie night, so off we went.

I had taken the lead when I heard a splash and looked around. No Pete. I peered over the edge of the seawall and saw, dimly lit by the lights on shore, a couple of chair handles and a head sticking out of the water. This appealed to my sense of humor, and I couldn't stop laughing, especially when Pete tried to cover his blunder by blaming it on his chair, which he said had "stumbled."

The area was deserted, so I went back and shouted for Sue on *Yemanja*. She brought me a rope, then ran to fetch some of the men working a late shift in the Globe workshop. Meanwhile, I threw one end of the rope down to Pete, who tied it to his chair. Then he swam to the trot, fighting against his spasm and weighed down by a thick white sweater that now was sodden with water and the harbor's perpetual oil slick.

The water was about 55° Fahrenheit, so we had to get him out quickly. Sue returned with three or four men, who pulled Pete up onto the trot. He was shivering violently and his legs were wild with spasm.

"Stand up," one of the chaps said.

"I can't," replied Pete. Well, that set off a panic, and they wanted to call an ambulance until Pete explained *why* he couldn't stand. He was so cold his spasm wouldn't stop, so they loaded him into a van, tossed his chair in the back, and rushed him to the yacht club, where he rolled straight into the showers, clothes and all, and sat under a spray of hot water for a very long time.

While he was there, a couple of members wandered into the men's room took one look at the kook in a wheelchair, showering with his clothes on while his legs kicked at everything in sight, and promptly left. This couldn't have enhanced the "paraplegics really do have intelligence" image we were striving for; rather, it surely bolstered the "crazy cripples and scruffy to boot" image we already had at the Royal Cape Yacht Club.

We made many friends during our stay in Cape Town. Particularly special were Paddy and Mike Briant, who were building a ferrocement junk in their backyard to replace the wooden one they'd cruised on for years. Mike had been an officer in the merchant navy and was currently marine manager of a trawling company, so his knowledge was extensive. Pete loved having someone to brainstorm with, and Mike was a perfect fit. Paddy and Mike sometimes took us home with them for dinner, a drastic change from our usual canned corned beef or whatever was cheap and quick to prepare. Except for the bread we bought at a little kiosk around the corner, we spent little money on food.

Max Leigh continued his good press coverage; in addition, he and his wife Charlene had us over and once took us to the theater. Peter Willis continued to be wonderfully thoughtful, periodically turning up with groceries and other goodies, much like a Cape Town version of Tassos. On one occasion when he stopped by to see whether I needed anything from the supermarket, I mentioned three items; imagine my astonishment when twelve bags were delivered. Peter was as kind as he was generous, with a sense of humor as warped as mine.

Mike and Bev, our neighbors on *Cirrus*, dispensed invaluable knowledge and were generous with their time whenever we needed a hand. When Mike took a navigation course, he photocopied all the written material for me and gave me a mini-version of the course. Lionel, who ran a workshop at the end of the basin where all the trash washed up, took an interest in *Usikusiku* and often brought bits of stainless plate when he dropped by for a cup of coffee. People stopped by so often for coffee that *Usikusiku* could have been renamed the *Coffee Stop*.

When I had finished my major projects, most of the remaining work required Pete's skills rather than mine, so it seemed logical to let him carry on with the boat while I brought in some money to pay off our debts. A regular job would be a shock to my system, but what must be must be, I told myself. I answered an ad for a receptionist and was invited to come in for an interview. I set off so full of enthusiasm that the five steps at the building's entrance, steps I'd have to negotiate twice daily if I got hired, didn't faze me; I could work that out later. In the meantime, I accosted an unfortunate passerby to get me up the stairs.

The interview went well; I persuaded the manager that I was exactly what he wanted, wheelchair and all. Then I asked about the loos—and everything screeched to a halt because they were down a hallway and up several steps. The women in the office said they'd help me whenever I needed to go—an incredibly kind offer—but I knew the novelty would wear off, especially when they found out how often I went. What wonderful people they all were, though, and what a great place to work that would have been.

I don't know whether it was my wheelchair that made people uncomfortable or the misconception that paraplegia is caused by a head injury rather than a spinal injury. Whatever it was, given the usual reaction, it took a lot of courage for me to wheel into every employment agency in Cape Town. I had few qualifications and just one reference, from Saint Giles Rehabilitation Centre. *I* knew I was a conscientious, hard worker, but my prospective employers didn't, so I'd have to bluster my way in.

Every agent I met with wanted to know how I'd get to work. Well, I'd pushed in today without trouble, hadn't I? But any job I took had to be in town, since I couldn't get onto trains or buses. A few agents refused to deal with me at all. I didn't have a work permit, they said, and getting one would be a big problem. Max got me the necessary forms, however, and I submitted them to the Department of Internal Affairs, hoping the paperwork would be sorted out by the time any interviews came up.

During the month that passed before I heard from any agents, I had a stroke of good luck. I'd had an article accepted by *Boote*, a German yachting magazine, and the editor said that if the check went to South Africa, as I'd requested, rather than to Rhodesia, I'd need an income tax number. I paid a visit to the tax office. No problem, they said, here's a tax number. Just like that, I was legal. Sort of. Enough to feel confident when one of the employment agencies contacted me about Buirski, Herbstein and Ipp, a prestigious Cape Town law firm looking for a three-month temp. Nothing like lawyers to sort out any problems that might crop up! What they needed, however, was a computer-literate bookkeeper, and what I knew about either bookkeeping or computers was only enough to be dangerous. Still, I agreed to an interview.

After a year and a half of living in paint-spattered jeans, it felt weird to dress semi-smart again. I set out early, unsure how long it would take to push to the law firm, and arrived before the appointment time. I went to investigate the loos. They were on the fifth floor, whereas the firm's offices were on the ground floor and the ninth, but to my relief they were wheelchair-accessible (as long as the elevator didn't hold me up). Moreover, I must have used my best bluster: the interview went well and the office manager asked if I could start then and there.

I was nervous, very nervous, because everything I was supposed to do was all new to me, and after only a month of training I was to take over on the Audit 6 computer while the regular bookkeeper went on vacation for two months. It all looked pretty complicated, but I made it through the day, then pushed home and told Pete we were in the money again.

Doing something constructive about our lack of money gave us a sense of control over our lives again. But even with me bringing home a salary and Pete working on *Usikusiku* full time, the realization slowly sank in that we couldn't finish the boat and pay off all our debts by the end of the year. Now, when the inevitable *When are you leaving?* came up, we swallowed our pride and answered, *Next year.* The resulting looks said, *You'll never leave.* The port was full of people who had been "leaving" for five or ten years and are probably still there. Pete and I definitely were not going to be in that category. We *had* to finish next year, for our own morale if nothing else.

Light at the End

THE HARDEST PART OF MY NEW JOB turned out to be getting off *Usikusiku* in the morning. Fortunately, a few men walked along the seawall around 7:00 A.M., taking a shortcut to their jobs, I think, and whoever was unfortunate enough to pass by got drafted into giving me a hand up. No one seemed to mind; at least I never saw anyone sprint off when they saw me waiting on deck.

The two and a half miles from the yacht basin to the top of Queen Victoria Street took me an average of forty-five minutes—the first fifteen through the obstacle course and around to the yacht club. There I picked up the road coming from the commercial docks, which had asphalt shoulders as far as the customs gate, but when I turned onto the main road I became just another vehicle in the rush-hour traffic. A half-mile farther on, where the shops began, were proper sidewalks, but between the curbs and the foot traffic, it was easier to stay in the street most of the time. In 1979 nothing in Cape Town was yet wheelchair-accessible.

If a sou'easter was blowing, I'd see how fast I could get my "crate" to go. My record commuting time was thirty minutes, and I was tempted to see how many minutes I could shave off by putting up a sail. Cape Town gales are notorious. The wind gauge in the yacht club sometimes showed a steady 40 to 50 knots, with gusts up to 60. Three or four people a year were killed or injured by being blown off the sidewalk and into the road.

Going downwind in a wheelchair could be hazardous; one time I couldn't stop until I directed my skidding chair into a wall. Moreover, downwind in the morning meant upwind in the evening, and often it would be absolutely howling when I set off for home. The last mile was hell. Sand pelted my face, and after every push forward my chair stopped dead when I let go of the wheels to grab for another push. I was like a cruising boat; I didn't go well to windward.

For the most part, though, I enjoyed the exercise, especially in the fresh, early mornings when I wheeled "beneath the moody grandeur of Table Mountain," as Jan Riebeeck had phrased it when he landed a party of sixty settlers in 1647. Sometimes I fantasized about climbing this imposing monolith and exploring her forests. Then I'd shake myself out of my reverie. What in hell was I thinking about?

Pushing eventually became so monotonous that I took to reading on the way, much to Pete's horror. I assured him that I read for only the first mile, quitting when I reached town. I tied a string around my legs, pinned the book underneath, and used clothespins to keep the pages from flapping. It was great to be able to read again, something I hadn't had time for since we'd starting building the boat. I felt a real banana, though, when I had to back out from under an enormous semi parked on the side of the road—the book must have been exciting because I'd gone straight under. Another time, I noticed to my embarrassment that I had a curb running between my wheels. I had to back up about six feet to get clear, while three old African men shook their heads in pity. One day I crashed into the back of a taxi. This happened right in front of the customs building, and the officials didn't know whether to laugh or hide. Once again I was failing to promote our "people-in-wheelchairs-have-intact-mental-capacities" message.

Because I worked straight through the lunch hour, I was able to leave the office at 4:00 P.M. When I got home, I cooked dinner, washed dishes, hand-washed the laundry in a tub on deck, hung it on the railings to dry, and then got down to work on the boat. One horrible job was making a wooden grate for the cockpit floor. You could get these prefabricated, but we couldn't afford that, so I made one myself—a dreadful, fussy job that required notching each strip for all the cross strips. I wouldn't care to make another.

Pete made new steel winch plates that bolted to the deck outside the cockpit, configuring them to house the propane bottles and plumbing the gas down to the galley. Because the one diesel tank had ruptured during our trip from Durban, we couldn't trust the other or the three water tanks, so we had five new ones made out of mild steel and then galvanized. Swapping them over was a real pain because we'd installed the originals into a bare hull and built the interior over and around them. Now one diesel tank was under the lift hydraulics and our bed. The other was under the shower and toilet. Pete also made a day tank for the engine that held about a gallon of diesel and had filters and a water trap. He never again wanted to suck on a fuel line at sea.

We tried to figure a way of getting home that Christmas, but the cost and time involved were prohibitive, since the cheaper modes of transportation such as the bus weren't available to us. So once again we prepared to celebrate away from home and family. Pete requested that instead of the usual clothing I give him a knife he could clip on his belt when we went sailing. I found him a super one with all kinds of tools on it. I also got him a wrench to replace one missing from his set, plus a new set of instrument screwdrivers and plenty of candy for his stocking. Knowing how curious he was, I kept everything at the office—a good thing, because he later confessed he'd searched the boat, trying to find out what I'd gotten him. Sneaky chap. Since I kept track of our every penny, he tried to earn money on the quiet so I wouldn't know how much he spent on me. I found out about these odd jobs, one of which, by coincidence, was making a new masthead fitting for *Galway Blazer*, the boat Blondie Hasler had sailed in the OSTAR against Val Howells and Sir Francis Chichester.

In February 1980 we won a sheep. The Protea Sports Club and six other clubs for sportsmen with disabilities were given twenty sheep to be raffled off in their annual fund-raising event. Someone bought a ticket in our name and it was picked, along with one bought in Protea's name. Peter Willis came up with the idea of increasing our winnings by spit-roasting the two and throwing a party, then splitting the earnings. We organized a wild sheep *braai* that included a cash bar, an auction of donated items, and a few raffles. Protea gave us all of the proceeds from the party, rather than just our half, and we ended up with better than 200 rand. Although I still wasn't used to accepting charity, having the moral support of so many people was wonderful.

February also saw the climax of extreme political change back home. After two decades of fruitless negotiations, fifteen years of worldwide sanctions, and civil conflicts that generated more than a million refugees, Ian Smith's government had finally capitulated. In 1978 Smith reached an accord with the nonviolent African nationalist leaders. A transitional government took over, and then-Bishop Muzorewa was voted into power in Rhodesia's first democratic election. But because the bush war then escalated rather than ended, the new government wasn't recognized and sanctions weren't lifted. Britain pressed for new elections. Just about the time we were having our sheep roast, Robert Mugabe became the first prime minister of independent Zimbabwe. Rhodesia, a country established during my great-grandparents' lifetimes, ceased to exist during mine.

Half the white population would leave Zimbabwe by 1987, taking with them an abundance of skills, expertise, professionalism, and money. Pete and I worried terribly about our families during our two and a half years in South Africa. Were they safe? Would their businesses continue to operate? Were their investments sound? Would they stay or leave? My brother-in-law, Ian, had been well off, but during the transition he and Joan lost everything they had. With two children in tow they moved to South Africa to begin again from scratch. Other friends and family were staying put for the time being. After all, it was their country too.

An unexpected effect of all this upheaval was that the $12,000 deposit required to guarantee *Usikusiku*'s return fell away when the government changed hands. When we learned of this sometime later, it took an enormous load off our minds. If the political situation became such that Pete and I were better off not returning, at least we wouldn't be punished financially.

When I'd started work at Buirski, Herbstein and Ipp, the woman I was subbing for had been way behind on the computer entries. Once I learned the system, I got everything up to date. I also became friends with Mr. Buirski, and when my three-month contract came to an end, he asked me to stay on. I figured that if Pete and I kept up the same monthly payments on our debts for another year, we'd have cleared the decks. We lived as cheaply as possible and I saved whatever I could, making sure we had enough material to keep us going until each coming payday. Pete, as usual, left the finances to me. I just kept him posted, especially if I could give him a boost by telling him that Scrooge here had saved a little boodle.

As April turned to May, we dreaded the approach of a second Cape Town winter. Thank goodness it was going to be the last. It had to be! Pushing to work under the moon and stars was a new experience because at home, a thousand miles farther north, the hours of daylight didn't change appreciably with the seasons. And there was that the freezing wind again—oh, for some of our beautiful Rhodesian weather! At night we worked as close as possible to the heater Paddy had given us. Then, because Pete didn't come to bed until around 2:00 A.M. and I couldn't wait that long for him to warm me up, I preheated our bed with my hair dryer.

At least my morning commute had gotten easier. After Pete put railings on the ramp, I found that, except at low tide, I could get myself up and down without assistance and without getting out of my chair. Then a man named Bernard started picking me up somewhere along the way and driving me to the office almost every morning. It was marvelous to get there warm and dry! When I first met him, Bernard told me he was an accountant for the Cape Gas Company, but I later learned he was the financial director. Sometimes someone gave me a ride home as well. On one memorable occasion the commodore of the Royal Cape Yacht Club stopped and offered to give my shopping a lift. I told him he could do the same for me. He was flabbergasted by my impertinence, but I got the lift, which was the main thing.

I'd become a familiar sight as I pushed through the streets of Cape Town, and traveling along the same route every day, I often saw the same people. Eventually I developed a set of regulars who greeted me and helped me up particularly high curbs. And it made the papers when a rough-looking man followed me and Adderley Street's taxi drivers guided me home like a school of concerned dolphins.

Many people—on the street, at work, and in stores where I shopped—were curious enough to inquire about what we were doing. Most stared in disbelief when they heard our plan. Some asked unbelievably inane questions. The most common was, "How will you go up the mast?"

"The same as everybody else does," I'd answer. "I'll winch Pete up in the bosun's chair."

"What happens if the engine stops?"

"Well, seeing as Pete is good with engines, that shouldn't be a problem. Besides, we're a sailboat."

"What will you do if the boat is sinking?"

"You don't need legs in a life raft." Honestly, sometimes I could have screamed. There was such a lack of awareness in South Africa about the capabilities of wheelchair-bound paraplegics; in fact, I don't think most people had seen any. I never did, which made me wonder where they all hid.

When people showed a genuine interest in us, I didn't mind conversing with them, but when they were ignorant and intrusive, I could be blunt to the point of rudeness. Once, as I waited at a corner for the light to change, a car screeched to a halt, blocking the cars behind it. The driver jumped out and ran into the inter- section, waving his arms to stop the five-o'clock traffic. Brakes squealed and horns blew. The man rushed over and tried to usher me across the road.

"Get lost," I said, mortified by suddenly finding myself the main attraction in this disturbance, but no, across the road we went. Unable to tolerate being pushed about even at the best of times, I lost my temper. "You're an ignorant peasant!" I steamed. "You've needlessly embarrassed me. If I'd needed help I could have asked any one of the people standing next to me." I'm not proud of that outburst, but I simply could not abide that degree of insensitivity. If something like that happened to a new para- plegic making a first solo visit to town, it could keep him or her home for life.

After I'd been in the Cape Town work force for a while, I devel- oped more confidence about being an oddity in public and could better tolerate these encounters, looking for the humor in them instead of spouting off. For instance, I could manage one or two steps on my own by tipping back onto my rear wheels and easing myself down, but to onlookers I seemed about to tip over backward. When frail old men or women came rushing to the rescue, I found it hard not to laugh. What did they think they could do?

One elderly man who worked in my building gave me nightmares at the elevators. Whenever he saw me approaching, he rushed ahead and held the doors open by standing between them with outspread arms. I wasn't sure just which way he wanted me to go, over him or under him. After missing many a ride up, we came to the understanding that he'd move out of my way and maybe even allow me to push the button for my floor. He was such a sweet old guy that I couldn't get mad at him, only frustrated.

I did need help getting up a particularly high step, and since people have diverse ideas about how you get a wheelchair up a step, the results could be awfully funny—or dangerous. Some think you push on the back wheels. Others think it requires two people, one to lift the front and the other to lift the back. A few will ram you up against the curb and nearly tip you over. Pete once asked a passerby to help him down a flight of stairs in front of a building. "Sure thing," the man replied, and pushed him straight down the steps. Pete managed to hang on until the chair hit bottom, at which time he splatted onto the sidewalk. Fortunately he got only bruises and a cut lip from his encounter with the pavement.

One time when Pete and I were heading out and couldn't get up the ramp without getting out of our chairs and dirtying our good clothes, I hailed the first man who came by. "Can you give us a hand?" I asked.

"Um—ah—" He seemed to be hunting for words.

"It won't take long and it's quite simple," I said. People sometimes needed persuading.

Pete shot me a look I couldn't fathom. "Never mind," he said to the man. "We'll wait for someone else."

"Come on, you can give us a hand," I chided, wondering why Pete wasn't backing me up.

"I can try," the man said, "but one is all I have."

Pete had noticed he was one-armed but I hadn't and was mortified by my blunder until the man began to laugh. Pete joined in and so, ultimately, did I; the three of us had a good old howl. Then the man went on his way while Pete and I waited for a two-armed person to happen by.

At the yacht club Pete met Ken and Molly Warr, both professional yachties (Molly had skippered the first all-female crew in a Cape Town to Rio race). They invited Pete on an overnight sail with them to Saldanha Bay to get more experience. It was difficult for him to do much, and he couldn't go below at all, but he learned a lot by observing. That someone from the yacht club was willing to see if Pete could survive on a boat represented a real breakthrough. A couple of times he also sailed with our friends on *La Niña*. I went along once, but since I couldn't get below to use the loo and couldn't pee over the side like Pete, I didn't repeat the experience.

Work continued aboard *Usikusiku*. One piece of equipment we absolutely had to have was a self-steering apparatus to relieve us from helming every minute of the day, but, as with most marine gear, buying one was out of the question. Pete studied every one he saw until he found the design he thought would work best on our boat. He made a replica, with its own rudder and a trim tab activated by a wind vane.

When Lionel hired a crane for a job he was overseeing, he asked the driver to pull our mast. Pete riveted on the parts he'd made for the furling gear, the tracks and slides for the running poles, and handholds so he'd be able to take some of the weight whenever I winched him up in the bosun's chair. His arms ached after all that riveting, and his body took a beating from negotiating the steps from the upper part of Globe wall to the lower, where the mast lay across sawhorses. Then he wound up having to sand and paint the mast twice because the first time, it rained before the paint was dry. When we stepped the mast again, though, *Usikusiku* looked really smart. Our sails were ready, too. Our old No. 1 headsail had been demoted to No. 2, outranked by a larger headsail we bought secondhand. A sailmaker recut both for roller furling, enabling us to have twin poled-out sails for downwind work. After I paid the huge bill for having the wire cable put in the first headsail, I decided to do the other one and the mainsail myself. First I sewed canvas sleeves around the stainless steel wire, and then I hand-basted the sleeves into each luff. I don't think my little hand-cranked Singer appreciated the abuse, nor did my fingers. For a nominal fee I found someone with an industrial machine to do the final stitching.

By October the main jobs were finished, and for the first time we saw a glimmer of light at the end of our four-year tunnel of labor. Pete began looking for work to help build our travel fund. When a shop near us advertised for electricians, he pushed over to put in his application, but the foreman asked to see his union card, which of course he didn't have. The union man was coming around the following day, the foreman said, and he'd send him over to the boat. No one showed up, so Pete took his qualification papers directly to the union offices, got himself a union card, and returned to the shop. But now the shop foreman said there were no vacancies! That hurt. We'd heard through the grapevine that there *were* openings, some for bench jobs Pete could easily have done. It was amazing how formidable a wheelchair was to some people.

I began phoning instrument workshops. When one turned out to be affiliated with the workshop Pete had managed back home, someone who knew the owner and had read about Pete in the newspapers came by the boat to offer him a job. The following Monday Pete took off in the opposite direction to mine. He returned angry and humiliated because, despite his qualifications and experience, he'd been put on an assembly line. Would they have given him such a degrading job if he'd been able-bodied? Still, he stuck it out because we needed the money. With his first paycheck, however, came another shock. Too shy to ask about money, Pete had assumed his wages would be comparable to what he'd made at home, but what they gave him for a month's work wouldn't even buy the new tires he needed after wheeling so many miles. He gave his notice, reckoning that if he did odd jobs for the international sailors who were arriving to prepare for their transatlantics, he'd make better money and still have time to finish up his projects on our boat.

It was time to haul *Usikusiku*. To lend us a hand we recruited Lionel, Mike, and Bev from *Cirrus*, and Reg and Maggie McCullogh, fellow Rhodesians from a boat down the way. We expected to see weeds hanging to the ground, but even after nearly two years of sitting at the dock, the bottom growth was minimal (the water in our corner of the harbor was probably too polluted to encourage growth). But the original epoxy we'd used to fair out the hull had blistered badly below the waterline. Mike Briant rented an industrial grinder. Willing to go any distance for something that was free, I pushed for miles to borrow another two. The following day Mike Briant, Pete, three African laborers, and I worked like mad to get rid of as many blisters as possible.

The third and last day we had on the slip was a Monday. I had taken vacation time, but Mike Briant had to go back to work, and Pete was in the middle of a project on another boat, which left me on my own to organize the painting. It was a rush job, and the topsides could have used a second coat, but *Usikusiku* looked good when Lionel came to help with the launching. Of course, a howling sou'easter had sprung up to give us a little trouble getting out of the cradle, but we eventually extricated ourselves and made it back to the jetty, where Pete was waiting to take our lines.

Now for the interior. The following weekend, when we both were off work, I scrubbed out the bilges while Pete roared through the boat turfing out junk. Before long, *Usikusiku* gleamed, inside and out. It was time to go sailing.

USIKU

LEFT: *OK, Pete. Stop playing footsy and let me down.* RIGHT (TOP): *In the Durban yard, the scissors lift was a terrific improvement over the tire; now the challenge was getting from the platform to my chair.* RIGHT (BOTTOM): *Pete was at my mercy when I lowered him over the transom to work on the self-steering rudder; we also performed this exercise mid-Atlantic.*

ABOVE: *Usikusiku's foredeck, showing the route through the deckhouse to the cockpit.* LEFT: *The appearance of Pete's pipe signified a successful sea trial in Cape Town.*

D-Day

FOR OUR FIRST SEA TRIAL in Cape Town we invited a crowd. Although Mike Briant was the official skipper, he and our other guests came along as passengers, not crew. The idea was for Pete and me to do everything ourselves. We'd planned every move in advance because with one boat docked behind us and two abreast in front of us, we needed to be well organized when leaving from and returning to Globe wall. Pete was stronger and more agile than I, so he would handle the forward lines and push off any boats, docks, or walls that might decide to get in the way. I would take the wheel. We had often seen couples doing the reverse: he at the helm because he was the "captain," the old girl trying to fend off as he roared toward the dock at full speed, hit reverse a bit too late, then yelled at her for screwing up. They just didn't seem to have the right idea.

I put the engine in forward and gave it a little gas, keeping tension on the stern line until the bow swung out. Then I slipped the line, at whose end we'd spliced an eye; we'd pick it up with the boathook when we returned. Pete had a better view from the foredeck than I had from the cockpit, so he directed me when to turn and how much power to use. He faced me when he spoke and reinforced his directions with hand signals. Having seen countless blunders in the yacht basin, and knowing we'd be watched more than others, we were determined not to make any mistakes.

Already I could feel the difference in the new engine controls Pete had made. And the wheel—it was large and in the open, a huge improvement over the tiny, useless thing that had once been ensconced in the wheelhouse. Conditions were just what we needed for our initial sail: light winds and a gentle sea. Unfurling sails was easy, as was trimming them, and I could do both while staying within arm's reach of the wheel. Even going to the loo was painless because of the false floors we'd fitted in place just before leaving the dock. I'd made them of plywood, with two-by-four supports that slotted into U-brackets on the bulkheads. The forward one was the same height as our bunk and the loo, and the one in the galley was stove height. The lift accessed both, so we just stopped at whichever level we wanted.

We experimented with every point of sail except running down-wind. *Usikusiku* was a dream to handle compared with the first time we'd sailed; in fact, she was a different boat from the one that had arrived in Cape Town nearly two years earlier. Pete and I were different too: more experienced, more confident, and eager to see how all our changes worked out. I felt a bit awkward at times, but I knew that with practice I'd find the right places to put my body to be able to do what was needed.

Even docking went without mishap. I was in the clouds! And how proud Pete must have felt that his sail plan and rigging turned out so well. To celebrate our success, he met me for lunch the next day in the park across the street from my office. Afterward he did some shopping, then met me again so we could push home together. During the sixteen months I worked at the law firm, Pete sometimes came all the way into town just to keep me company on the push home. It was wonderful to be that much in love and cared for after nearly six years of marriage.

Christmas 1980 approached, our second in Cape Town. Also our last. If we were to ride the Golden Highway across the Atlantic, we needed to leave while the winds were still favorable, and that meant before April. Most of my family planned to come for the holidays. Shortly before their arrival date, Pete's brother John unexpectedly turned up, having made the four-day drive on his own. He'd grown heaps since the day, four years earlier, when he'd jumped on our railings to coerce them into the right shape. Now eighteen, John was more man than boy and a tremendous asset during my frenzy to make *Usikusiku* presentable. I laid new linoleum in the galley and carpeting elsewhere, trying my best to make the boat brighter and more homey so that for once the family would visit us in a home rather than a workshop. The day John left, Pop arrived, and two days after that everyone else descended upon us: James and Kath, their four daughters, and Mom. Nearly all the family together! Paddy and Mike thoughtfully had offered the use of their travel trailer, a neighbor who was going away had offered us his boat, and Mike and Bev had asked if someone would stay on *Cirrus* while they went home for Christmas, so our family spread out over three boats and a trailer.

Of course, we wanted to take everyone sailing. The wind was stronger this time, which meant a lumpy sea, and I soon started to yawn—a bad sign. Then queasiness set in. Just what I needed! Soon Paddy started to feel poorly. Kath went below to fetch my camera, and *she* turned green. Thankfully, three of my four nieces, who ranged in age from five to twelve, fell asleep, leaving us only one to keep from going over the side. Apart from these physical reactions, everyone seemed impressed. James, in particular, couldn't get over how a cement shell in a hole in the ground had turned into a yacht that floated and moved with the wind.

The rougher conditions, though uncomfortable, fulfilled our need to put *Usikusiku* to the test. We found that when we reefed the mainsail, the clew (aft lower corner) rose and the luff (forward edge) pulled away from the mast in an arc, both problems ruining the aerodynamic shape of the sail. Pete and Mike Briant put their heads together. The clew problem would be easier to fix, they declared. We could make some large wooden beads and thread them onto a rope, pass this oversized necklace under the boom, and fasten it to the clew. The necklace would keep the clew down, and the beads would allow it to roll easily along the boom as we pulled the sail out or in. For the luff Mike suggested brail lines at two different heights. They would go into the mast, come out at deck level, and lead aft. Pete would have to cut three holes in the mast and rivet in rollers, and the sailmaker would have to put a couple of cringles in the sail, but we'd be able to control the brail lines from the cockpit.

We hadn't yet tried out the downwind running poles, so Mike and Paddy went forward to put them up. They had a lot of trouble, which got Mom fretting about how Pete and I would ever be able to manage if two experienced, able-bodied sailors couldn't. "Don't worry, Mom," I said. "Pete will devise a system to make everything more workable." I knew he could, yet dealing with those poles looked awfully hard. The exhaust system still plagued us, too; the smell turned my stomach, and Pete didn't feel comfortable with how hot it got despite the commercial-grade asbestos lagging. He and Pop put their heads together and designed a water-cooling system that Pop would make up when he got home and send to Pete to install.

For our third sea trial, Mike from *Cirrus* signed on as skipper. We were going along nicely when suddenly the jib started flapping and snapping—the sheet had come untied. I slid over and winched in the control line that furled the sail. Pete went forward to the mast, released the halyard, and dropped the sail, which fell to the deck all nicely rolled up like a big sausage. After retying the sheet, he hoisted the sail, and I let off the control line and pulled in the sheet to open and trim it. The fact that none of this proved difficult sent our confidence soaring. We'd learned an important lesson, though: we must check everything continually.

Since Christmas comes in midsummer in the Southern Hemisphere, we had a *braai* on the beach—an unusual setting for us
Rhodesians, but the only thing anyone missed was the tree. Later in
the day James took us for a drive along the coast, high up on the
cliffs from where we looked over an ocean stretching away into the
haze. Apart from a few dinner invitations and the occasional Friday
night movie at the yacht club, Pete and I rarely got out just for
pleasure. Doing so now, especially with family, was a real treat.

Saying good-bye was extremely hard. When would I see them
again? Where would Pete's and my adventure take us and for how
long? Where would we end up? These were the great unknowns,
but that's what adventure is all about.

D-Day minus two and a half months. Pete and I worked flat out to
amass as much money as possible. Once again Mom had managed to withdraw money from our Salisbury bank account and
convert it to rand. Now that sanctions were over, the annual
holiday allowance had increased from $280 to $600 Zimbabwean
(US $950) each, a more reasonable amount. Pete was taking as
many odd jobs as he could, and I was putting in overtime on
Saturdays. We'd nearly finished paying off our debts, but we still
had no life raft or dinghy, both of which were expensive items.
We were prepared to leave without the life raft, if that ended up
being the only thing holding us back (they cost several thousand rand, which was why a lot of cruising people did without
them), but the dinghy was a necessity.

During January and February we sailed nearly every weekend,
always taking friends along. A lot of people asked if we planned on
doing any sea trials on our own. We would have loved to, and I'm
not sure there was a specific rule against it, but since we had to sign
out at the Royal Cape Yacht Club, we decided not to push our luck.
Besides, the port captain might get jumpy, and we didn't want to
stir up trouble with him this close to our departure. Anyway, Pete

and I did all the sail handling ourselves, so there was really no difference. We needed help only in doing the untying shuffle with the boats outside us when we left, and in jumping ashore with lines when we returned—procedures we'd rarely have to do once we took off, because we expected to be anchoring most of the time rather than docking.

Actually, we were becoming adept at leaving and coming back to the jetty, although I never got used to not knowing what was happening up front. Pete issued orders, and I had to obey, which was really hard for me—I didn't like taking orders. To complicate matters, the yacht behind us now had an eight- by ten-foot raft tied alongside it and a dinghy trailing from that. As I nosed my way toward our spot one day, Pete signaled me to move in closer. "I don't think so, buddy," I muttered to myself, then, "Geez, I'm going to crush that dinghy for sure!" I took avoiding action.

Arms flailed on the foredeck. "TURN!" Pete bellowed.

"I'll hit the dinghy!" I yelled back over the roar of the engine.

"I'm here and you're not, so do as you're told!" It took some real jostling and hot-tempered yelling to get us in the right place. At the postmortem Pete asked why I hadn't turned when he told me to. "Because I would have hit the dinghy," I said.

"Rot. I can see, you cannot, and you must trust me and follow my—um—ah—*instructions*." Well, I had to laugh. Pete knew that "instructions" would be more palatable to me than "orders."

D-Day minus one month. We had a full house again: Pete's mom, his sister Mary with her fiancé, and his sister Sylvia with her two kids. Pete's mom was dying to go for a sail, so we went out on Sunday. We had a brisk sail out, then came about and hardened up. But why was the headsail sheet so hard to winch in? Was it the wind, which had picked up? A nasty sound came from above. No, it wasn't the wind. The sail had snagged on the jumper strut and ripped the stitching along its leech. Pete's mom got all worried about how Pete would prevent a repeat occurrence and about how much it would cost to get the sail mended. Pete and I, on the other hand, were relieved this had happened now, when we could correct the problem, rather than later, when we were at sea. After all, this was the purpose of sea trials.

That family visit allowed Pete and me to relax—a good thing, too, because once they left it was all go, with no time to spare. Back in June I'd told the law firm I'd be leaving my job in February, which I did. I spent a week cleaning out the entire boat, including lockers, and then restowing everything. When that was done I began shopping for charts, navigation books, a plastic backup sextant, spare engine pump and rigging parts, medical kit components, flares, and hundreds of other articles.

After one of these long days in town I hurried home to winch Pete up the mast. We'd spent a couple of evenings making baggywrinkle to keep the jib from tearing again, and he wanted to fasten it onto the spreaders and jumper struts before dark. I arrived to an ebbing tide and a steep ramp. Typical! I was tired and just couldn't face getting out of my chair, moving the shopping from the back to the seat, lowering the loaded chair down the ramp with a rope, sliding down on my bottom, bringing up the lift, persuading the chair and packages to get onto it, and getting my body back into the chair after unloading it in the galley.

Instead I backed onto the ramp (if I'd gone down forward I would have slid out of my chair), grabbed the handrails, and started easing myself down. The next instant my chair was off down the ramp on its own. It hit the deck with a crash and then fell over from the weight of shopping on the back. Pete came up to see what all the racket was about. He found packages scattered over the deck and me on my knees on the ramp, hanging from the railings. "You're a crazy fool," he laughed.

"I was just making sure you knew I was home."

Cirrus Mike asked Pete to make some fittings for his boom and some parts for his steering system, and he suggested a swap: Pete's work for an old inflatable dinghy he didn't want. This eased one expensive headache. Then Mike Briant scored us an enormous twelve-man life raft salvaged from a fishing trawler that had caught fire. One of the companies authorized to service these happened to be on Globe wall, so Pete and I went over to see what exactly was in the enormous canister and to watch it being repacked. Because we didn't plan on sinking with twelve people on board, we had them remove some of the stores and pack everything into a ten-man container, but even that was so big and heavy that we had no place to put it. Pete ended up mounting it on brackets at the starboard side of the deckhouse, cutting away part of the railing to accommodate its width. If we needed to abandon ship, we just had to lift two levers and the raft would roll overboard. Bingo, another expensive headache gone.

D-Day minus two weeks. I went to the law firm to say goodbye to Mr. Buirski, who informed me his office manager had resigned. He didn't want to pressure me, he said, but if we decided not to go, I could have her position at double my previous salary. Was he joking? No. What lousy timing! Before we left he brought us a case of wine. "The world is a small place," he said. "If you have any hassles, let me know."

Press coverage intensified, generating some bizarre responses. A letter arrived from America marked "Please Deliver Emergency" and with the correct spelling of *Usikusiku*, which was rare. Inside were two newspaper clippings about pirate attacks in the Bahamas and an unsigned note asking us to reconsider making a trip to that area "in your condition." What condition? Did they think we were pregnant? I was touched when total strangers worried about us, but so often they didn't have a clue. Did this person think you had to be able to stand up in order to defend yourself?

Sometimes strangers stopped us on the street. A woman approached me during one of my shopping expeditions and said, "Please, would you consider taking someone with you?"

"What for?"

"You will never make it, dearie."

"Why not? Have you done any sailing? Have you seen our boat?"

"No, but you get big waves out there."

Arguing was pointless. "Don't worry, we'll take someone along if we feel we can't manage," I said. At least people like this came to us outright. Too many others, particularly yachting types, presented a smiling facade and then, behind our backs, dismissed us as crazy or became outspokenly skeptical—often to reporters. I could get really heated up about this stuff, but I tried to ignore it and get on with more important things. Pete, although he inwardly seethed, maintained his composure better than I. "We're not out to commit suicide," he quipped to a reporter. "There are cheaper and easier ways of doing that." At times I felt we had not only an ocean of water to cross but also an ocean of doubt, criticism, ignorance, and prejudice.

D-Day minus one week. I had one major task left. Most cruising women complained about what a chore provisioning was, but after two years of watching other boats loading up, I looked forward to it; I'd been making a list for the past two months. Bernard, our Cape Gas friend had been transporting me around town for some of my shopping. He now dropped me off at the supermarket, where I happily filled half a dozen shopping carts. Mike Briant arrived to help with the bill, which came to 800 rand! He had tried to find a supermarket that would donate food if his trawling company agreed to match the donation, but all he'd come up with was this store, which promised to give us some damaged cans that couldn't go on its shelves. The manager, though, after noticing that Mike's company was paying half the bill, kindly threw in another 40 rand worth of goods. Mike and I got back to *Usikusiku*, after finishing our errands, to find that the provisions had arrived before us and were spread all over the deck and down below. I didn't get my head out of the lockers for the next two days.

An international television company that had come along on one of our sea trials asked to come out again. I refused. We'd just wasted a day taking out a *National Enquirer* photographer, plus a reporter and a photographer for a local afternoon paper, and didn't have time to go out again just to please the press. We were down to the wire. I didn't feel nervous, but I was so excited my words sometimes came out backward. For instance, I went into a chandlery and asked, "What is the price of your rows?"

"Rows, Madam? I'm sorry, I don't know what that is."

Idiot, I thought. Aloud I said, "You don't know what rows is? It's what you rows a dinghy with."

"Oh, you mean *oars*, Madam."

I couldn't get out of there fast enough.

Letters and telegrams poured in from family, from other yachties we'd met and stayed in contact with, and from strangers who'd seen us on TV. The most touching telegram came from London: FROM OUR WHEELCHAIRS TO YOUR WHEELCHAIRS GOOD WISHES—DIAN CLARE ANDREW MARTINDALE SCHOOL HOUNSLOW.

How they found out about us, I'll never know.

D-Day minus one day. The *Cape Times* chief reporter, Roger Williams, and chief photographer, John Rubython, had been doing some really good articles about us. They behaved like real people rather than vultures, and Roger would write what you'd actually said in an interview. The day before D-Day they arrived early, followed by a stream of others. I made everyone else wait until Roger and John had left; then we took the rest one by one. This was not what we needed to be doing, but we figured it was best to be cooperative and get it over with. Not that being pleasant was easy. One reporter walked on my wet varnish. A photographer, while we were dutifully posing for him, asked me to feed Pete a banana. "Pete isn't a monkey," I huffed, "nor do I hand-feed him." Pete was in convulsions laughing. Just when we thought we'd gotten rid of everyone, up trotted a woman who wanted to write an article about us because this was the Year of the Disabled. "What's your main concern?" she asked. "Reporters," I said.

About noon, Roger Williams returned with catastrophic news: Bill Hillstead, the Table Bay port captain, had told him we'd be stopped if we tried to leave port. I was spitting mad. How could this man, who'd never met us or seen our boat, dictate to us? Why had he waited until the last minute? And why hadn't he told us directly rather than let us hear secondhand? I became even more enraged when Roger pointed out an elderly couple who, he said, planned on sailing across the Atlantic. I nearly choked! They looked to be in their seventies, weren't at all agile, and couldn't even tie up their boat properly, but because they could stand upright they'd be allowed out of the harbor with no questions asked.

Mike Briant, who was a licensed ship's captain and a well-thought-of yachtsman, went off to plead our case. So did Roger, who phoned Captain Hillstead from his office. "Are you going to deny the Fordreds permission to sail, without even seeing their boat?" he asked.

"Yes," Captain Hillstead replied. "Oh—are you going to print that?"

"Yes, I am."

"Hold off awhile," Captain Hillstead said and headed down to see us just as I was on a mission to see him; we practically collided. Together we went to the boat. He didn't inspect anything, just talked to us for a short time about nothing in particular. "All right, you can go," he said at last, "but it will go on record as being against my better judgment." Fair enough.

What a day—I was up, then down, then up again. Thank goodness for Mike Briant and Roger Williams! Pete and I phoned our families from the yacht club. If the weather still held, we told them, we'd leave in the morning. We'd call from Saint Helena in about three weeks.

Amazingly, Pete and I slept like logs that night.

D-Day: March 26, 1981. Pete hanked on the staysail and prepared things on deck, all the while bombarded by the press. I stayed below, putting in the false floors and hanging fresh vegetables in nets. Then we went to the yacht club, partly to enjoy one last shower but mostly to get away from our probing audience and be alone for an hour. On the way back Pete and I raced each other through the obstacle course for the last time. That was one thing we wouldn't miss.

We were excited and tense but not afraid, just anxious to be on our way. (Actually, I was afraid of one thing, that I'd hit something on the way out, in front of all those photographers.) We pulled out amid cheers and streamers and the clanging of the Royal Cape Yacht Club bell.

"Good luck!" Paddy called out from the end of the breakwater as we exited the harbor. "Don't come back!" Mike shouted, referring to the difficulty in returning against the wind and current. Three days out could mean seven days to get back.

Departure Day couldn't have been more perfect: clear sky, flat sea, and a gentle sou'easter to help us clear the coast. We motored slowly toward the channel, allowing *La Niña* to catch up. Her decks swarmed with reporters, photographers, and television crew. Pete put up the staysail, the only sail that required hoisting, then went below to stow his chair. On the way up the lift stopped. We couldn't believe it! For two and a half years it had worked nonstop with only one malfunction, and just in case it felt like breaking down, Pete had changed the brushes in the motor. Yet the minute we pulled away from the dock it decided to quit. A good start!

After hand-cranking the lift, Pete joined me in the cockpit. I turned into the wind to make it easier for him to pull out the mainsail and jib, then I shut down the engine and fell off onto a course that would take us out of Table Bay. *Usikusiku* slowly picked up speed. *La Niña* followed us for another two miles and then gave us a last "Good-bye and good luck!" and turned back. For the first time ever, Pete and I were sailing on our own, down the Golden Highway.

MARCH 26, 1981. *Distance to Saint Helena, 1,700 miles.* Looking back over the waves I could see Table Mountain in her grandeur. She would provide our last sight of land until we reached St. Helena.

"Let the sheet out a little," Pete said. From my position in the leeward corner of the cockpit seat, with one leg down alongside the wheel and the other crossed in front of me for stability, the mainsheet winch was but an arm's reach away. I gave the sheet plenty of slack, but the traveler took no notice. On most sailboats the traveler is mounted on a track on the deck, the cockpit coaming, or the cabintop. Ours had to be overhead so it didn't block our wheelchairs when we were in port, and now that we were on our bottoms, that 54-inch-high roll bar was out of reach. How could we get up there to untangle the snag?

While I pondered, Pete jumped, so to speak, into action. He hoisted himself up onto the winch plate and, keeping his legs locked in their lotus position, reached overhead to the roll bar and went hand over hand across it. Hanging from one arm, he reached up and untwisted the block. The traveler slid to the far corner of the roll bar, where it was stopped by the eye welded there. Pete worked his way back across and dropped onto the cockpit seat cushion.

"Well done!" I said, my confidence soaring. Together Pete and I could do anything. Instead of letting our handicaps serve as obstacles, we found ways to work around them. When women began sailing, especially single-handedly, they'd learned to use ingenuity and the boat's motion to compensate for their lack of brute strength. Pete and I did the same to compensate for the parts of our bodies we couldn't use—although sometimes we needed brute strength as well.

Late that afternoon the wind picked up until *Usikusiku* seemed to be straining. A headsail change was in order because the No. 2 was smaller and made of heavier material, better for stronger winds. I eased the No. 1 headsail sheet while Pete winched in the line that rolled up the sail. Then he flicked open the jam cleat to free the furling line for the No. 2 headsail, and I pulled the sail out. Pete eased around the wheel, removed the washboard at the back of the cockpit coaming, and lowered himself the six inches to the aft deck to engage the self-steering trim tab. No matter how he adjusted the wind vane, though, our "third crew" couldn't cope with the confused beam seas. A long night of helming lay ahead.

Well, then, we'd better eat. Pete took the helm and I maneuvered myself into the deckhouse and onto the lift, which didn't require the motor to go down because all the "down" button did was release the pressure in the lift cylinder and allow gravity to take effect. I descended to galley level, thankful that I didn't have to prepare a meal from scratch; all I had to do was heat up the stew I'd made the day before and stashed in a Styrofoam cooler. I sat cross-legged at the stove, one hand holding on and one doing the job. Then I ladled the hot stew into deep, lidded, plastic dishes I could take up the lift and move ahead of me across the cockpit without anything slopping over. We didn't eat much—too excited, I suppose. And I didn't know about Pete's stomach, but mine was starting to churn.

Hoping I could get control of it, and because Pete seemed too tense for sleep, I asked him to take the first watch. I headed below and tucked myself into our bunk, setting the canvas leeboard to keep myself from rolling out. The sound level was astonishing. People who haven't sailed imagine it to be silent and peaceful, but instead you hear a symphony of noises: halyards slapping the mast, sails flapping if the wind is light, water gurgling past the hull, things clunking about in lockers and cupboards. That concert, plus the apprehension of our first night at sea, kept me wide awake. I also felt awful.

March 27. Pete called me at midnight. When I finally arrived in the cockpit, after using the loo and hand-cranking myself up to deck level, he announced that sleeping below was not going to work because getting to the cockpit took too long; in an emergency we could end up in a real pickle. He grabbed a couple of blankets from the deckhouse, lay back down on the cushioned cockpit floor, and waited patiently while his legs went through their familiar antics of slowly stretching out and then violently shaking. When they relaxed, nearly a minute later, he wadded one blanket into a pillow and pulled the other up for warmth.

My first night watch was one long battle to hold up my eyelids. Once, I drifted off while sitting straight up, and *Usikusiku* drifted off as well—off course, that is—until the wind sneaked behind the mainsail and slammed it across the cockpit in a jibe.

While I struggled to stay awake, Pete's attempt at sleep was futile. Then, just as he began snoring, I had to wake him so I could visit the loo. Going below made me feel sicker than ever, and having to hand-crank the lift back up didn't help. Halfway, I dropped the handle. This happened twice! The first time I lay down on the platform and reached down for the handle, which I eventually

ABOVE: *Off at last. One mile down, the South Atlantic to go.* CENTER: *Liz on the false floor cooking dinner.* BELOW: *Pete plotting course to Saint Helena.*

TOP: *For once Pete's self-steering apparatus is doing its job.*
CENTER: *The skipper balances on the winch plate to take a sight. All he had to do was touch the sun to the horizon. He then let me get sick doing the rest.* BOTTOM: *On our approach to Ascension Island, a friendly booby dropped in for a chat.*

snagged, but the effort was too great. The second time I let the lift down, but then I had to crank it the whole way up again. Going down there every time would never do, I decided, so I brought the bedpan back up with me. Now I could just wriggle out of my pants, roll onto it, and afterward toss the contents overboard.

Pete took the helm at 0600. He woke me at 0900 because the boom was flogging around a bit and had caused the mainsheet block to twist again. Up the roll bar he went, cussing the block makers to hell and gone. I'd have given anything for my camera while he was hanging like a monkey in his underpants and sweater.

After he rigged a preventer from the end of the boom to the gate stanchion and back to the winch, I got out the South Atlantic chart to see where we were. I drew a line along the compass heading we'd been steering and measured off the ninety miles that the SumLog told me we'd covered: theoretically, that's where we were. That small mental and visual exercise made me feel worse than ever. Oh, la-la, this seasickness was for the birds!

After installing the lift's spare starter motor, Pete felt awful, too, so he went back to sleep. "Sir Francis Drake must have been nuts to do this all his life," he moaned when he awoke. *We* might not have been having fun, but a half-dozen porpoises were enjoying the wave action, zooming alongside *Usikusiku* and then shooting ahead and across her bow as if laughing at her mere 5 knots.

I had a freshwater sponge bath and changed into clean clothes, then took over from Pete so he could do the same. We had to push ourselves to do that daily, no matter what the conditions, because paraplegics are susceptible to chafing sores. Our success partially rode on avoiding sickness, sores, and injuries. Besides, it felt great to be free of the salt we collected on our legs and bottoms when we moved around on deck.

In the dark that evening the waves took on a surreal quality, seeming to loom up all around us—it was better not to look at them. Whenever we rolled to leeward, water washed along the outside of the cockpit coaming and swished through the spare gas bottles that lived under the winch plates. We shortened sail until *Usikusiku* settled down. At the end of my watch I stretched out on the bunk we'd built in the deckhouse and tried to sleep. No luck. It was no good being tired, I told myself. I needed to fall asleep soon because I didn't think Pete would last his six hours (we wanted to take long watches at night so the other person could have a decent period of sleep), but it took me ages to drop off—unless I was on watch, and then it was everything I could do to stay awake. Something wasn't fair in this arrangement!

March 28. "It still takes you too long to get here," Pete said when I next took over. "You'll have to sleep in the cockpit."

"Okay, I give up," I grumped. "From now on I'll sleep outside with a jacket and gloves and three blankets." I slumped moodily at the helm, feeling nauseated and now fighting to stay awake. What was I doing out here? Four years of backbreaking work to do *this*? Surely not! That didn't seem fair, either.

The self-steering finally seemed to have learned what it was supposed to do. Since nothing was in sight, I lay down behind the wheel and dozed, checking the compass and horizon every fifteen or twenty minutes. Well, I thought I did. At 0900 Pete woke me and asked what I was doing. Sleeping—what did it look like?

Midmorning, when we'd been out for nearly forty-eight hours, Pete wanted to take a sun sight. He reached into the deckhouse and pulled out the sextant box. He lifted his body onto the cockpit seat and then onto the cockpit coaming and winch plate, retrieving his legs and crossing them to give himself a triangular base for stability. Taking the sextant out of the case, he hung its lanyard around his neck as a precaution against dropping it. Meanwhile, I'd gotten out paper and pencil, dividers, parallel rules, the chart, the nautical almanac, and the sheet of Plexiglas that served as my portable chart table. Also the bedpan, because I already felt rough.

I sat poised with our ship's chronometer, a 10-rand digital watch that was all we'd been able to afford. But it kept good time, and we had Pete's wristwatch as a backup, so what more did we need? Pete leaned against the railing for balance, swaying comfortably with the motion of the sea while he looked through the scope. "Mark!" he called out when he'd brought the sun down to kiss the horizon. I wrote down the time and his sextant reading. After several more sights that obtained similar readings, he put the sextant back in its box and swung down.

"Right," he said, shooting me a look that meant he'd done his bit and now it was time for me to do mine. "Where are we?"

I tried my best to work out the numbers, but all I did was feed the fish.

A noon sight seemed prudent; if nothing else, we could determine our latitude. Getting the sextant reading took longer because Pete had to keep taking sights until the sun reached its highest angle, but the calculations were simpler, and this time I managed to do them without getting sick. But 35° south? That was the same latitude as Cape Town! What the hell was going on?

Pete went over everything and discovered that we'd forgotten to correct our course for magnetic variation, which in this part of the world was so huge (30 degrees) that instead of steering 310 we should have been steering 340 degrees. So the jokes people had made about being careful not to head for the South Pole weren't that far off—we'd been heading more west than northwest. Once I got over the shock of making such an enormous mistake, I wasn't all that sorry, because the accidental westing took us farther offshore and out of the shipping lanes. But I'd been given a wake-up call to get it right, sick or not.

We knew we should set the running poles so as to steer in a more northerly direction, but felt so awful we decided to wait. Just before my night watch Pete set the self-steering in an attempt to make *Usikusiku* steer higher, and then went to sleep. He didn't seem to have a problem dropping off. No way could I make the stupid boat steer higher, but Pete needed sleep, and what did it matter that we were doing only 3 knots? Seven or eight extra hours on a 1,700-mile trip wouldn't make much difference. Speed and duration weren't important. Arrival was the name of the game.

March 29. "I'm taking a bus from Saint Helena back to Cape Town," Pete said when I woke him at 0100 to change watch. A while later I lifted my head and found the skipper keeled over on the seat, fast asleep. "What's this?" I said. "Sleeping on the job?"

"Fire me."

It wasn't even light yet when he woke me; he wanted to set the running poles, he said. Why the hell did he have to want this at 0500? The exercise promised to be fun, since he had done it only in port and I'd never tried it at all. He went through the deck-house to the mast, where the poles stowed vertically on tracks. He unclipped the lower end of the starboard pole and shoved it over to the railing. I eased the headsail sheet enough for him to get the sheet into the pole end fitting. Back at the mast again, he pulled the uphaul to raise the outboard end of the pole, which of course caught on the railings. He hopped back there and lifted it over. While I kept just enough tension on the sheet to keep the pole from swinging back and forth, he adjusted the uphaul and down-haul to make the pole the height of the headsail clew and perpendicular to the mast. We repeated the process on the other side, which was easier because he could clip in the sheet before I pulled open the sail. It always amazed me how Pete had worked everything out, right down to the tiniest details, during the designing and building stages, and he'd obviously practiced mentally exactly how he'd perform each procedure.

Once we'd furled the mainsail, we were sailing comfortably wing-and-wing—"reading both pages," as the schoonermen used to say. What a team! Pete dropped the staysail and lashed it to its boom, then tightened the lashings on the anchor. He returned to the cockpit jubilant but tired. I was glad to have him back. He got out his pipe and had a smoke, a sure indication that he was in good form and not seasick, then went aft to set the wind vane. If *Usikusiku* steered herself with the running sails set, everything would be perfect. She did! Oh, you wonderful girl! Pete lifted himself up onto the cockpit seat and lay down with his head on my lap.

"Ten points, my love," I said, stroking his hair. "I couldn't have done all that."

The previous day we'd learned the hard way that nude sunbathing causes sunburn in all the wrong places. We wouldn't have that problem today, though; the temperature had dropped, and the sky was filling with dark clouds that seemed to be marching over us in formation. "I wonder where they're going," I mused. "Cape Town," replied Pete.

We hoped to get a noon sight through the clouds. A stroke of luck: the clouds parted by 1200. Eighty sights later we discovered that noon happened at 1320 at this longitude—in my befuddled, seasick state I'd forgotten I had to figure out *local apparent* noon. Oh well, it was good practice, fairly interesting and there wasn't much else to do. At least we got a latitude: 32° 15' south.

I had made porridge for breakfast. Pete, who was feeling better, requested lunch and dinner as well—a tough order, when spending time below turned me green. The pump flask I'd bought in Cape Town was a lifesaver because I could make a large amount of soup or cocoa at one time. Getting it to the cockpit was another matter, though. When the boat rolled, the flask didn't want to stay upright. Whenever it fell over, the button on the lid invariably bumped against something and squirted hot "whatever" all over me; and when I grabbed the errant flask, I would accidentally push the button again, which sent out another hot gush. It became a matter of pushing it ahead of me and getting it to the cockpit as quickly as possible. Though it wasn't an ideal container for moving about, it was best for us because we didn't have the abdominal and back muscles to hold a cup and pour from a thermos, all the while balancing upright on a rocking boat.

March 30. The self-steering was functioning, thank God. The sun broke through the morning clouds so Pete took a sight. Later he got a noon sight, so I was able to get a fix. Figuring out our position made me sick to my stomach again, but it had to be done. Glory, glory, it worked—except then I found out we were in a new time zone. I had recalculated everything before I realized that the time zone didn't matter because we used Greenwich Mean Time for navigation. Something was wrong with my brain. I didn't seem to think so well at sea.

Pete was grumbling, too. He'd come for a vacation, he said, not to search for his pipe, tobacco, pencil, book, or whatever else had wandered off. The cockpit was our anything-goes area and seemed to swallow stuff. To keep trips below to a minimum, I kept it stocked with oranges, cookies, and candy. In the deckhouse, which was like a sheltered extension of the cockpit, were charts, navigation books, sweaters, hats, wet-weather gear, blankets, books, and more. With this much gear floating about, things got messy in a hurry. I stripped away the cushions and gathered everything into a heap in search of the five pencils I'd lost. Found three. Where did things go?

I saw a bird, flying low—ah, a flying fish. Yahoo! I saw a flying fish flying!

Pete saw a whale, or rather he heard one spouting, first on one side of us, then on the other. Having read too many books about yachts being sunk by whales, he nearly croaked once he realized what it was. He told it to go away, off toward the horizon, if it wanted a look at us. Damn, I missed it! I was dying to see a whale, in spite of Pete's jokes that from underwater *Usikusiku* probably looked like a whale, and it might be mating season.

Again I had cooked porridge for breakfast because it was quick and about all I could handle. I made more soup for lunch, then washed the dishes and got out the Bactrim for Pete, who thought he had a bladder infection. I refilled the cockpit water flask and urged him to drink. For entertainment while I was below, I switched on the radio and tuned in to the BBC World Service. Someone mentioned Mother's Day. I knew it wasn't Mother's Day at home, but I began thinking about Mom. She must have been thinking of us, too, and wondering where we were.

Uh-oh, a nasty smell. My nose led me to the cooler with the remaining stew. I put it on the lift, scooted it onto the foredeck, and tossed it overboard. Oh, my retching stomach! When my belly had settled down, I got around to the apples. Back in Cape Town an elderly man had turned up one day with a box of apples and introduced himself as Elgin Curry, a name that meant nothing to us. Later we found out he was one of South Africa's largest fruit growers. Just before we left, he appeared with another box, which I hurriedly stowed away. Now, when I opened it, I found not only apples but an envelope of money. I never knew how to thank these people who stepped in out of nowhere to help us.

March 31. We were beginning to get used to the motion of the boat and didn't keep falling all over the place. Learning to live at sea was, in a way, like being a new paraplegic again because we had to relearn each task. Take getting dressed: it was complicated for us at the best of times, but now we had to do it on a rolling boat. To put on my tackies, I used one hand to lift my foot and the other to put the shoe on it. My foot would curl up with a spasm and refuse to go all the way in. Then the boat would lurch and I'd end up lying on my back with my leg in the air, still trying to get the sneaker on. Eventually, we learned to use the motion of the boat to help us do things and get places. It was hilarious watching each other dress or slide about, especially when the cockpit floor cushions were wet and we could move really quickly. We just had to make sure we ended up where we wanted to go.

In the late afternoon we ran the engine to charge the batteries. While I sat at the helm, choking on exhaust fumes, I heard Pete whistling away down below. What was he up to? He popped up and asked what I wanted for dinner. I fell over in a mock faint. How could I get him to do that more often? After we'd eaten, I washed the dishes. I was becoming an expert at getting water: sitting on the winch plate, tying a rope to the bucket, leaning over the railing and plunking the bucket into the sea. Sounds easy if you've never tried it on a moving boat where, if you simply toss the bucket, it lands upright and skips along the surface. You have to throw it down with enough force that the rim enters the water first. Then, when the rope snubs, the bucket digs in and practically yanks you overboard because the boat is sailing away from it at several knots. The ocean must hold thousands of buckets that have been ripped from hands unprepared for the sudden drag. Luckily, I had built-in ballast. Old Fordred proverb: Never use too big a bucket.

April 1. It had taken a week, but I finally had my sea legs and felt energetic enough to get some real work done. I made scrambled eggs for breakfast, rice and curried meat (the canned variety) for lunch, worked out Pete's morning and noon sights, washed my hair, and did some laundry. The latter was an archaic process, done by hand in the plastic washbasin, which I filled with buckets of seawater, using a small amount of freshwater for the final rinse. I felt like an indigent woman on the banks of the Ganges. Today it was bloody infuriating because I lost my newest pair of jeans overboard—how, I don't know! When I was finished, Pete refilled the basin and got in it. He whistled and sang and sloshed about while the orange tub, with him in it, slid around the aft deck. He said he was playing the fool.

We were making good progress: 110 miles in the last twenty-four hours, compared with our usual 90. I no longer had trouble working out sights, but we'd have to find Saint Helena to see just how good I was. That was the problem with this navigation lark—you didn't find out whether you knew what you were doing until you got there.

April 2. Pete found a flying fish in the scuppers. "Hey Liz!" he called out as he flipped it into the cockpit. "Look, breakfast!" The days were lovely and warm now. We'd caught the trade winds at last: a gentle southeast wind and a blue sky adorned with cottonball clouds. We were naked and loving it. Our all-over tans saved on the laundry, which saved on changing clothes, which could be difficult. We were tired but happy, getting used to this new life, I suppose, but feeling good was always easier when the weather was beautiful. We lazed about, playing chess and reading. Even though not much was going on, time flew.

April 3. Another lovely day. In love, made love, and what a laugh it was with the motion of the boat rolling us about. We kept collapsing in fits of laughter. For the rest of the day we felt lazy and lethargic, but happy. Seven hundred miles down, a thousand to go. If it all could be like this, I'd do ten thousand.

April 4. Sailing certainly was a life of contrasts. Just as we began enjoying the good, the unpleasant reared its ugly little head. The self-steering quit, so we had to steer by hand. Lumpy seas, boat speed 6 to 7 knots, which may not sound fast but it was too fast for *Usikusiku*, whose cruising speed was 5 knots. In keeping with our policy of sailing conservatively, we shortened sail to bring our speed back down. The sailing was invigorating, except when a wave turned us beam to the wind, which then howled through the rigging. Pete struggled to steer while I struggled to sleep. When I took over at midnight, the wind had started to settle and a soft rain had flattened the sea. How did such fine drops do that?

A headsail sheet had been chafing against the railing and was worn almost through, requiring Pete to perform his most dangerous feat yet: repairing it while the sail was set, because furling the sail put the clew out of reach. He went forward, climbed onto a drum of water that was lashed to the railing, cut the sheet at the damaged site, and tied the two ends together. While he balanced at railing height and used both hands to tie the knot, I had moments of heart failure. Risky business, that was.

"Sell this rolling bitch as soon as possible," I wrote in the log that afternoon. The boat's motion was violent, and we both felt yucky again. I really had to push myself to wash the dishes in the rain. Why were we doing this? "This is not my scene," said Pete. Hear, hear! A life of feeling sick and having to hold on all the time was just plain crazy. Oh, for a log cabin in the mountains! On second thought, forget the mountains. Too many steps.

April 5. Still raining, but I was happy because I beat Pete at chess. He was happy because the self-steering was working again—just as well, because he'd been threatening to throw it over the side if it gave him any more trouble. *Usikusiku* drifted along at 4 to 5 knots. When things were going well, this was an easy way to live. Except that I started to do the laundry and lost the bucket overboard. Bugger it. At least we had a spare.

April 6. Still raining. Pete made lunch (probably the cause of all the rain). We saw some dolphins, always a beautiful sight, but what were they doing out here in the middle of nowhere? We also saw our first light in ages, though it quickly disappeared. I thought it was a ship—it couldn't have been anything else—but Pete kept making references to bad navigation and how the African landmass might be closer than we realized.

April 7. Because the ocean can be such a vast and lonely place, a bird casually hitching a ride on a yellow 44-gallon drum was a great reminder that animals and people still existed. I wanted to take a picture, but my camera was below, and we'd have been miles away before I could have fetched it. Oh well, couldn't think about things like that or I'd go crazy.

April 8. We turned our wristwatches back for the second time. Incredible—your watch said 10:00 and you just turned it back to 9:00, even though you didn't feel you'd gone anywhere. You had just been sitting on a boat. We were now the same time as England—I couldn't get over it. Also, in Cape Town we'd gotten used to a sun that set in the northwest. Each day of this trip it went down more toward the west. The water temperature was rising, too.

I siphoned freshwater from one of our spare drums and had a lovely bath on the foredeck with the sun shining and the deep blue sea all around. It was a good time to reflect upon what we were doing. I realized that everything worthwhile has both good and bad components, and overall, I appreciated experiencing things I previously had never felt or known. After my bath I washed our clothes in the bathwater and tied them to the railings. Pete reckoned if anyone ever wanted to find us, they just had to follow the trail of laundry.

April 9. A dollop of water splatted into the cockpit and rudely woke me, probably as a reminder we'd finished our second week at sea. Pete found it uproariously funny until later, when one got him in his sleep.

My fix put us too far east, so we decided to reach off until the next day. After all the work getting the running poles down, something about the decision nagged at me. I took another look at the books and chart, and sure enough—"Ummm, Pete, it looks like I forgot the bloody variation again."

"Oh? Let's see."

"Well, you see, we should actually still be running, but with the wind more off our quarter."

"Trust you!" he snorted. Hop, hop, hop he went to put the poles back up.

"Sorry!" I shouted after him. "I just thought you might be bored and need something to do!"

No answer from the foredeck.

April 10. Five degrees out on a position line? I checked my calculations and decided it was the person who took the sight, not the person who worked it out. We'd have to wait a day to see, because neither of us felt like doing it again. Other than that, nothing to report. Nothing going or coming. Pete and I were as lethargic as the weather, which was balmy. *Usikusiku*, too, slowed her pace, creeping along at 1 or 2 knots. Apparently it is like this all year round at this subtropical latitude of 19° south—an amazing change from Cape Town's perpetual storms.

April 11. I worked out Pete's sight, and all was okay. Only 140 miles to go. That meant two days, unless the wind picked up, which was unlikely. We prayed Saint Helena was where it should be. Pete was devouring the pilot book.

We threw a fishing line over the stern, a bit late in the trip but we hadn't felt like it before. Pete woke me to show off the two-foot hake he'd caught, although something had gotten to it before he did, so there wasn't much left. No fish, no dinner. We'd have to rig a bell to alert us when a fish struck. He saw another whale and where was I? Down below making dinner. Damn! Pete, who didn't like whales while he was sailing, had now seen two, while I, who was dying to see a whale, hadn't seen any. That just wasn't fair. This one sounded, then surfaced next to *Usikusiku* and swam so close its barnacles were visible. Pete told it to go away. It went, but I don't think because he told it to.

April 12. The pilot book said that Mount Actaeon, which is 2,684 feet high, can be seen from sixty miles away on a clear day. Well, the day was clear. Where was it? We scanned the horizon until our eyeballs were sunburned. Just as the stars were beginning to appear, a few birds flew past—was that a good sign? We squawked at them, which made them circle over us. In case my navigation was off, we doused the running sails and reached so that we wouldn't hit the island in the dark. Mind you, with this wind we weren't going far. I spent the night worrying, not about *Usikusiku* climbing up Mount Actaeon but about my navigation. The chart had a line of neat little x's marching across the Atlantic toward Saint Helena. What if we were there but Saint Helena wasn't?

April 13. "Get the anchor ready!" Pete's voice woke me at 0600. Was he kidding? No, there among the clouds was Saint Helena! My navigation worked—it really worked! Yahoo! Yahoo! Pete kept shaking his head in disbelief. Seventeen days at sea without seeing land and then out of the clouds, dead ahead, loomed the blueish outline of a mountain. We could have danced for joy on the deck.

Making History

HEADWINDS HIT US on our approach to the volcanic island of Saint Helena, so we furled our sails and motored around to James Bay on the northwest side. Flocks of petrels and hundreds of little brown birds circled us, and a pair of boobies—our first—dropped down for a look before flying off again. I guess they all hoped we were a fishing boat. Pete hoisted the yellow Quarantine flag to the spreaders to signify that we were coming from a foreign port, then tied our garish Zimbabwean ensign to the backstay. Bloody hell—that sure rubbed me wrong! I was tempted to cause a stir by putting up the green and white Rhodesian flag instead. Afterward, I wished I had, because no one we met in Saint Helena had yet heard of Zimbabwe.

James "Bay" is a mere indentation in a rocky coast. Jamestown, Saint Helena's only town, spills down a crack between two mountains, giving the appearance of houses and buildings riding an old lava flow to the sea. Before we got close, a dinghy headed our way. "Pete," I said, "that looks like Horst, hey?" I scanned the harbor with binoculars until I spotted a funny-looking orange boat bobbing at anchor. Yes, it was Horst, whom we knew from Cape Town. He was so excited to see us that he took our bow line and started to row in front of us, even though we were motoring and still had a good way to go. Horst pulled his engineless yacht around by rowing his dinghy, so I think he had the same idea with us. He led *Usikusiku* to where the other cruising boats were and secured her fore and aft to moorings. Other dinghies approached, and yachties clambered aboard, bubbling with questions. How many days had it taken us? What was the weather like? Did we have any problems? We'd briefly met some of these people in Cape Town, but because they'd been moored at the Royal Cape Yacht Club rather than Globe wall, our paths hadn't crossed much. Now, having negotiated the same 1,700 miles of water, we all felt an instant camaraderie.

A longboat brought customs and immigration officials, who joined the party. A man with them introduced himself as Pat Williams of Solomons, the company that ran most of the shops in town. Cape Town had informed the island we were coming, Pat said, and Solomons wanted him to squire us about and offer any help we needed. Were we ready to go ashore? Give us a couple hours to tidy up and collect ourselves, we said, and we'll be ready for anything. What a welcome!

After everyone had left, I removed the false floors and handed them up to Pete, who stowed them alongside the deckhouse. We tidied up the boat, put on clean clothes, rigged the mainsheet block and tackle to the middle of the boom, and swung the boom out over the water like a derrick. When the longboat returned, we passed down our chairs and then lowered ourselves using the bosun's chair. The longboat headed to the town landing—steps chiseled into solid granite. A swell always made its way into James Bay, and although on this day it was only moderate, according to Pat, to me the landing looked formidable even for the able-bodied. How could they ever get Pete and me safely out of the longboat onto those slippery stone steps? "Even the Queen came ashore this way," Pat assured us.

The teamwork that followed was awesome. Helping hands

fended the longboat off the steps while it rose and fell with the swell. Our chairs were handed ashore, and then it was our turn. Pete insisted I go first; I wasn't sure whether this was chivalry or not. Two of the men in the longboat put their arms around my back and under my knees and scooped me up while I tried to relax by telling myself that if we ended up in the drink, at least all three of us were going together. Another two men ashore, holding onto knotted lines that hung from a gallows-like frame, leaned out over the water to help support and balance us while my bearers stepped across to safety. They carried me up the stairs, and placed me in my waiting chair.

The islanders, I gathered, hadn't seen anything like this before. I hadn't seen anything like them, either. The Saint Helenians have a wide spectrum of skin color, black hair that ranges from straight to kinky, and a hint of the Orient in their eyes. They are descendants of a real mix: British settlers sent by the British East India Company a hundred years ago; the settlers' African slaves and indentured workers; various sailors who were left on the island to recover from scurvy before being picked up by the next ship to come along; and Malaysians—how they got there I'm not sure. They warmly welcome visitors, even though yachts are a poor replacement for the hundreds of clipper ships that once used the island as a waypoint on the South Atlantic's tradewind routes.

Pat drove us a long way up the valley to the Briars, an inn where Napoleon had spent his first night on the island 166 years earlier and where the main telephone exchange was now located. First I called Mom. When she heard my voice she gave an enormous sigh, as though her worries were at last over—at least for a couple of weeks. She promised to telegraph Joan and Ian, who had just moved to Cape Town and would carry on worrying until they had news of us. Then Pete phoned home. His parents were more or less speechless—not that the Fordreds ever did much talking—whereas Kath and James, whom I called next, went to the other extreme and wanted to know about every detail of our trip. I ended with calls to the *National Enquirer* and to Roger Williams at the *Cape Times*.

I didn't think my happiness could have been greater—until Pat took us to a hotel for baths and dinner. Heavenly! It was late that night before Pete and I got back to the boat, overwhelmed by such kindness and generosity. We fell into a blissful sleep, uninterrupted by tossing and pitching. I woke up only once, to change watch, then realized it wouldn't be necessary after all.

Word of our arrival must have spread through Africa by bush telegraph because letters and telegrams began pouring in. My favorite came from Elgin Curry, the Cape Town apple man: WONDERFUL NEWS BEST WISHES ENJOY THE APPLES STOP YOUR CRUISE MORE IMPORTANT THAN COLUMBIA SPACE SHUTTLE STOP GOOD LUCK. While I didn't think we deserved being put above the very first shuttle flight, that was a real compliment.

The Saint Helenians are affectionately known as the Saints, a nickname derived from their island's name but one that also acknowledges their amazing hospitality. For two and a half wonderful weeks, Pete and I were treated like royalty. A doctor drove us to his house for cocktails. A South African couple took us in for the weekend. We were treated to a night at the Briars and were taken to a brass band concert on Easter Sunday. We had so many invitations we couldn't possibly have accepted them all. Pat drove us around the forty-seven-square-mile island. From a fort high on the barren, wind-eroded coast we looked down at *Usikusiku* floating upon magnificent, deep blue water. Beyond her was nothing, just an eternity of ocean. Had we really sailed all that way? Two miles inland we discovered another world, green and lush. Cows, sheep and goats grazed on steep mountain pastures; ferns and lilies grew wild in the forest. All that green was a welcome change after seeing just sea, sea, and more sea.

We paid a visit to Longwood, the estate where Napoleon lived in exile from 1815 until his death in 1821. The house, preserved as a museum funded by France, demonstrated that Napoleon had been given everything he could possibly need—except generals to run a war. Since toilet accessibility is a top priority in my life, I got a charge out of Napoleon's loo, which stood about three feet high; short as he was, he must have had to get on a box to reach it!

The yachties we met were super. We toured a posh American power yacht (as much of it as we could) that was all French polish and high-tech equipment. We met Frank, Dawn, and Simon on *Beryl-Jean*, beginning a deep and gratifying friendship that would grow over the miles and years to come. Bernie and Sue, a couple from Liverpool, took us snorkeling over the *Papawui*, a ship that caught fire in 1911 and was run aground in order to offload its three hundred passengers. Afterward, everyone got together for a *braai*.

To pass our message of inspiration and endeavor to all 5,000 Saint Helenians, we did an interview for the local radio. In addition, Pat brought on board a chap disabled by polio who scooted around on his bottom like Pete and was fascinated by how we'd adapted *Usikusiku* to our needs. I've often wondered whether we made any impact on his life, just by opening his mind to possibilities.

Some days Pete and I stayed on board and did nothing but read and nap, occasionally sliding off the deck into the warmest, clearest water we'd ever seen. Val Howells had been right: there was far more to cruising than the miserable parts. Pete thought that enlarging the rudder and trim tab on the self-steering might make the exasperating thing more efficient, so the islanders helped him bring his tools ashore and set him up in a workshop on the waterfront. I sat nearby and wrote dozens of postcards and letters, or went swimming in the hotel pool.

On an island too mountainous for an airport and too far from anywhere else for helicopters to reach (Angola, 1,100 miles away, is the closest country), a single supply ship represented the only regular physical link with the outside world. The *St. Helena* came every three weeks or so to transport goods and mail to and from Cape Town. Its crew turned out to be a jolly bunch who gave us 50 gallons of diesel, some hydraulic oil, and their ship's plaque. A number of sea cadets from Jersey's training ship *Undaunted* were on board, and they too presented us with a plaque. Some had seen us on TV in England so were full of curiosity about *Usikusiku*. We showed them around and explained how we sailed her.

Pete fell so in love with Saint Helena that he could have been tempted to stay, but since we both had a hankering to see more of the world, it was time to move on. On our last day he developed a case of "leaving nerves," which many yachties get before a passage. "It's just as well one of us worries," he said in response to my teasing, "because you barge along and go where angels fear to tread. Mind you, if we followed just me, we wouldn't go anywhere. So we complement each other." I wasn't sure whether that was a compliment or not.

April 29. Distance to Ascension, 700 miles. The other cruising yachts had left before us, but a crowd of islanders turned up to wave goodbye as we weighed anchor. We set our sails for a reach and skimmed away from some of the warmest people we'd ever met, our eyes turned toward Ascension, the next stop on the Golden Highway.

Pete connected the self-steering, but guess what? It was worse than ever. It had worked before on a reach and he'd modified it to work even better. What had gone wrong? And how demoralizing! We had to helm all night, taking two-hour stints.

April 30. By morning we both felt vile. The self-steering continued being such a bloody cow that Pete wanted to chuck it overboard. He could see something trailing from the trim tab and thought it might be a piece of fiberglass that had come loose, but we felt too yucky to do anything about it. I helmed most of the day, letting him sleep, until at 1500 I finally said, "Come on, Pete,

I've had enough. Let's do something about that self-steering." With a great groan he sat up and headed for the aft deck.

For an hour he tried to dislodge the fabric with a boat hook. No luck—the whole damn rudder would have to come out of the water. He tied a rope around the brackets, brought the rudder up over the bar between the two davits, and took the rope to a winch. Then I cranked while he heaved, with *Usikusiku* going wildly off course every time I let go of the wheel. Finally he got the thing halfway onto the deck, where he cut off a three-foot length of fiberglass that had delaminated from the trim tab.

That was the easy part. The hard part was the reinstallation. The top and bottom rudder pins had to be lined up and simultaneously slotted back into the eyes on the transom, which was difficult at the best of times and nearly impossible while under way. The water rushing past us buffeted the rudder and kept trying to steal it from Pete. I'd never heard such swearing! I asked if I could help.

"No, there is nothing you can do," grump, grump.

I suggested that I support the rudder's weight on the winch while he guided it and told me how much to ease it down, but oh, la-la! Wives should be seen and not heard! Eventually, though, he got tired and gave in to my idea. Miracle of miracles, it worked, and when I secured the wheel with a bungee cord, *Usikusiku* helmed herself. Yahoo! I danced around the deck and did handstands—well, I thought I did—and made the most out of ragging him about what a good crew he had.

May 1. We both felt much better after a good night's sleep. We were making an honest 4 knots and didn't have to steer. We must have been near Napoleon Seamount, a volcanic rise that, unlike Saint Helena, hadn't reached the ocean surface. Millions of fish were leaping out of the water—a beautiful sight, but I felt sorry for them because something big, a shark or dolphin, was chasing them from below and sea birds were swooping down from above.

I was feeling better, so I went below to wash, change, and make breakfast. Bad idea—I had to get back on deck fast. Before I dared work out Pete's morning sight, I took an Australian seasick tablet given to me by the mate of the fancy American yacht and lay down until it took effect. It worked better than anything else I had tried but made me way too happy and gave me the shakes. I almost preferred being seasick—which was easy to say when I wasn't.

May 2. We'd been married for six years but I was still learning about Pete. He pulled in an 18-inch tuna and asked me how to gut it! I explained, and he did it, but afterward he declared he was done with fishing because he didn't like killing a living creature and the blood and mess just weren't worth the effort. Besides, then you had to go below to cook it. We made an agreement that whoever put the line over had to gut and cook the fish. I guess that meant me.

May 3. I was writing to Mom. "Do you think I should mention that I think we must be mad to be doing this?" I asked Pete.
"Don't bother," he replied. "She already knows."

May 4. The self-steering worked like a dream—except in light winds. Then Pete would sit for hours, trying to get it to helm. He'd be swearing and cursing, until eventually I'd say, "You know, I haven't slept because you've been bitching at this boat the whole time. Just go to sleep and I'll do it." Within ten minutes I'd be nodding off behind the wheel while the boat steered herself. You only had to tweak it a little, but he never had the patience.

May 5. Ascension Island popped up—need I say it?—dead ahead. Bloody good show! Discounting the self-steering repair, we hadn't done more than trim sails on this passage. What more could we ask for? Actually, getting in before dark would be nice.

We must have asked for too much. OK, we'd spend the night milling about.

May 6. Birds were swarming around us. A large booby flew over, so I began quacking. He circled us for a better look, then landed on the lazarette hatch and hopped up onto the winch plate. When I saw how long his beak was, I stopped quacking because I had the distinct impression he might try to sit in my lap. I offered him a banana, which he halfheartedly pecked at: I suppose what he really wanted was fish. He must have liked our company, though, because he stayed with us for an hour. It was great to see something alive other than Pete.

We prepared for our first attempt at anchoring, and of course the depth-finder chose this inopportune time to die. The bottom looked close, too close. I kept encouraging Pete to drop the anchor, and he kept motioning for me to go nearer to shore. I steeled myself for a grinding sound. At last the hook went over and I reversed slowly to let it dig in, then hit full throttle to check its staying power. Yes! We stayed put. Pete put a lead line over and found we were in forty feet of water. Sure fooled me—the water was twice as clear as at Saint Helena, and you could see every detail of the bottom.

Within half an hour a lighter bearing four men came toward us. "Would you like to come ashore?" they asked.

"Yes, please."

"Who else is on board?"

"We're the only crew."

They kept peering about. We finally took them below, where they looked in every cupboard and locker. They finally seemed satisfied we weren't hiding an invisible deckhand and helped us transfer to the lighter.

If we'd thought going ashore in Saint Helena was difficult, Ascension was a paraplegic's nightmare—the concrete dock was close to twenty feet high with steep steps going up the outside. But we hadn't reckoned on the ingenuity of these mid-ocean islanders. The lighter motored straight to a crane that lifted us, boat and all, from the water and gently set us in a cradle. "How are we going to get down?" I whispered to Pete. The answer roared toward us: a forklift. With what seemed like the island's entire population watching the show, Pete and I worked ourselves onto a platform attached to the "forks" and were lowered to wheelchair height. Despite my embarrassment, I was grateful for how organized the operation was. I was also aware that when you're the first to do something, you have to deal with the curiosity it arouses.

Because of the high security surrounding this island's joint American-British tracking station and missile base, yachtsmen were vetted by the officials in Saint Helena, who then informed Ascension who was coming (Saint Helena, Ascension, and the Tristan da Cunha group form a single British colony). Visitors were allowed to stay for just three days, needed permission to go ashore, and had to leave the island before dark.

After our phone calls, Pete and I were loaded into the back of a pickup and taken on a bumpy tour. I hadn't thought anyplace could be more desolate than Saint Helena, but Ascension, with its forty-four distinct volcanic craters, looked like the moon. Only one of the many mountaintops had a faint green covering at the top; they called that one Green Mountain. On our second day we did an interview for the BBC, which broadcasts from the island to Africa and Latin America. We were one of ten items for a BBC World Service program on the Year of the Disabled.

The population of Ascension comprised about 850 Saint Helenians, 100 Americans, and 350 Brits. All those we met were extremely friendly and went out of their way to help us. I asked one of the men in the lighter where I could buy some bait. On our return ride to *Usikusiku* he produced some bread, which he broke into bits and threw over the side. The water immediately became a black, seething mass. He thrust in his hand and flipped several black fish into the lighter. I asked him how his fingers fared, and he held them up to show where part of a finger was missing. He told me to fish only after dark, otherwise these black fish, which weren't good eating, would demolish my bait. That evening I threw my line overboard, using the black fish for bait. Within an hour I had six good-sized grouper and snapper, the easiest fishing I'd ever done. But six caught meant six to clean—what a pain. I cooked what we could eat now; the rest I gutted, rubbed with salt, and hung up to dry. When we were at sea, I would soak them in water for a couple of hours and cook them as if fresh.

Ascension serves as a jumping-off point for South America, the United States, and the Caribbean. By the time we left Cape Town we'd settled on the Caribbean and had bought the appropriate charts, but in Saint Helena we'd learned that if we went straight there, we'd arrive during hurricane season. Our friends on *Beryl-Jean* were going to Natal, Brazil, which sounded like a reasonable place to pass the time until it was safe in the Caribbean, but we hadn't bought charts of the South American coast. I ordered some, including the cities of Natal and Fortaleza, through the crew of the *St. Helena*, who would see that they were put on a plane to Ascension. I assumed that the charts would beat us here, but they didn't, so when our allotted three days were up, we had to wait on the boat. On the fifth day the charts arrived and were brought to us by the guys on the local ferryboat. Since we had no more business in Ascension, and couldn't go ashore again, it was time to leave.

May 13. Distance to Brazil, 1,500 miles. Pete strained his arm getting our 60-pound anchor onto the bow roller because he had to pick it up with one arm, using the other for hanging on. He'd have to adapt the fitting to make it easier for himself. The sky behind us was a mass of birds diving for small fish that were being chased by bigger fish that were being chased by even bigger ones. The water was alive with them. Having discarded my clothes, I must have looked like a demented photographer as I skittered around on the foredeck with my cameras. *Ciné* in the nude. I couldn't believe how much energy I had at the start of this trip. Was it because I wasn't seasick?

May 14. Pete was all right, but I felt awful. When I was sick I just wanted to stop.

May 15. The drain for the bathroom sink seemed to be blocked. The great plumber had failed again! I got some wire out of the forwardmost locker (impressed that I managed to get all the way up there) and pushed it down, down, and down to see if the drain would unblock, but no such luck. I hated that feeling of failure, especially when I'd put a lot of effort into something. Maybe if I'd stayed at it longer—no, I had to get up on deck, because I was green.

May 16. Naked and loving it! We were six degrees south of the Equator, following this imaginary line of latitude west, and it really was hot. We were nut brown all over.

May 17. It rained heavily at lunchtime, so Pete had a shower in the cockpit and washed the dishes, singing away the whole time. He kept surprising me: one minute he'd be quiet and conservative as usual, the next minute he'd have me in fits because he was sliding around on the soapy cockpit floor cushions, going back and forth with the boat's motion. If we hadn't done this, I never would have seen the side of him that could be such a card.

May 18. This downwind stuff across the ocean was pretty boring. Nothing happened all day. At least we were past the halfway point, thank God. This was not my scene. Or Pete's. Still, it was a good experience—not the sick part, but the rest of it. Once should be enough, though.

All of a sudden I wasn't bored. The hum of engines woke Pete, and lo and behold, not a hundred yards astern was a ship towing another ship. Yeow! Did that give us a fright! It was my fault; I was dozing on watch. We'd heard that a ship could come from beyond the horizon and be on you in minutes. My mind reeled with the possibilities of what could have happened.

May 19. Didn't sleep, watching for bloody ships. Just one more appeared—hardly worth losing all that sleep for.

I bruised either my ribs or a kidney on the back rest while trying to get on the bedpan. Without stomach or back muscles to lift myself, and with a carnival ride rolling me about, it was tricky getting it under me. Beat going down to the loo, though.

May 20. Two ships last night—an improvement. Both were huge tankers, and Pete woke me to turn on our navigation lights, which we generally didn't use in order to limit battery charging. The swells were enormous and incredibly long, without the usual small ones in between. They lifted *Usikusiku's* stern and gave us an exhilarating surf down. The motion unblocked the sink drain.

My back was killing me; every time I leaned over I got a sharp pain, and my spasm went mad, jumping in my stomach. Fortunately, Pete's arm was better. It came back to us that we couldn't afford injuries or illness.

May 21. Pete was reading yachting magazines. "People spend a lot of money to be uncomfortable," he said. "Bloody stupid, if you ask me." I also heard him say, when he thought I was asleep, "Don't worry, Boat, I will sell you as soon as I get someplace." Brazil wouldn't be the end of it though; we still had to get to the Caribbean, but at least the trips would be shorter. We confirmed with each other that we both must be crazy. We were craving steak, apple crumble, ice cream, and a few cold beers for Pete. Since we had no fridge, everything we drank was the same temperature as the air, which at this latitude was damn hot.

May 22. No sleep. The boat was rolling badly, the wind was inconsistent in strength and direction, and a thick cloud cover was dumping rain. Pete was helming with one hand and swishing his other hand in front of his eyes like a windshield wiper. All the while he was singing, "Rock-a-bye boat on the sea top, when is it going to bloody stop?"

May 23. I was getting a bad feeling about Natal; why, I had no idea. I didn't like being silly about things like that, but vibes were vibes. I spoke to Pete, and he suggested we go to Fortaleza instead, even though it was 150 miles farther along the Brazilian coast. I felt better immediately. The course change meant taking down the running poles, though—Pete's favorite drill. In Ascension he'd put lengths of hose on the headsail sheets to stop their chafing in the pole-end fittings, and one had jammed so the pole wouldn't release. He had to lower the sail, go forward to free the pole, then haul the sail up again. Bare-bottomed and salt-licked, he was awash much of the time in the water coming over the deck. Really foul language came from the bow.

Doing all the foredeck work was tiring for him. Because he was stronger and more agile, while I was stronger on the helm, this was the only sensible division of labor, but it meant he was saddled with all the really exhausting work. I always worried about him and often felt sorry for him. I tried to make up for it by letting him have extra sleep and rest.

May 24. When I awoke I smelled the most delicious smell of wet earth and vegetation, exactly like a mossy, fresh morning on the veld. I just couldn't stop breathing it in deeply. So the stories of being able to smell land were true. Some pretty butterflies blew past, another indication that land was close. The sea was calmer but the wind veered, which meant putting the poles up again. More swearing from up front. Then we got into an argument about furling the main. It was more complicated than the headsails because, in addition to rolling up the heavy sail, we had to ease the sheet, raise the topping lift, release the clew outhaul, and take up the slack in the brailing lines. More than one sequence was possible, and Pete insisted on doing it his way. He tried twice, then said, "You bloody well do it your way then!" which I did, and it worked! Ha-ha! I loved it when I was right, which wasn't often—or should I say, wasn't as often as I would have liked.

May 25. When the sun came up we saw land, with a big city on our port bow. We dropped the sails and started motoring in, partly because the batteries needed the charge but mostly because once we saw our destination, I became impatient and started to nag. We could see a few yachts so I headed in that direction, giving wide berth to a wrecked ship. (Wrecks always made me wonder how they happened, and so far there had been one in each port of call.) Yes! There was *Yemanja*, our neighbor in Cape Town, and Sue was waving madly. Yahoo! We were here!

We arrived without fanfare, not that we needed any. Apart from transoceanic races, that's how crossings end: no spectators, no press, no cheers, bands, or balloons. Not even a crowning moment; in fact, it's tough to pinpoint just when the trip ends. When you see land? Hours, sometimes even days, pass after that first hazy shape appears on the horizon. When you drop the anchor? Sailors don't mentally or physically stop when the hook goes down, because a mountain of tidying up awaits. When your feet—or wheels—touch the soil? You might not go ashore right away, and when you do, you don't necessarily whoop it up; you just enjoy being with other sailors and swapping yarns.

A crossing is more than a landfall, just as running a marathon is more than crossing the finish line. The endeavor is what's important: the sweat, the anguish, the push to keep going when you're exhausted and discouraged. In other words, the thrill is in the pursuit, not the finish, and the achievement is personal, not public. Pete's and my goal, after all, wasn't to cross an ocean; it was to travel—as independently as possible. We did feel a deep satisfaction now that we'd completed a 3,800-mile voyage from Africa to South America, but it was tempered by the knowledge that the same distance again lay ahead of us and the sailing promised to be far more dangerous. Challenges would continue to surface daily.

After we'd gotten ourselves anchored to our satisfaction, and after we'd spent a few hours with Sue and Hector and their daughters, Pete and I were able to crawl into our bed for the first time in two weeks. We cuddled quietly, lost in our own thoughts. "Well, Liz," Pete said after a bit, "we made it."

"Of course, my love. Was there ever any doubt?"

Up the Coast

PETE AND I HAD ALWAYS SAID that sailing *Usikusiku* would be a piece of cake compared to building her. We'd also said that getting ashore would be our biggest cruising challenge. Doing it totally on our own for the first time here in Fortaleza was bound to be a laugh, considering we'd never rowed a boat as paraplegics. I lowered myself into the dinghy, then Pete passed the folded wheelchairs down and joined me. No problems there—it just took time. We paddled off with great enthusiasm, but sitting in the bottom of a rubber inflatable and reaching out over its wide sides with our paddles was not particularly efficient, and the offshore breeze soon put us behind *Usikusiku* rather than in front of her. Fits of laughter further offset the effectiveness of our already poor performance. "Paddle harder, you lazy dog!" said Pete. "No, you moron, we're swinging to the right, which means *you* must paddle harder!" More fits of laughter, although by the time we got ourselves tied up at the yacht club's pontoon dock, we were swearing.

Now for the tricky part. I held us firmly against the dock while Pete sat on the side of the dinghy, which already had half deflated. Putting his hands behind him on the dock, he hoisted himself up until his bottom touched down. My turn. I had to face forward, the same way I got into my wheelchair. After pulling myself into a kneeling position on the side of the dinghy, I gave a hard push with my arms and got my chest and stomach onto the dock. I worked myself forward until my hips were on, then turned onto my back and sat up. Pete kept a grip on my trousers in case I needed a boost. Success! Once in our chairs we needed help, because from the dock there was a step up onto a ramp, then three more steps at the far end of that. But since the yacht club was right there and yachties were sitting around on its verandah, willing hands materialized.

We phoned our families, initiating a storm of telegrams from family and friends. I wished we could have called Tassos, Val Howells, and everyone else who had lent a hand in our venture, because without their contributions of time, money, and encouragement we could hardly have succeeded. I phoned Roger Williams at the *Cape Times* and had a lovely, sane conversation compared with what came next: contacting the *National Enquirer* as our contract demanded. Its reporter couldn't accept that two paraplegics had crossed an ocean without any life-threatening occurrences. I tried to explain that we'd spent two hard years in Cape Town making sure nothing bad *would* happen, but judging by the way he embellished the story, he required sensationalism.

When the article came out, we read how we'd spent thirty-eight "peril-packed days at sea . . . battling 40-foot waves and struggling to repair our boat in the midst of furious storms." We were "flung about the cabin without any control." Our close encounter with a ship had become even closer: Our "ears were filled with the drumming of the mighty engines of the ship, which towered 10 stories above us. It missed us by a few yards." I can't say we didn't need the US $1,000 they were going to pay us, but I was relieved that we hadn't experienced their version of the crossing, or been in America when that pumped-up story was published. And I was especially grateful to Mr. Buirski, who'd gotten us out of our obligation to do a second story for the *National Enquirer*.

After our phone calls we joined the other yachties on the verandah for a beer or two—more than two in Pete's case, which meant that on our way back to *Usikusiku* we traveled mostly in circles while he serenaded me. The following day we got our paddling more organized, although we still couldn't go in a straight line. On the third day all boats had to move out of the bay while the navy took soundings. This put us about a mile out. "Do you think we can make it?" Pete asked after we'd already gotten into the dinghy. "The wind is up."

"Yeah, Pete."

"I'm having less and less faith in this 'Yeah, Pete' of yours."

"Has it failed yet?"

He mumbled something through his teeth that I couldn't catch. Of course we made it in; we were becoming expert paddlers. Getting out at the other end remained the hard part. One day Pete must not have been paying attention because when I leaned against the dock for balance, the dinghy shot out from underneath me, and into the water I went. I bobbed to the surface to find Pete and everyone on the yacht club verandah laughing their heads off. I heaved myself back into the dinghy, loudly cursing Pete—until it struck me that I'd gotten into the inflatable on my own. What an achievement! If someone had told me five years before that one day I'd be able to get myself from the sea into a dinghy, I wouldn't have believed it.

Having left South Africa with just US $600, much of which we'd spent on phone calls, telegrams, and postage, Pete and I badly needed to beef up our "bank" account. This time I stayed home and began writing our story while Pete went off to work for Hector. Sue, Hector, and their daughters spoke fluent Portuguese and had settled in for a while. The girls were enrolled in school, and Hector was managing an opal-cutting company called Orion. I think he created a position for Pete: designing a security system to prevent the employees from pocketing so many opals during

We received an amazing reception on Ascension Island.
TOP TO BOTTOM: *A lighter picked us up. A crane lifted
the lighter out of the water. A forklift unloaded its freight
from the lighter into our chairs. The look on my face says
it all, but in spite of my extreme embarrassment I appreciated the service.*

This sequence shows how we got into and out of tiki-taki, our dingby, using the side davit Pete made for this purpose. When going down (*left and below*) we didn't need the bosun's chair.

"Hey, get your hands out of my pants!"

Photos this page by Klaus Gehrig

ABOVE: *Going up, I wasn't exactly graceful, but then you can't have everything.* RIGHT: *Pete controlled his spasm by keeping his legs in a lotus position.*

the weighing and cutting processes. I'm not sure how legitimate Orion was or even how much Hector knew about cutting gems, since he often asked Pete's advice.

One day Hector stuck a three-pound lump of opal in front of Pete and asked how best to tackle it. Pete went at the project like an engineer, lugging home books that he read cover to cover, and then scrutinizing the rock before suggesting the best approach. But mostly Pete reckoned he really did nothing all day. The company supplied a large lunch followed by rum and coke, and around 4:00 P.M. they sent out for more food accompanied by more rum and coke. Several times Pete came home totally bombed. He was bored, but I thought the change would do him good, and the pay, though appalling, meant we didn't have to touch our small capital. It also saved on the cooking, which made a nice change for me, too.

Pete was such a worrier, though. He'd coped with my wheeling to work and back in Cape Town, but when he was the one to go off and leave me behind, his mind went wild with all the trouble I might get into. If we'd had two-way radios, I think he would have had me contact him hourly to say I hadn't drifted, died, cut my hand, broken a leg, had a fire, or drowned. He certainly didn't lack passion!

Anyway, I could take care of myself, even defend myself and my man if need be. We'd moved into *Usikusiku's* aft cabin, where the bunk was larger and the ventilation better if we opened the lazarette hatch and the door at the far end of the bunk that opened into the lazarette; at three degrees south of the Equator we needed as much air as we could get. The first night we slept there, a bump against the hull woke Pete. The next minute an arm came down into the lazarette and started digging around in the fenders and rope. Pete made a grab for it, but in a flash the intruder was out, back into his *jangada* and rowing off.

The next day when we were shopping, I spotted an array of machetes used for cutting cane. I picked up the most enormous one and slashed the air with it. "This would be great for thieves," I said to Pete. "Next time I can cut that guy's arm off." Too big, said Pete. He talked me into a smaller one, but an 18-inch blade was as short as I'd go.

Pete claimed even that was way too big; when we got back on board he asked me to demonstrate how I was going to use it. I lay down on the bunk, pretended to wake up, grabbed my machete, swung it around, hit the ceiling, and whacked the light fitting. Eventually I did get the weapon into the lazarette; all I needed was some practice! Pete promised to keep his head down while I got it.

Three weeks later we again heard someone climbing on board. Boy, was I excited. This time I'd get him! I waited at the door with my knife, ready to cut his arm off (actually, just to scare him), but nothing ever came down through the hatch—maybe he'd heard or seen us. We weren't troubled again, which was just as well, because I probably would have chopped up Pete.

Maybe he was right to worry about me, because I certainly knew how to get into trouble. One day I had just stocked up at the supermarket and was sitting in the bottom of the dinghy in the ever present pool of water, ready to go home. Because the inflatable had a mania about pulling to one side as though it had a flat tire, I faced sideways, with my folded wheelchair on one side of me and three cardboard boxes on the other. I started toward *Usikusiku*'s bow and the rope we always left hanging down, and I was working hard to approach at the right angle because the land breeze had strengthened; if I missed my target I'd be swept away.

Just as I got there, a gust pushed *Usikusiku* back. She pulled against her anchor chain, which rose as it went taut and came up under the corner of the dinghy, flicking it away like a pesky mosquito. I paddled like mad to get back but made no headway against the wind. Off I blew toward the open sea—next stop, Africa! I made for *Yemanja*, yelling for Sue, but she didn't come up. I ticked off my options, all two of them: I could make for the fishing *jangadas* moored to my left, or I could bail out and swim back. Blast! I wasn't prepared to lose my groceries, wheelchair, and dinghy without a fight. *Jangadas* it was. Just then Eduardo, an Italian yachtie, appeared on the deck of his boat. "O mama mia!" he shouted, throwing his arms wildly as he jumped into his dinghy and came to my rescue.

Beryl-Jean arrived from Natal, and now we spent our evenings with Dawn, Frank, and their twenty-one-year-old son Simon, playing cards and chatting. During the day, while Pete was at work, Dawn and I would go to the supermarket and on to the local vegetable market, where it was impossible to barter because we didn't know enough Portuguese. We bought a dictionary, thinking that would sort us out, then found that most of the people we dealt with couldn't read.

The Brazilian government had good intentions during this Year of the Disabled, but its implementation wasn't always well thought out. The newly built wheelchair ramps we saw were either extremely long with too gradual an incline or so short and steep you'd never be able to push up them. Making toilets accessible would have been a better use of money; builders, at least those in Fortaleza, had a real knack for toilet stalls with narrow doors. While ashore I drank as little as possible, and if I did need the loo, I went from one place to the next until I found one I could get into. I learned to fly about four feet from my chair onto a toilet, if necessary. Reversing the procedure was tricky because I had to half-fold my chair to get it through the door, then transfer into it and get back out the door before opening the chair all the way.

Whenever Pete and I pushed through Fortaleza, we drew a crowd. If we stopped to buy something, especially food, people stood around us three or four deep and gawked as though they couldn't believe that people in wheelchairs needed to eat. One day on our way to town, which was six or seven miles from the yacht club, we encountered a horse pulling a cart filled with old car parts, with an exhaust pipe quite rightly sticking out the back. "C'mon, Liz, let's catch a ride," said Pete. We tore along until we caught up and grabbed onto the back of the cart. Of course we drew stares, which at first the old man with the reins couldn't fathom. Slowly he turned and looked back over his left shoulder. I greeted him and waved. He grunted, took a second look, and whipped his horse up. After a while he looked over his other shoulder. Pete grinned and waved. It must have been too much for the old guy because he ignored us the rest of the way into town, even when we shouted our thanks and let go.

I couldn't imagine being a new paraplegic in Fortaleza. At the yacht club we met a lawyer who wasn't allowed to drive a car because he used a wheelchair. The disabled needed to unite, I thought, and bring awareness and change to their society. Pete and I did our best to reach everyone we could. We were on television as well as in the newspapers, which was pretty amazing, considering that the reporters who interviewed us spoke no English. As a result we encountered many people in the street who pointed to us, pointed to their eyes, and drew a square in the air, indicating they'd seen us on TV. We then had long discussions about what we were doing— at least I think that's what we talked about.

In August, *Beryl-Jean* left for Paramaribo, Suriname, a sad event because we'd become very fond of that family. When would we see them again? Saying good-bye to friends was one part of yachting we didn't like. We would have loved to join them, but because of our money situation it was logical for Pete to work another month.

Dawn wrote us from Paramaribo that everyone was friendly and spoke English and that they'd met a man named Jim Healy who would help us with a place to tie up. Just like that, Paramaribo became our next destination. It would be easier there than here in Fortaleza to slip *Usikusiku* and to build a proper dinghy.

In preparation for leaving, we took all of our diesel and water cans ashore, and while a helpful chap was filling them, we strung a rope from the jetty to *Usikusiku*'s railing. With the jerricans back in the dinghy, we pulled hand over hand to the boat. I went up in the bosun's chair, Pete sent up the cans, and I poured their contents through deck fittings into the proper tanks. Then Pete went back on his own via the rope to fill up again, making four trips in all. It was a time-consuming but successful drill.

September 26, 1981. Distance to Paramaribo, Suriname, 1,400 miles. Usikusiku departed Fortaleza amid shouts and the blowing of horns, which always sent shivers up my spine. "We look forward to moving on," I'd written Mom. "This sailing is addictive." I must have had a short memory. We were embarking on a trip nearly the same length as Ascension to Fortaleza, and it wasn't going to be tradewind sailing.

September 27. Being sick and uncomfortable and getting bashed around at great expense was just plain crazy. My navigation was nearly a disaster, for I was continually sick into a pan between putting lines on the chart and doing the calculations. The bloody self-steering wasn't working and dollops of water kept splatting into the cockpit so that we were continually damp and encrusted with salt. Why were we doing this? In Fortaleza, Pete and I had talked about looking for a place to stop, find decent jobs, and build our dwindling bank account. We'd heard we could get work in the States and were determined to stop sailing once we got there.

September 28. What a night, helming all the time. The damn self-steering was going in the ocean soon. It had worked previously in similar conditions. Why not this time? The only thing we could figure was that our bottom must be dirty. Pete had scraped off the prop and self-steering rudder before leaving, and I had scrubbed the hull as far down as I could reach from the dinghy, but that still left a lot of surface area. Whatever the cause, it meant going back to the grind of steering all the time.

September 29. Nothing went right today, and we were both fed up. The "chronometer," our cheap digital watch, conked out. One headsail wouldn't roll up properly because the furling rope had stretched, which meant turning the drum by hand—not a difficult job but one that required some effort. The running pole's uphaul caught on the mast rungs. The compass light broke for the second time since leaving Fortaleza. More went wrong in one day than during the entire Atlantic crossing.

September 30. As the sun rose, I saw land on our port bow, and the water, which had been blue, was murky again. What had happened? We'd gone straight out from the coast for two days before changing course to parallel it. Was the current pushing us in? Whatever it was, I said a prayer of thanks that daylight came in time for us to see the land and said a second prayer asking that we be spared from meeting up with any of the countless underwater obstructions shown on the charts.

The self-steering was back on duty, but the watch had lost its marbles again. Pete found a loose connection.

October 1. We crossed the Equator and entered the Northern Hemisphere for the first time in our lives. Pete said he would celebrate with a rum and coke but later decided against it, as his stomach didn't appreciate alcohol when at sea.

Log: Pete's a bit crabby.

October 2. So much for the eight- to ten-day trip we'd expected to need to reach French Guiana's Îles du Salut, our one planned tourist stop on the way to Suriname. We made only sixty miles in the last twenty-four hours. Seven days and not yet halfway there.

Log: Pete still grumpy.

October 3. I went to the foredeck for a shampoo and bath, then did nine days' worth of laundry: three shirts, one pair of shorts, and two pairs of underpants. Perhaps sailing had some advantages after all.

Log: Pete still bitchy.

October 4. At sundown the bell we'd rigged on the fishing line rang, indicating a strike. As Pete was pulling in the 60-pound line we used, it slashed through his finger, flew out of his hand, and broke. It must have been a mighty big fish. And most likely it spelled the end of Pete's short fishing career.

Log: Pete in a filthy temper.

October 5. It was so hot that Pete hung a partially full jerrican over the side to cool some drinking water. Two hours later he noticed that it was no longer banging against the hull but was bobbing in the distance, about half a mile away. "Let's go and fetch it," he said, and fired up the engine—which promptly died each time he put it in gear. We'd seen a lot of fishing trawlers, so Pete thought we might have picked up a piece of line or net around the prop— the only thing to do was go over the side and have a look.

He got into the bosun's chair and tied a rope on it, which I passed over the support pipe between the davits. I led it to a winch and slowly lowered him into the water. He submerged to his chest and put his head under to look at the prop, taking care that the stern, which was gently rising and falling with the swell, didn't bash him on the head. He went under several times but saw nothing, so I winched him back up.

He headed straight below, where, after tinkering around for an hour and a half, he discovered that the packing in the stuffing box, where the propeller shaft went through the hull, had become silted up with mud in Fortaleza. He loosened the gland to allow a steady drip of water to come through and lubricate the spinning shaft, then I started the engine and put her into gear. She kept running, and I silently thanked Pete for being so mechanically inclined. By this time, though, the jerrican was long gone. Moral of the story: don't trust Pete's knots.

Log: Beat Pete at chess again. Four nights running.

October 6. Pete woke me at 0300, concerned because he could hear waves lapping or water rushing and was afraid we'd again gone too far inshore. The sea was almost boiling and sounded like a fast-moving river, complete with waterfalls. Were we near shallow water? Surely not! Could it be some sort of tidal race? The meeting of two major ocean currents? It seemed forever before morning arrived and showed the water to be still a royal blue, but the surface was covered with little wavelets, all lapping against each other. This continued all morning.

Then the water changed from blue to dark green, and the entire sea, horizon to horizon, filled with thousands of dolphins. Those near us danced on their tails and dove and showed off, and there were also lots of small fish swimming next to us. The scene reminded me of the hymn "All things bright and beautiful, all creatures great and small." In so enormous an ocean, for us to be there at that moment was such an incredible experience that all the discomfort and seasickness seemed worthwhile.

As we angled in toward the coast and came under the influence of the Amazon, the water became dirty. Satellite photos show a greater spread of silt off the Amazon mouth than from that of any other river, which must be why the pilot book warned us to watch for "floating logs and debris that can be found far out to sea." Just what we needed. At 2200 we saw the loom of Îles du Salut's signal flashing on our port beam. Having been warned not to rely on the lights along this coast, we reduced sail to wait for morning.

October 7. We must have been farther off than we thought, because by noon we still hadn't sighted the islands, though my fix put them about twenty-two miles away. So after slowing ourselves all night, we had to speed up. Then a rainstorm came through and with it a wind shift that ruined any chance of making it in before dark. As much as we dreaded a night entrance, we didn't feel safe hanging around all night in these unpredictable currents, so we headed in. It looked simple enough—we just had to go around to the other side of the island group and enter a little bay. We were nearly there when torrents of rain dumped down. Great. Zero visibility. Just what we needed when trying to make our first night entrance. To make matters worse, the engine quit.

"Get some more sail out," Pete said as he scrambled below. Just as I'd done that, we were bombarded by the wind behind the rain, and I had to trim the sails. Shortening sail on my own was easy in light winds but a bear in wind like this. The five minutes Pete was gone seemed like ages. By now I was a competent sailor, but this was the first time I'd had to make a decision and shorten sail on my own in a hurry. I felt alone and just a little frightened, and realized how much I relied on Pete's guidance and physical strength.

When he got back to the cockpit, we searched in vain for the light. Where had it gone? A sickening feeling grew in the pit of my stomach. Were we lost? What if we ended up on the other side of the islands with a current pushing us onto the rocky shore and the wind on our nose to prevent us getting off?

Finally, one of the harbor's leading lights appeared out of the wet blackness. We edged our way toward it, hoping to find the other. Then, as if someone flipped a switch, the rain stopped, the clouds shifted, and a brilliant full moon spotlit the small islands. Dead ahead, with the moon's reflection like a silvery path drawing us in, was the harbor entrance. It was magical.

Pete went forward with a lead line and took soundings as I eased us forward. "That's enough," he called back to me. "My nerves can't take any more. We can move in the morning." Down went the anchor.

I was passing the false floors up to Pete when a dinghy clunked against our hull and a familiar voice called out, "Velcome!" We'd noticed another yacht in the anchorage but never dreamed it would be *Dorianna*, belonging to Heinz and Doris, who had left Fortaleza long before we did. Having friends to explore with would be way more fun than being here on our own.

The Îles du Salut, part of French Guiana's infamous former penal colony, comprise three islands: Île Royale, Île Saint-Joseph, and Île du Diable, or Devil's Island, the name most familiar from the Dreyfus case and the movie *Papillon*. We were anchored at Île Royale, the largest.

We always arrived in new places with a nagging anxiety: could we get ashore? No single method was foolproof because we had to adapt to each landing's peculiarities. For our first attempt here, Pete and I got in the dinghy and paddled as fast as we could toward the small slip. We hit with a thump, followed by a grinding noise as the dinghy bottom gained a few more holes. We thought the next wave would give us a lift and a push up the ramp, but instead it leaped into the dinghy. Failed! For our second attempt, the following day, Heinz ran a rope from a mooring buoy to a post on shore, the idea being that Pete and I would pull ourselves far enough up the slip to get our chairs and ourselves out of the bow, staying dry. Well, sort of dry, anyway, as the dinghy took on an inch of water in no time. But when we reached the slip, we couldn't pull as high as we'd anticipated. OK, wave, come and get us. Failed again! We needed wheels on the dinghy or, better yet, a wooden dinghy. We were sick and tired of pumping this one up, fixing punctures, sitting in water, and going ashore wet.

Heinz and Doris proved a godsend because the roads, which had been paved with gray stone blocks cut and laid in place by a century of prisoners, were so steep we couldn't have gone anywhere on our own. Heinz and Doris got a real workout pushing us up the rutted track that led from the anchorage. The island was beautiful, with huge old mango, banana, and papaya trees, flowered creepers overhanging the track, and a dense mat of ferns. On the way up, I needed to go to the loo. Typical! I shot off onto the side of the steep road and went picnic style, hanging over the edge of my chair. Of course the chair fell over as I was trying to get my pants up.

"Have you hurt yourself?" Doris called out.

"Just my pride. You have to expect odd things like this if you associate with us."

After more heavy going that required stopping for a breather every ten minutes or so, we reached the top. Prowling through the ruins of the prison buildings was eerie, as if we were walking among ghosts. Had men really been imprisoned here for decades? We went on to the small hotel, at one time the warden's mess hall, where we met a few islanders and learned that only fifteen people lived permanently on the island and that a daily launch from Cayenne brought visitors.

Pete and Heinz celebrated a little too much and on the way home launched us off on a shortcut that was cobbled, full of potholes, and even steeper than the main track. It was pitch black by then, and we had but one flashlight among us. Heinz, who believed that the faster we went, the more bumps we'd miss, actually pushed my chair instead of holding it back—I got friction blisters trying to keep the brakes on. "Don't vorry, Liz, ve get you down okay," he laughed whenever I yelled for him to slow down. Behind us I heard Pete and Doris crashing along, also in gales of laughter.

We went by dinghy over to Île Saint-Joseph, which was now used by French Legionnaires taking a break from the jungle around Kourou, where they made roads. Before I could make a move to get out of the dinghy, an enormous black Legionnaire with a weight-lifter's build strode over, picked me up in his arms as if I weighed nothing, just like in the movies, and gently placed me in my wheelchair. If only we could have taken him with us!

This island was flatter around its base. We pushed along a track that narrowed to a path overhung with vines and coconut trees, leading to a small pool where the prisoners had built a low stone seawall to keep the sharks out while they or the wardens swam. It was an enchanting place to sit and listen to the island sounds: the sea breaking against the rocks, palm fronts rustling in the wind, and macaws squawking and flitting about. Heinz and Doris had seen the solitary confinement cells on top where Papillon spent years after one of his escapes. Pete and I would have liked to see them too, but the path was too steep for us to get up, even with assistance.

Our planned three-day stay in this tropical paradise stretched to a week. Our only complaint was the anchorage, where the boats rolled so badly that we got seasick. Most evenings we spent up at the hotel, going back on board only to sleep.

We weighed anchor at noon on October 15 and almost immediately got a new aquatic treat: a huge ray shot out of the water several times and soared, completely airborne, before bellyflopping back in. We also saw our first shark since leaving Cape Town. *Dorianna* left after we did but easily caught up and overtook us; our hull must have been awfully dirty. On the second morning, dawn's light unveiled the mile-wide entrance to the Suriname River. Just inside, looking like a Dutch village plopped into the jungle, was New Amsterdam. As the tide was in our favor, we carried on and motored twelve miles upriver to Paramaribo, Suriname's capital.

A pilot boat approached. I explained who we were and asked the captain if he knew Jim Healy. Well, that's all it took. "Oh, yes, I've been expecting you," he smiled, and escorted us up to where the other cruising boats were anchored. Once we were settled he offered to have his chaps clean our topsides, and when I declined, saying we planned to haul the boat, he said he'd bring them there! I couldn't get over the receptions we got now that we were proven cruisers. All it had taken was a few thousand miles to make the critics vanish.

Dorianna had beaten us in. *Blue Haze*, a South African boat that had been in Fortaleza, was there too, and her crew, Rob and Lynn, came to visit. While we were chatting, we saw two men waving on the jetty so Rob went to collect them. One was the Jim Healy Dawn had written us about, an American who, curiously, was the Honorable British Consul. "I've organized a place farther up the river where you can tie up," he said.

Never one to be shy, I asked, "What about that little dock over there? It's level with the road—no steps! Would it be possible for us to tie up there?"

"That's the president's dock," he said, "but I don't see why not. He only uses it on the odd Sunday when his boat picks him up."

"What will he do if we're here?"

"It's just going to be rough on him for a while."

His friend Jim Robbins, an American marine insurance agent, asked, "Where are you heading?"

"Well, America somewhere. We haven't decided yet."

"I have two jetties outside my house in Fort Lauderdale, Florida. If you'd like to use one, let me know."

Hmmm. Florida sounded good.

Paramaribo was another tidy Dutch town surrounded by jungle. Compared with Fortaleza, its cleanliness and its well-kept lawns and gardens were impressive. Better yet was the harmony among the people of East Indian, Creole, and Javanese descent who lived there. Best of all were the wide loo doors and the wheelchair-accessible buildings. We planned to stay just long enough to slip the boat, clean out the fuel tanks to get rid of whatever it was that kept clogging the fuel line, and build a dinghy. We figured that would put us in the Caribbean in mid-November, at the tail end of hurricane season.

We went onto the slip almost immediately. Because Pete and I stayed on board for the three days we were up, having decided it would be too risky to attempt getting down, Heinz took pictures for us before the shipyard workers cleaned the hull. No wonder we'd been moving so slowly—an inch-thick layer of barnacles covered the bottom. So much for the antifouling we'd put on in Cape Town.

When we returned to our commandeered dock, we discovered that Jim Healy had had the railing at the end removed so that at high tide, with the aid of a board, we could roll right off *Usikusiku* and straight to the road. Though staying at that dock simplified life, it also meant we were on show. The questions never stopped, and they were generally the same ones, but the people were so friendly and so genuinely interested that we tried to answer all their queries. But one night Pete was too tired to be diplomatic. Before coming to bed he went on deck, as usual, to check our mooring lines, have a smoke, and enjoy the marginally cooler evening air. From where I sat in bed, reading, I heard, "Hello, you sleeping?"

"Yes."

"Where you coming from?"

"I don't know. I'm asleep."

"OK, me come back, just I knowy, yes OK, bye-bye me."

"Bye-bye," said Pete, and, after the footsteps had faded, "Bloody twit."

A short time later: "Hello mister, me bring you some food, cigarettes. Good, no? Chinese food, you eat him." Pete, now more meek than cranky, managed a thank you.

Early the next morning: "Hello, it's me. I bring you some food, ya." A middle-aged Indian man with a front tooth missing stood on the dock. Pete invited him on board, where he introduced himself as Mr. Bhagwondian. We showed him around, and Pete explained that we had plenty of food, so please not to worry.

Mr. Bhagwondian looked crestfallen. "You no like, Mr. Pete?"

"Oh yes, it's delicious, thank you."

"Good, I bring more." That afternoon he showed up with oranges, eggs, and more Chinese food. I was really embarrassed and tried to get him to stop, but he wouldn't hear of it. "No, no, no, me I got plenty money, look my car. You no worry, I give you food every day."

Then how about bringing just one portion of Chinese food, I suggested, because we hadn't yet finished what we already had.

"What? Liz! One no, two is good."

So two it was. We fed the other yachties for days.

Pete drew up plans for a new dinghy. In addition to the main seat in the stern were two gunwale-level side seats that would give us a higher perch from which to get onto jetties. A backrest could be attached to the middle seat to brace us if we needed to row rather than motor. A bow compartment held both folded wheelchairs, and the painter was attached inside the bow rather than outside, so we could get to it without having to clamber over chairs.

Mr. Bhagwondian desperately wanted to help out. When Pete learned he owned a transport business, he asked whether Mr. Buggy, as we found it easier to address him, could collect our wood, because none of the merchants delivered. Not only did Mr. Buggy transport the wood, he paid for it himself and insisted we build the dinghy at his house, under cover from the equatorial rains. He said he'd pick us up in the morning.

When we got to the Buggies' house they dragged the kitchen table outside into a sand lot where cars parked. Mr. Buggy snapped his fingers at his daughter, who brought out a full bottle of Chivas Regal and tumblers to pour it in. Pete and I didn't cope well with sitting in the equatorial sun drinking hard liquor! During the two weeks it took us to build and fiberglass our dinghy, Mr. Buggy kept us company, periodically shouting to one of his many children or relatives to bring cool drinks or beer. Mrs. Buggy, a feisty, scrawny little thing, kept us well fed with her blistering-hot food and explosive chutneys.

A woman using carpentry tools was hard for Mr. Buggy to accept. Whenever I picked up the saw or plane, he took it from me. I'd take it back, he'd take it again, and on and on we went. When other Indian men came by to see what we were doing, I had to wrestle them, too, for my tools. Although Mr. Buggy seemed to do nothing but watch us all day, he in fact was a prosperous businessman. In addition to the transport business, he loaned money, owned several properties in town, and had a hotel behind his house, a garish affair that was mint green with hot pink trim where guests paid 20 guilders per night or 13.50 for an hour and a half. What a business! All day long, couples traipsed up the stairs carrying bedsheets and electric fans and guilders eager to pay their 13.50 guilders.

If any of the Buggies' friends saw us pushing around in town, they'd wave frantically to us. Later in the day Mrs. Buggy would stop by and ask exactly where we'd gone, what we'd bought, how we'd pushed so far, and why we hadn't phoned her so she could come and take us. She knew all about our business—everything we did, everywhere we went, everything we bought.

We named our dinghy *Tiki-Taki*, one of Mr. Buggy's nicknames, and also a variation on Taki-Taki, one of the local languages. Mr. Buggy and his relatives and neighbors loaded it onto his pickup and brought it to the river. Much cheering broke forth when *Tiki-Taki* floated (I don't think they expected it to). They all took turns sitting in it, trying unsuccessfully to row against the current. This worried Mr. Buggy tremendously, and he wanted to give us his spare outboard motor, but it was enormous and we declined. Then he wanted to buy us an outboard, but I put my foot down.

Actually, an outboard would have been wonderful. I had phoned the *National Enquirer* upon our arrival in Paramaribo and asked them to send the US $1,000 they owed us for the article. Knowing money was on the way, when we heard of a secondhand outboard for sale, and after Pete dismantled it and found it in good condition, we decided to splurge. Then Mr. Buggy insisted on paying for it and wouldn't hear any differently, his reasoning being that what we were doing would help others.

That reminded us that maybe we needed to give a little, too, so while we waited for our money, which was taking an awfully long time to arrive, we visited a school for handicapped children. There we met Dr. Gever, the head of rehabilitation in Suriname. He had a friend of his make a video showing how Pete and I got in and out of our wheelchairs and from the boat into the dinghy. It was shown on television in Suriname, and Dr. Gever planned on showing it to his paraplegic patients and to medical students.

The $1,000 from the *National Enquirer* took two months to reach us, and by then it was just a week before Christmas. Rather than being alone, pining for our families, we stayed to celebrate with our friends. On Christmas Eve Pete and I were visited by nearly everyone we knew, both yachties and locals. On Christmas Day we had a *braai* that spread from *Usikusiku* out onto the dock. We saw in 1982 with Jim Healy and his family, and I'd never seen so many fireworks; the noise was deafening and a smoky pall hung over the entire city.

Then it really was time to leave. A crowd saw us off. A couple of miles down the Suriname River we spotted the Bhagwondians' van parked on the riverbank with the entire family standing alongside, forlornly waving.

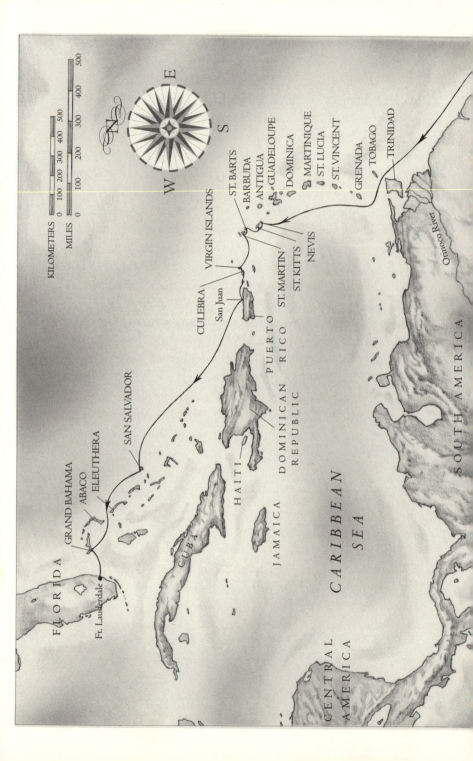

Just Cruisin'

W HAT WE THOUGHT would be a four-day trip to Tobago turned into a 14-day marathon that missed half the islands we'd hoped to visit. To begin with, this part of the South American coast was a sailor's nightmare, thanks to the continental shelf, the muddy water disgorged by the Orinoco River, and a current that ran 3 to 4 knots. The wind got into the act by swinging to the north, against the current and against us. What a way to start: pounding into the waves, helming all night, throwing up in the bedpan while trying to navigate, and getting drenched by continual squalls. Oh, for a log cabin with a fire and some peace and quiet! "But it's great!" Pete kept saying. "Isn't sailing wonderful?"

On days five and six we zigged and zagged to avoid oil rigs belching smoke and fire and to skirt Trinidad, which we'd decided not to visit because it had little to offer yachts. With *Usikusiku* sailing no closer than 60 degrees to the wind, and the current sweeping us along, we made hardly any headway. A helicopter flying from one oil rig to another flew over us and the pilot waved. Why couldn't he have dropped a line and plucked us out of this rolling sea and deposited us on dry land?

On day seven we were still tacking up the coast of Trinidad but at least could see where that island ended. Tobago was just eighteen miles away, hidden in clouds. The current sped up as it squeezed between Trinidad and Tobago, and we had to fight for every inch of northing. We beat and tacked for twenty-four hours. We even threw on the motor for a few hours, but we didn't dare waste much fuel. Like fools, we hadn't filled up with diesel in Suriname; we were waiting to buy it in Tobago, where it was cheaper. But though we got close enough to see the houses in the town of Scarborough, we eventually quit fighting the current and let it take us west through Galleons Passage and into the Caribbean. We would go to Grenada instead.

The wind veered a little and eased enough that we could use the self-steering. We even managed a game of chess. I was making dinner and minding my own business when BANG! over we went—my head ended up in the cupboard. A tremendous squall had hit from the opposite direction to what the wind had been and had caught behind the mainsail, which couldn't jibe because the preventer held it to the side that was now windward and very much uphill. I turned myself around and hauled myself and my legs onto the lift. When I pushed the button to go up, the face of Brian Gowans, the naval architect who'd given us such a hard time in Durban, materialized in my mind like a hologram, saying, "This thing will never work at an angle." I swear I could see his mouth moving as he spoke. But it did work, and at an angle that wasn't far from 90 degrees.

Pete, in the meantime, was climbing up to the port side of the cockpit and letting off the sheet for the headsail, which was backed against the inner forestay, so by the time I got to the deckhouse we were a little closer to upright. He waited for me to pull the slack out of the mainsheet before he released the preventer. The boom dropped to starboard and we sprang up some more; then I eased the sheet and *Usikusiku* came all the way up. In torrents of rain we partially furled and then sheeted in the headsail, which had been loose and flapping, and put a reef in the main.

When we'd finished, the adrenaline still coursing through my body left me shaky. The leg that had feeling was trembling, and odd sensations ran up and down the other leg. Nothing like a good fright to get the blood moving! It was a good test, though, that showed we didn't go to pieces in a crisis. We worked as a team, and Pete made the right decisions to sort everything out.

Minutes after we'd gotten back on course, the wind went back on the nose. Give us a break—we've been beating for a week! And where was Grenada? Ten miles to windward, as yet unseen. With all the sails up and the motor helping, we knocked ourselves out going against the wind and current, plowing into the waves, taking water over the bow, and getting nowhere. Through the haze we caught a brief glimpse of the Spice Island and then she was gone. Bye-bye, Grenada! Pete and I spontaneously waved, then burst out laughing at our absurdity. Next stop—who knew? As long as we got there safe and sound, who cared?

On day eleven we were reefed down and still beating. Oh, la-la! Why are we here? Dear God, let this wind ease! "We're going to live inland from now on," Pete said. Four-day trip to Tobago? By the look of it we were going to end up in Puerto Rico, or at the Panama Canal, or maybe just wandering around these waters for the rest of our lives. Would we become the next *Flying Dutchman*?

On day fourteen the first lump appeared on the horizon. Land, glorious land! An hour later we saw lumps all over the place. Good grief, what was what? We poured over the landfall sketches in the pilot book until we reckoned Montserrat was on our starboard beam, Redonda Rock farther forward, Nevis dead ahead, and Saint Kitts on our port bow. That other lump would be either more of Saint Kitts or all of Saint Eustatius. Montserrat was the closest, but to windward. Nevis was next, so we aimed for her and beat for our lives, praying we'd get there before dark.

Just as the sun went down, the wind eased. For the past ten days, every time the sun had set, the wind had picked up, and now, when we needed it to pick up, it eased. Should we risk going in at night? No, we'd sworn after Îles du Salut not to do that again. One more night at sea wouldn't kill us. We did a 180 and sailed for five hours, then turned around and sailed back. When we got to Nevis, we dropped the anchor and just slept and lazed about for two days without going ashore. Then we went on to Saint Kitts, a mere hour and a half away.

Most of the jetties in the town of Basseterre looked too small and rickety to contemplate, so we anchored. After some radio calls and a visit to the deep-water dock, we got permission to tie up at the sugar mill's pier. In the morning, Allen Dickinson, the mill's electrical engineer, came down to meet us. He came back that evening with his wife, Marguerite, and asked whether we'd like to tour the sugar mill and see some of their island. We were also adopted by Jim and Maureen Curran, who were Irish and had lived in Zambia; it was great to meet someone from that close to home. During our six-week stay in Saint Kitts, both couples toured us around and entertained us in their homes, and Marguerite and Allen organized a small surprise party for our seventh wedding anniversary. We took Jim and Maureen on a weekend jaunt to Saint Barts and discovered the fun of sailing with other people. On the way back the steering went, and we had to change over to the emergency tiller. It was heavy going, but with our renovated cockpit seating arrangement I had no trouble steering. I even brought us alongside the pier without hitting anything. Another crisis coped with.

Then came one we didn't handle so well. I returned from shopping to find that the wind had come up, a huge swell had developed, and *Usikusiku* was bouncing against the pier despite the anchor we'd put out to windward to hold us off. Pete was anxious to move. It was going to be tricky, though. Could we do it without mashing the dinghy, which was hanging from the davits? We stalled, hoping things would quiet down, but instead it got so rough that the swell began throwing us into the pier. Three of our older mooring lines snapped and the railing got mashed in two places. While Pete tied a fender onto the anchor rode and threw it over the side, I fired up the engine. Just then Allen roared up in a car—knowing what the harbor was like in a blow, he'd driven down from the sugar mill—and cast us off. Pete and I learned another lesson that day: we should have acted sooner.

A boat flying a Zimbabwean ensign on her backstay and a green-and-white Rhodesian flag on her forestay sailed in and dropped the hook. It was *Spar*, with Pete Addison. We'd all come a long way since he'd taken us to the international jetty in Durban right after our launching: we'd crossed an ocean and he'd sailed with his brother in the Cape Town to Uruguay race. In Uruguay he'd met and married Christina, who now was sailing with him. I couldn't get over how small the cruising world was. With millions of acres of ocean and thousands of boats sailing it, we had the most improbable encounters and reencounters.

While in Saint Kitts we originated "flying wheelchairs." Pete raised the boom until it was at a 45-degree angle to the mast, then clipped four wire strops onto his wheelchair and onto the boom's block and tackle, which he'd unshackled from the roll bar. Meanwhile, I tied a line to the end of the boom, threw it over the deckhouse, rolled through to retrieve it, and took it up forward. Pete hoisted himself up off the deck. When he was high enough to clear the railings, I pulled on my rope until the boom swung over the pier. I didn't have much leverage, so one second he was over the pier and the next second he was back amidships. On the following swing he lowered himself and unclipped in a hurry. My flight was more sedate because Pete controlled the boom from the dock rather than the foredeck. He always insisted on going first, worried about my safety, he said, but I think he wanted the fun of the riskier ride.

At the beginning, he didn't always get all four strops off in time. Once he was yanked off the pier before he got fully unclipped, so that his chair hung sideways over the boat, but he managed to keep hold of the block and tackle until I got him over something solid. Sometimes when I was coming back on board he'd let go of the control rope and allow the boom to swing all the way to the other side so that I was dangling over the harbor. Then he'd say, "Bye!" and disappear down the lift. We had to make it fun; otherwise it would've been a drag every time we wanted to go ashore.

Once we'd refined the operation, we went flying just for the heck of it. Timing our descent so we'd hit the jetty while the boom was still moving gave us a good ten-foot run during which to free up as much mainsheet as possible, hit the brakes, and unclip—all before the boom changed direction. It was like landing on an aircraft carrier.

Saint Kitts was another place where you didn't see wheelchairs out and about, and people often had such absurd reactions to the two of us that I wished I could photograph their faces. Older people in particular sometimes stopped in their tracks and stared, absolutely agog.

On one occasion I was sitting on the sidewalk waiting for Pete when an ancient, bent-over woman hobbled down the street toward me, pulling a small shopping cart and breathing heavily. She stopped in front of me, unrolled herself, and looked me up and down. I greeted her, thinking, Well done, old girl, keep it up. She took a few more shaky steps, then stopped again and stared fiercely at my chair. "I could do with that; it's a good idea," she said. "No, ma'am," I replied. "You stay just as you are. The exercise is good for you." She blew me a raspberry and shot me a look that plainly said, You insolent, lazy pup, get up and give me that chair!

Another time Pete and I were pushing along the road when a woman stopped her car and asked, "Are you doing that for fun or what?" My favorite, though, was the rumor Marguerite heard that we were a setup and could be spies. That one topped them all.

A letter arrived (via my mom) from *Beryl-Jean*, saying that Frank and Simon would be in Tortola, Virgin Islands, while Dawn went to England. OK—next stop, the British Virgin Islands. We left Saint Kitts with gifts from the islanders, new friends to keep in touch with, and great memories.

Not in the mood for another long passage, Pete and I made a stop at the half-French, half-Dutch island of Saint Martin (Sint Maarten). A swell was running and all the jetties were high, so we required help getting ashore, but the dockmen came forward without our asking—you'd have thought it was an everyday occurrence for two people in wheelchairs to arrive in a dinghy. After clearing customs we went window-shopping, or perhaps I should say window-gawking, because we couldn't believe what was available in the shops. Realizing how starved of goodies we'd been in Rhodesia and since leaving Cape Town, we longed to get to the States to see what they had there.

Next we set off for Tortola. We cleared in at Road Town, then toured the packed harbor in search of *Beryl-Jean*. Where was she? Rereading Dawn's letter, I realized that they'd gone to Trellis Bay on Beef Island, which was linked by a bridge to the east side of Tortola. We headed off again, unaware that Frank and Simon had heard of our arrival and hitched a ride into town to meet us. From the top of a hill they saw us leaving. So now they were in Road Town and we were in Trellis Bay, anchored next to an empty *Beryl-Jean*. Hurry up, you guys! Come on back!

They did, and the wine flowed.

Pete was amazingly agile. Whenever he lowered the dinghy into the water, he then swung down into it on a rope, pretending he was Tarzan, I think, although he'd never admit that. Other times he seemed like a rabbit, with all the hopping he did on his backside (he credited his hopping ability to the quantities of greens I fed him).

Sometimes I think he forgot he was supposed to be a paraplegic. Our first morning in Trellis Bay we got up early for a swim. I was already in the water when I noticed that Pete, instead of getting out of his chair, had wheeled to the open railing gate. "I'm going to dive from my chair," he announced. Two splashes followed, first Pete and then his chair. The sight of the wheelchair sitting upright on the sandy bottom, as if it did this every day, set us both off laughing. Then we noticed that *Usikusiku*, blowing gently back and forth on her anchor, was passing back and forth over the chair. The unlikely pairing of a sailboat's bottom and an underwater wheelchair, with the dappled light flickering on both, was worthy of an art show. Eventually I got back on board via the bosun's chair and threw Pete a rope. He dove down and tied it to his chair, which I hauled up into *Tiki-Taki*. Pete climbed in after it, and while he was hooking it to the block and tackle I heard him reprimanding it, explaining that because it couldn't swim, it must stay out of the water.

We all four walked (well, you know what I mean) to the airport to meet Dawn when she flew back from England. After a few more days of play in Trellis Bay, we sailed in tandem to Road Town for water and shopping, then over to Saint John (in the American Virgins). The wind got so light that Pete and I got bored and motored ahead into convoluted Coral Bay and its Hurricane Hole, inside of which are four separate inlets with hillocks between. The first two were taken, but the third was free, so we claimed it and anchored deep inside. When *Beryl-Jean* entered Coral Bay, there was no sign of *Usikusiku*; they had to poke into every little cove until they found us. Who ever thought you could play hide-and-seek with sailboats? Well, I guess the privateers did, and for a brief time we'd felt like one of them.

Our secluded hideaway was surrounded by mangroves and so still that the anchor chain hung straight down. The first morning, braying donkeys woke us. Pete and I sat in the cockpit with our coffee, watching them chase each other, then we swam over to *Beryl-Jean*. "Ahoy! Put the kettle on!" we yelled. While we waited for them to stagger out of bed, Pete got into *Yellow Peril*, their wooden dinghy, and I surprised myself by doing the same. I don't think my maneuver was very elegant, but then, we can't have everything. Simon rigged *Yellow Peril* for sailing and took Pete and me out. The three of us, with the scanty wind, didn't go fast but we had fun. Another day Simon towed us behind his windsurfer.

We could have stayed forever in this peaceful Caribbean paradise, but June 1, the official start of hurricane season, was three weeks away, and we still had a thousand miles between us and Florida. We and *Beryl-Jean* made another hop west, to Saint Thomas.

Pete and I loved watching the various stages of shock people went through when we arrived someplace new. He sat by the windlass, ready to drop the anchor. That drew looks because it seemed he was sitting down for fear of falling overboard. When we both appeared on deck in wheelchairs, heads poked up through hatches and binoculars came out. When we hoisted our ensign, flag books came out. Zimbabwe was too new to be listed, so many people jumped into their dinghies and paid us a visit. We met some great yachties this way.

Technically, we should have cleared customs in Saint John, which is part of the American Virgin Islands, not the British, but we'd all rationalized that since we hadn't gone ashore, we could wait until we got to Saint Thomas. Pete and I set off in *Tiki-Taki* to find a dock low enough for us. All we found was an earthen bank—we wouldn't stay clean, but a bit of earth would be a change from the usual greasy jetty. Pete got out, and with some difficulty I passed him the chairs, which kept trying to roll down the slope into the water. They were infuriating! And before I dared get into mine, I had to work myself well up the incline, of course in my best slacks. I didn't like pushing through Charlotte Amalie with a dirty bottom.

Saint Thomas gave us our first look at the American influence: ramped sidewalks, ramps into some of the shops, accessible loos, and more money in yachts than I could believe was possible. We went crazy seeing all the beautiful—and often inexpensive—goods available. The variety was incredible, even in the supermarkets, where you could choose from a dozen kinds of bread and six varieties of apples. We'd never seen anything like it. Everything we did and saw opened our eyes to how provincial Rhodesia was. We were enthralled with the sophistication of the outside world— the advancement, the efficiency, the *knowhow*. The radio service alone gave unbelievable amounts of information. Events took place and goods were available that we'd never even heard of at home. Pete liked being places where he could get anything, even if he didn't have the money to buy it.

We were fed up with always being down to our last penny, with being seasick, with not being able to get ashore or go places once we were there. It was time to stop sailing, to settle down for a time. We wouldn't have changed anything about our experience (except the seasickness), but there were still so many other things we wanted to do. We couldn't sit on a boat forever.

When we returned from customs clearance and shopping, a southerly had come in, a swell with surface chop had developed, the tide had come up, and the slope was awash. I eyed *Tiki-Taki* crashing about against the bank. "Who goes first, Pete?" I asked.

"You, Liz. It's easier for me to lift the chairs in."

"You mean you want to see how I mess up, so you can do better." I slid down the muddy bank on my bottom. Now what?

"I think I'll put my legs in first, then I'll have a 'foothold,'" I said. "Laugh, you! That was supposed to be funny." He did laugh, because the dinghy, with just my legs in it, went up and down with the swell, pushing my knees into my face. With nothing to hold onto, I had to be quick, which for me was always laughable. The next time the dinghy went down I pushed my body forward until gravity took over. I'd hoped to get my arms back in front of me to break my fall, but no such luck. My bottom landed on the gunwale as planned, but my upper body had another destination in mind, and I ended up face down in all the water that had slopped into the dinghy. My bottom stayed in the air seemingly forever, until my spasm released and dumped me. Pete was laughing so hard he nearly slid down the bank into the drink.

"Okay, Superman, come and do *your* bit."

Right. Chairs in, shopping in, bow and stern lines untied. The heavens chose that moment to open and Pete let loose with his favorite song, "Come to the Sunny Caribbean." That entertainment almost made up for his getting in without mishap, the lucky bugger. I started the outboard, he pushed us off, and we were clear.

In Suriname he'd mounted a small davit amidships, at the railing gate. It had its own block-and-tackle system, with a hook on the end that we could attach to the bosun's chair without messing with the boom. I writhed around in the bouncing dinghy, trying to get the bosun's chair under and around me.

"This really improves your balance," I said to Pete. "Maybe we should suggest it to the physiotherapists back home at Saint Giles." Now all I had to do was connect with the hook while *Tiki-Taki* went up and down like an elevator, *Usikusiku* pitched like a rockinghorse, and the two of them sometimes collided. After much swearing I did it and pulled the rope. Nothing happened; I still sat in the dinghy. No, I was in the air. Then the dinghy came up underneath and smacked me on the bottom and once again Pete got to laugh.

I quickly pulled myself up the rest of the way and swung over onto the deck. Pete took the hook and connected it to my wheelchair, which swung wildly once it was airborne and hit him on the head, knocking him off the seat. Yes! There was justice in the world! I tried to stifle my laughter because his legs were shaking in spasm and he was trying to sit up again, which with the dinghy's motion wasn't easy. Besides, he wasn't laughing. My chair's name was dirt, but we got it on deck, where *Usikusiku*'s next roll promptly toppled it. It really was trying its best to be difficult! The other chair came up, followed by the shopping and then Pete, who again broke into his favorite song: "Come yachting in the Caribbean, with its wonderful blue skies and flat seas."

Beryl-Jean was going to the Turks and Caicos, then up to the Bahamas and finally to some as yet undetermined destination in the States. We said our good-byes one evening after dinner and cards. Early the next morning Frank sat on his deck and watched us sail away. I hated leaving friends! When would we see them again? I reminded myself that we'd asked ourselves that once before about these particular people, then found ourselves together again here in the Virgin Islands. Maybe that history would repeat itself.

After a day's sail to Culebra, a small island just east of Puerto Rico, and four days there waiting for the rain to stop, Pete and I headed for San Juan. It was supposed to be an eighteen-hour sail, and we timed our departure accordingly, but we went faster than expected and picked up the first light at 0100. It resembled nothing on any of our charts. The next, a big one, had to be El Morro lighthouse, but it too resembled nothing on our charts.

The new chart said El Morro was group flashing 3 in 40 seconds and the two older charts said group flashing 3 in 10 seconds, but this one wasn't flashing group anything—though what appeared to be a promontory extended from it, and a light on the end of *that* was group flashing 3 in 10 seconds. Nothing made sense, and with so many shore lights added to the stew, we couldn't tell what was what. We saw a ship go in, seemingly behind the promontory, so at 0400 we dropped our sails and slowly motored closer in hopes of picking up the entrance markers.

A big swell was running. "I don't like it," I said. My words were followed by a bump. "What's that?"

"What?"

Bump, bump. "That!" I brought the wheel down hard to get *Usikusiku* around, but she didn't budge. The next swell picked her up and dropped her. BANG! She fell to one side, then slowly came upright. "Call the harbormaster, Pete, quickly!"

Hop, hop to the deckhouse. Where were we? asked Puerto Rico Radio.

"Next to a group flashing 3 in 10 seconds."

How big were we? What was our draft? What were we made of? Then, "We'll be with you in five minutes."

Eternity. Each swell picked *Usikusiku* up and dropped her with a crash that set the mast vibrating. Then she'd lean over and groan, as though she were dying. Dear God, we need your help! We don't want to lose our *Usikusiku*! I kept the engine at full revs and tried my best to point into the swells. I didn't know if that was right, but it felt right. Oh thank you, God! Someone is here!

"It's a pilot boat, Liz," said Pete, "but he can't get close enough. He says we must be in about four foot of water." My mind often went strange places in a crisis. This time it was: Old Chinese proverb say 6½ feet into 4 feet don't go!

A U.S. Coast Guard speedboat with a 140-horsepower engine arrived about twenty minutes later. Pete hopped forward to catch their line, which he made fast to the bollard. They took up the slack and laid on the gas. So did I. *Usikusiku* went forward a little, then began hammering on the bottom again with awful, shuddering jolts. The speedboat pulled us one way, then the other, but every impact stopped us dead.

They handed off the line to the pilot boat, threw a second line to Pete, and the two boats pulled simultaneously. It felt as if they were ripping our keel off.

"Check your bilges!" The last series of bumps already had sent Pete scurrying. "Liz," he called up to me, "tell them we're still all right." I was relieved until he reappeared with an ashen face, carrying our passports and money; then the direness of our predicament struck me. Our lives weren't in danger—I'm sure we could have swum ashore if necessary—but to fail now, to lose our home and everything we possessed, all because of a stupid mistake that had nothing to do with our handicaps, was an ending we'd never envisioned and one too awful to contemplate. Dear God, you've let us get this far and helped strengthen us in the past, so this can't be the end. Let's get it sorted out. Please!

A third rescue boat arrived, a Coast Guard cutter with a 600-horsepower engine, three hours after our first bump (they'd had trouble mustering the crew so early on a Sunday morning). They threw us a new line to attach forward. The speedboat came alongside and offloaded a man who climbed onto our boom, tied a line around the mast about a third of the way up, then jumped back aboard his boat and fastened the other end to his stern. The speedboat drove straight out abeam of us. "Keep your helm straight!" came the voice. They hit full throttle, straining until *Usikusiku* was all the way over on her side. The cutter pulled forward. Our deck was awash and from my position at the wheel I saw Pete dangling from the uphill railing.

Bump! Bump! CRASH! Dear God, we're going to lose the keel!

A swell lifted *Usikusiku*. I braced myself and waited for a jolt that never came. She was afloat.

"Check your bilges!"

Pete was halfway down the lift. "We're still dry," he reported over the VHF when he came up again.

"Good. We'll tow you into port."

"Thanks, but we can follow you. Our engine is all right, I think."

"No, we'll tow you. You're our responsibility until we have you anchored."

Now that it was over, fatigue overwhelmed us. As did gratitude—to God because we three were safe; to the U.S. Coast Guard, whose men had worked efficiently, without fuss and with extreme kindness; and to our VHF, which had just paid for itself many times over. As for Pete and me, we'd be mentally beating ourselves up for a long time. Why had we broken our vow never to go into port again at night? The wait would have been three hours at most.

That afternoon the pilot showed up to see how we were. Pete told him he'd gone under to check the hull and, miraculously, had found nothing more than a couple of chips in the cement. "What happened last night?" the pilot asked. "Did you have trouble with the lights?"

"Yes."

"You have an old chart?"

"We have old and new. Both show the El Morro light as group flashing, but it's not group anything."

"I will have a look tonight. This has happened before. The last boat, a Brazilian training ship, was aground for two years."

That made us feel less stupid—but why hadn't they fixed it?

19

Bahama Breeze

"THIS IS WHAT SAILING IS ALL ABOUT, hey
Pete?" The weeklong sail from Puerto Rico to San Salvador
Island in the Bahamas had been uneventful, as had been
the past two days from there. In other words, perfect: a soft breeze,
a flat sea, no queasy stomachs. On a mid-June afternoon, Eleuthera
slid past, surrounded by alluring turquoise water. Now, as we
entered the Northeast Providence Channel, darkness blanketed the
treacherous reefs on either side of us, but I felt secure about our
position because we'd taken simultaneous bearings on Great Stir-
rup light in the Berry Islands and Hole-in-the-Wall light on Abaco.

What a splendid way to end an 8,000-mile cruise! I basked in
the balmy evening and the gentle, downhill ride. Pete settled beside
me. He lit up his pipe and took a few puffs, then put it out; he had
to ration the last of his tobacco. Together we watched what should
be our last sunset at sea. Tomorrow we'd reach the U.S. mainland.

By midnight we were engulfed by lightning, wind, and waves,
all seemingly bent on testing us and *Usikusiku* to our limits. For
three hours we'd run with it, under bare poles. Then, after the wind
had changed and come down some, Pete had taken down the poles
and pulled out a headsail to handkerchief size. We now were claw-

ing our way off a lee shore. I ruminated over the damp, ragged chart and tried to figure out how far we'd gone and where. "How fast do you think we're going, Pete?"

"Hard to tell with no sail up, and the water's so disturbed I can't make out our wake." Since the SumLog had died just three days out of Cape Town, we'd learned to gauge *Usikusiku*'s speed by the appearance of her wake.

"How much should we allow for drift? Do you think we made the right decision by changing to this course?"

What a dirty look I got! "Well, I'm sure as hell not putting those poles up again!" he spouted, and I winced, recalling a time I'd had him do just that. I guesstimated our drift and placed a position line on the chart. During the first two hours of the storm we'd helmed a little high on our course to stay dead before the wind. At the time it hadn't seemed too radical—we couldn't go far under bare poles, could we? I hoped we weren't close to Little Bahama Bank, whose coral heads had mauled dozens of vessels over the centuries. I could almost feel it somewhere off to starboard, greedy for new victims. *Usikusiku* would be just one more statistic.

We hadn't slept since the previous night, and Pete looked bushed. "Why don't you have a rest?" I suggested.

"Thanks, Liz." He grabbed a blanket and lay back on the cockpit floor cushions, so close I could reach out and touch his damp, sun-bleached hair.

Dawn was a relief, even though the wind still howled and the water churned white all around us. Sometime later the sun poked through.

"Pete! Quick—get the sextant!"

Pete groaned in protest but managed to take two sights before the clouds swallowed the sun again. Then he took the wheel, and with relief I moved to the cockpit floor. My cramped legs shot out in spasm. The stretching felt good, although what I really wanted was a long sleep in a quiet, dry place that didn't move about. I propped myself up with cushions and folded one leg to help me balance, then started working out the sight, periodically looking at the horizon in a futile attempt to calm the ever present waves of nausea that accompanied the ever present waves of water.

"The clouds are lifting." Pete's voice yanked me from my calculations. "There's land on our starboard side."

"Heavens above, it's Grand Bahama! The chart says 'Dangerous bight in southwest winds.' Naturally, we have southwest winds." Pete and I didn't need to verbalize our worries about being blown onto a coral reef. Without a word, he brought the sail in tight and nursed *Usikusiku* as high as possible without sacrificing the boat speed necessary to drive us over the waves.

"I can see ships, Liz."

"The chart says 'Industrial Harbour.'"

"Can we anchor there?"

"I'm not sure. It's totally open and might not have facilities for yachts. And look at it. Either it's not completely built or else it's just a place for tankers to unload. What if we have to leave but can't beat offshore again?"

"The farther we stay from land the better, then."

In the early afternoon a tanker loomed out of the low cloud cover. It was hellishly frightening when an enormous thing like that suddenly appeared out of nowhere. But when Pete slid into the deckhouse and called it on the VHF, hearing another voice and knowing someone else was out here warmed us both. Because we'd failed to get a noon sight to cross with our morning sights, Pete requested a position, which I put on the chart. "Bloody hell, Pete! We've done sixty miles in fourteen hours, three of those hours under bare poles and the rest with just a handkerchief up. Sixty miles! That's practically our normal cruising speed!"

Pete was still in the deckhouse with his ear glued to the radio. "A reconnaissance plane says this is, quote, 'only a tropical storm'! They'll keep us informed. They've also reported several waterspouts in Miami."

When Pete and I switched places after my next stint at the wheel, I was ready to drop. Lying back, pulling the soggy blanket over my head to block out the spray and noise, I closed my burning eyes. It seemed like minutes later when Pete woke me. The wind had eased almost to nothing. "Is it over?" I asked.

"I don't think so. Let's fire up the engine and get away from the coast. If the wind should pick up again, we'll need the extra space." For three hours we motored due south from Grand Bahama on what felt like a roller coaster. Just when the land was receding, the black clouds piled up again. More vicious wind and rain blasted us. Oh, to be a landlubber again, steps and all! I could even savor the idea of having my wheelchair stuck in mud.

The swells grew, probably because a southwest wind was blowing over the shallows around Bimini and we were in that place where the charts said you shouldn't be caught. Clouds scudded by, reaching down to touch the sea, and the sea tried to devour us. But *Usikusiku*'s bow rose up proudly to meet each wall of water. Every once in a while we'd get a series of four or five colossal waves half the height of *Usikusiku*'s mast—I actually had to tilt my head back to see their tops. Each one pointed us toward the sky, thrust us up, then roared beneath us while we slid down its backside. We labored to point straight into these waves because when they came at us from the side, the ride wasn't incredible, it was hair-raising.

We'd untied our harnesses when the wind abated, but now we cleated them again so that if *Usikusiku* was knocked down, rolled, or pitchpoled, we'd still be around when she came back up. My greatest concern was where to stow the bedpan. What if a wave took it? In bad weather, mundane thoughts like this often nagged at me. Or maybe this one wasn't so mundane, since a small item like the bedpan saved me the torture of going below.

The wind wouldn't let up. As night descended, the Grand Bahama shoreline lit up. We had beaten nowhere. Throughout the night we sat in turns behind the wheel, cold, wet, tired, and apprehensive.

I seemed to wake up a bit with daylight, although I was cramped and stiff—if you have to be a paraplegic, you'd think you could be born with short legs that didn't get so tangled up. We hadn't eaten or drunk anything in ages, which was a bad plan. It was time to face going below. I dragged myself down to the galley, where I boiled water, filled the flask, and added instant soup mix—all the cooking I could handle while riding this roller coaster. Amazingly, I wasn't sick. Had I finally gotten my sea legs after 8,000 miles? Or was fear overriding the sensations from my inner ear and my stomach?

When I got back to the cockpit, Pete looked awful. "I've had it, Liz," he said. "I just have to get some sleep." So did I, but I seemed to hold out better than Pete. He needed more sleep than I and could sleep during the day, which I found difficult. He gulped down his soup and then dragged the cockpit cushions into the deckhouse. Just as he drifted off to sleep, the sun peeped through the clouds.

"Pete! Quick—the sextant!"

Pete hopped around on his bottom like a mad thing, getting the sextant to the cockpit and himself up onto the winch plate. He got three sights, not an easy task when we were lurching all over the place and he was dealing with a watery sun and a horizon that looked like the Himalaya. According to the position line I got, we were quite far west, but unless we could get a noon sight, only God knew how far north we were. We had to get a noon sight or find another tanker to give us our position.

The wind dropped to a steady 45 knots—Force 9. Pete went back to sleep while I watched the sky darken with more clouds. So much for the noon sight. Near noon I saw a tanker and woke Pete to radio him. Eventually someone answered and gave us his position, which was five miles farther west than my position line. Five miles off in these reef-strewn waters could be fatal. I'd had enough. "Should we make for Freeport, Pete? Fetch the pilot book and see what kind of entrance it has."

"No, the boat is strong and so are we. Land is what kills." A new onslaught of wind and rain reinforced the decision that avoiding land was best.

At last it was my turn for rest. I was too scared to actually sleep; though exhausted, I kept stirring, wondering where the land was and whether we were doing the right thing. Please, God, help us make the right decisions.

"Mayday! Mayday!" I nearly sat up without using my arms. The VHF crackled with an unfolding horror story: another sailboat was in distress and calling for help. Both Xanadu Marina on Grand Bahama and the U.S. Coast Guard in Miami responded, but the yachtsman wasn't receiving their transmissions. I jumped on the radio. "Vessel calling Mayday, what is your position?" I asked repeatedly, but he didn't hear me either. He just kept calling out his Mayday. After a while he was silent, and all we heard was Xanadu still trying to reach him. Our hearts went out to that yachtsman, who taught us a valuable lesson: always give your position. Even if you can't hear anyone, that doesn't mean someone can't hear you.

Later that afternoon another tanker materialized out of the rain and swirling clouds. Pete called. She was the *Chevron Antwerp*, anchored off Freeport and waiting to offload oil. The radio officer gave us a position and told us to call him any time. I could have kissed him.

We couldn't see land, but when darkness descended we picked up lights and looms. Bloody hell! Where had we been going all day? Shortly before midnight Pete called the *Chevron Antwerp* again because we were afraid of being swept by the Gulf Stream onto Little Bahama Bank, which wrapped around Grand Bahama and carried on to the northwest. The radio officer gave us a radar fix that put us farther north than we'd thought, close to the island. We must have been getting a lot of sideways drift, and I was sure we'd had some current too. "He reckons the storm is nearly over," said Pete, emerging from the deckhouse.

Time for another decision. We could go to West End on Grand Bahama, but we didn't fancy any of the entrances there. We could carry on across the Gulf Stream to Florida, but that would be dangerous if we couldn't keep track of our position. Or we could stay out here in the New Providence Channel until the weather cleared, then make for Freeport. That made the most sense. I didn't see how we could stay awake much longer and still function effectively, but we carried on until the wind eased and the visibility improved enough to let us head for Freeport and wait for first light.

A pilot boat led us in, and with help from a couple of men on the jetty we successfully tied up. Now all we wanted to do was sleep. But when customs came, we learned it would cost us $25 a night to stay in Freeport. Exhausted as we were, that was out of our budget. I went ashore and phoned marinas until I reached Xanadu, the one we'd heard respond to the Mayday; we could anchor there for free. Pete and I filled up with water, had a cup of coffee, and tidied up a bit. Then, in spite of our desperate need for sleep and a good meal, we headed out to sea again.

Xanadu was a man-made harbor eight miles down the coast. The closer we got to the entrance, the smaller it appeared. Could we get in? *Usikusiku* was 12 ½ feet wide; the entrance was 15 feet, which meant barely a foot of clearance on each side. *Usikusiku* drew 6 ½ feet; the entrance was 6 feet deep at low tide, 8 at high. Though it was close to high tide now, a large cross swell crashed against the boulders of the seawall. What was the depth in the wave troughs?

My hesitation made us lose steerage. "Forget it!" Pete shouted from the foredeck, but it was too late to turn back; we were committed. I hit the throttle and went for it. Riding the crest of a wave, *Usikusiku* shot down a passage so narrow that if we'd reached out we could have touched the rocks.

We were through! As I wearily steered toward the anchorage, a tiny woman on the bank waved. "Hello, there!" she called out cheerily. "Are you having a nice day?"

20

A New Life

JUNE 27, 1982. We were making a good four knots under power, in calm seas and under a blue sky. Was this the same ocean that had raged at us a week earlier? Tall buildings materialized on the horizon—our first glimpse of North America—and then four red-and-white smokestacks identified Port Everglades, Fort Lauderdale's commercial port. I called the Coast Guard and asked where we could anchor or tie up when we got in. They suggested Pier 66, just the other side of the 17th Street Bridge. The entrance into the Intracoastal Waterway and the port itself were like superhighways, jammed with Sunday traffic that ranged from dinghies to freighters. We bounced through all their wakes and then joined the other sailboats milling around, waiting for the first drawbridge we'd ever encountered to open and let us through.

The chap who helped us tie up at Pier 66 phoned customs and also Jim Robbins. We'd called Jim from San Juan and told him when to expect us, but the storm had put us way behind schedule and he now was in Bermuda on business. His wife gave directions on how to get to their house: north up the Intracoastal, left into the New River, left again into the South Fork, under the Interstate-

95 bridge and right at the first canal. While waiting for high tide, which we needed in order to keep *Usikusiku*'s keel off the river bottom, I pulled Pete up the mast to take down our VHF antenna, because the last bridge, I-95, didn't open.

Fort Lauderdale looked like a subtropical Venice, with canals going off in all directions from both the Intracoastal and the New River, and each corner posting a street sign. Houses and mansions lined the waterways, their beautiful lawns and gardens running right down to the seawall, giving us a peek into the lives and personalities of their owners. Restaurants and marine businesses fronted the water, and boats were everywhere.

The trip upriver took a good hour. A few people on boats shouted, as we passed, "Where does the name come from?"

"Zimbabwe—Rhodesia—in Africa," we proudly answered.

We had another four drawbridges to go through. You were supposed to signal the attendant with a horn: one long blast, one short. As we didn't have a horn, whenever we approached a drawbridge Pete bellowed, "Baaaaaaaar! Baaar!" while I prayed the attendant would hear him over the traffic noise on the bridge. I didn't fancy turning around in a narrow channel lined with boats.

The I-95 bridge came into view. It had a clearance of 54' 6" at high tide, while our mast was 53' 9" off the water. This was going to be close. The nearer we got, the lower the bridge appeared. What was it with us and bridges? Would this be a repeat of our trip through South Africa? Would we have to take down the mast before we could get under? I slowed until we were nearly drifting, and steeled myself for the grating of metal against cement. "You're OK!" called a voice from behind. "You have a foot to spare!" Thank goodness someone in the boat following us had a better perspective. Because I was losing steerage, I gunned it and we shot through. Now for the canal. I cut the corner too closely and for a moment felt the river-bottom muck sucking at our keel, and then we were through that, too. Ahead of us a woman was waving.

"Come to this jetty," she shouted. We did, never dreaming that *Usikusiku* would still be there eighteen years later.

Arriving in America with just $3 (not including the Krugerrand, which we still have), Pete and I didn't differ from many of the immigrants who had entered the country via Ellis Island, in an earlier era. We disembarked from our boat bringing with us nothing but ambition, drive, and a willingness to work hard. Two weeks after our arrival, Pete connected with Hardrives, a paving company in such need of mechanics for pumps and small engines that they were willing to sponsor him for a work visa. I immediately tackled the reams of application papers. By mistake I requested permanent residency rather than temporary residency, which meant we couldn't legally work until we got our green cards. Our priority date—the projected date for someone actually looking at our application—was nearly a year away. In the meantime, Pete took whatever under-the-table jobs he could find. I continued writing and got *Usikusiku* up to snuff.

Our priority date came and went, so I, too, began working on the sly. With both of us now working illegally, constantly scared of being caught, our nerves began to fray, especially when our priority date was postponed yet again. We were ready to throw in the towel and return home until James urged us to stay put because of the unstable political climates in both Zimbabwe and South Africa. He reminded us that while we had families, friends, and breathtaking landscapes to return to, we had few opportunities. We hung on.

After two and a half years of making monthly phone calls to immigration, we finally got our green cards. To this day I don't understand the logic of being offered a job but only being able to start it years later.

Pete went to work at Hardrives. Mel Mellinger at Headhunter, a marine plumbing company, read about us in the newspaper, tracked us down, and offered me a job as bookkeeper. I suppose it was fitting that, with all the trouble I had with loos, I ended up working for a company that made them.

I got pregnant but miscarried after a fall. Then, in 1987, the joy of our lives was born, a daughter we named Jane Elizabeth. Surprisingly, *Usikusiku* was a wonderful place for a baby. Pete built a little crib at the foot of our bunk, and the rest of the boat was like a big playpen, because without companionway steps to climb, Jane couldn't escape. As she became more mobile, however, she needed more space. At the same time, I was longing for somewhere to plant things. A house went up for sale two houses down from Jim Robbins'.

"Why don't we buy it?" Pete casually said, and from that moment on there was no stopping me. I was determined to have that house even if I had to do some serious negotiating in order to get the bank to accept a smaller-than-usual downpayment.

Moving ashore was bittersweet. *Usikusiku* had played such a significant role in our lives. We'd built her with our own hands, we'd lived aboard her for ten years, we'd brought our new baby home to her. She was a part of us, almost like we three were one being. She even had a personality and moods—at sea we'd learned she could be wicked, playful, or just downright content. She also, when we sailed away from Africa, was the vehicle that would return us home. Now, it seemed, that wasn't going to happen. There was never a moment of decision, a time when Pete and I looked at each other and acknowledged that we weren't going back, but buying a house and moving ashore said all that needed to be said. We had a new home now, not the one of our birthright, but the one where our American daughter would grow up.

What would we do with *Usikusiku*? We really didn't want to sell her, unless to a disabled person or organization, and so our attempts to market her were half-hearted. As a result, she sits dejectedly at the dock, chastising us for our neglect. While it pains me to see her looking so awful, in such desperate need of an infusion of cash and attention, I can't imagine driving down our street and not seeing her mast sticking up behind the houses. I still love that boat.

A year after we bought the house, Pete casually said, "Why don't we go into business for ourselves?" I went at that with a vengeance, too. With James's help we bought Power Center, a small-engine repair, sales, and service business. It has doubled in size since then, with a staff of seven who are like a second family, although the financial responsibility is daunting—I sometimes feel we've traded one type of cash-flow problem for another. At least we don't get seasick on this one!

Obviously, when inspired, I still grab something with both hands, shake it, and hang it upside down. This has been my greatest strength, yet also what most complicates our lives. After 25 years of marriage, Pete has learned not to casually toss out intriguing ideas such as "Let's build a boat."

Sadly, Jim Robbins, our American father, passed away before he could fulfill his wish to stand with us when we became American citizens. This is one step Pete and I didn't take lightly. That Rhodesia was no more and that we had no future in Zimbabwe prompted our decision to stay in the United States, but even so, we went through much soul-searching because we have such strong feelings for our heritage. My grandparents were in Rhodesia early in the country's history, while both sides of Pete's family go back more than 300 years in southern Africa. His mom, born Petronella Johanna Hermina LeRoux, is a direct descendant of one of the Cape Colony's founding families. The LeRoux were Huguenots, French Protestants who escaped religious persecution from Louis XIV by fleeing to the Cape in the 1680s. So, while we're proud to be Americans, like many other immigrants who are here because their homelands are in political turmoil, our hearts are elsewhere. We're Rhodesian till we die.

Looking back, I can see how Pete and I grew during our venture. Simple tasks like changing clothes had once taken enormous effort and brought on tears of frustration. Pushing around Mom's garden was a major expedition, while going a half-mile to the shops was out of the question. With hard work these became everyday actions and we could go on to overcome far greater obstacles.

Although I sometimes ponder over what we accomplished, the enormity of it has never sunk in because as far as I'm concerned, all we did was cast aside the expected role of paraplegics and try to lead normal lives (well, what *we* considered normal). But now, from a middle-aged perspective, I shake my head in wonder at some of our reasoning. Not the paraplegics-going-sailing undertaking, just certain aspects of it.

For one thing, at the time we ordered the hull there was no reason to think sanctions ever would be lifted. Where did we think we'd go when no country except South Africa recognized Rhodesian passports? The question crossed our minds, but we figured we'd deal with it later.

Why didn't we save our money first so we didn't have to scrape by each month? For the most ridiculous of reasons: we had never seen any old paraplegics. They all must have died, we thought. Assuming we, too, would have short life spans, we wanted to get going *now*.

Mom was horrified when we explained our reasoning. "Of course there are old paraplegics," she said.

"Then show us some," we countered.

We not only began building without much money, we took off cruising with just $600. Why didn't we amass a reasonable travel fund rather than being so strapped for cash that we didn't get to see and fully experience everything? Simply because we no longer could tolerate hearing about how we'd never leave.

In spite of our youthful naïveté and rashness, everything worked out. Was that due to our sheer bullheadedness or were we being guided in some way? It sounds odd even as I write it, but from the time we met Tony Turner I felt that a force beyond us was lending a hand and deciding the timing of every step. I'm not saying things happened like magic; we had to work for them. But everything fell into place with such simplicity when the time was right that it seemed we weren't being allowed to rush, that we were held back until *Usikusiku* was modified for us and we were competent to sail on our own. If we'd gotten that longed-for sponsorship, if a sugar-daddy company had stepped in to pay off our debts and shower us with gear, we might have left South Africa before we were knowledgeable enough and mature enough to succeed. We needed that time to grow and strengthen, both physically and mentally.

We fretted so about money, but it turned out that our money was always just enough, and when it was gone, more dropped into our hands, sometimes from the strangest sources. And then there's the navigation error we made when we left Cape Town. Both Pete and I knew about magnetic variation. We'd also had two years to daydream over the charts and plot our course. Yet we took off and headed almost due west, unknowingly avoiding terrible weather that we otherwise would have encountered before we had enough sailing under our belts to deal with it.

The guiding hand was always there. At first I thought I was imagining all this, but when I checked with Pete, he, too, feels we were being guided in some way.

The ultimate irony of our venture is that after everything we put into making our dream a reality, we didn't like sailing. We loved the lifestyle but we hadn't counted on the chronic seasickness that marred nearly every passage. I know people who prefer being at sea to being in port, but for us each passage was something to be endured in order to reach the next destination. So, after four years of backbreaking work to make our dream a reality, we spent just sixteen months living it.

On the other hand, look at what we gained from the endeavor: Because our success depended on teamwork, Pete and I forged a bond far stronger than most couples ever experience. We were exposed to a wider world and an astonishing kaleidoscope of people. We were led to a new life in a new country. Was the guiding hand involved in any of that?

I have continued our ambassadorship, speaking to schools, hospitals, yachting groups, and service organizations like the Lions Club and Civitans to educate the able-bodied about the capabilities of the handicapped. I address groups of people with disabilities and encourage them to take just one step beyond where they are now, a step that might be hard but that could spur them on to their full potential. Is this the reason I was born or why the guiding hand helped shape my path? The reason I've written this book? Or am I simply trying to give meaning to my loss?

Life is about how you respond to not only the challenges you're dealt but the challenges you seek. Some people avoid whatever they can because they're afraid of failure. Others, like Pete and me, need more stimulation than most in order to feel alive. To my way of thinking, success is measured not by the position you have reached in life but by the obstacles you've had to climb to reach that position. If you have no goals, no mountains to climb, your soul dies. That's the nature of who we are.

I'd be lying if I said I didn't miss running wild with my dog through a field until I'm tired, or galloping across the veld on a horse. On the other hand, if I hadn't had a tragic accident, I wouldn't have built a boat and sailed her across an ocean. There are plenty of satisfying things to do in life. You just have to look for them.

TOP: Usikusiku *at Jim Robbins's dock, her new home in Fort Lauderdale. We lived on board for another five years.* BOTTOM: *The Fordred family today—Pete and me with Jane, the joy of our lives.*

Acknowledgments

I'd like to express my eternal gratitude to the following:

In Rhodesia/Zimbabwe

"My Mom" for your constant love, guidance, support, and faith in us, and for letting us dig a fifty-foot-long hole in your backyard.

Pop, even though you're no longer with us, for all your hours of ingenuity and labor, and for always being there to make a "whatsit."

James—how can I even start? You stepped in where a father might have, giving us your love, sweat, and total trust. I'm proud to be your sister.

The rest of our family, whom we deeply love. Thank you.

In South Africa

Dear Tassos for the generosity that taught us, in turn, how to give of ourselves. I wonder if you know the impact you had on our characters and on the direction our lives took?

Val for the encouragement that changed everything and for your belief that we had a right to try. In Durban you took us in hand and introduced us as gently as possible to sailing life, a momentous step that with anyone else would have been jarringly different.

Mike and Paddy for your belief in us, the numerous dinners, and your clever ideas.

Peter and Max for the groceries, fund-raising, positive newspaper articles, and your steady faith in us.

Roger Williams for your influence with the port captain and for your great, accurate articles.

Duffy for the home-cooked meals that nourished our bodies and for your bouncy visits that nourished our spirits. You lit up what otherwise was a dismal time in Durban, while your superb photos have given us a permanent visual record of our early days on *Usikusiku.*

In America

Our American family, the Robbins: Jeanne, Karen, and Cindy for accepting total strangers into your home and family after Jim invited us, way back in Suriname, to live in your backyard; and Jim, wherever God has taken you, for becoming a father when we were far from home and beginning anew in a strange country.

Mark Cronje for making me haul my manuscript out of the bottom of the cupboard and for finding a publisher who believed in us.

Susie for your faith that this was a good story that needed to be told. For your hours and hours of research and writing, and for putting up with my strong-willed (we will not say *stubborn*) character. Without you this book would never have been finished. You should be proud to know that together we will help someone, somewhere, find hope out of despair.

Our editor, Jon Eaton, for your "defining moments" and for your gentle prodding whenever Susie and I bogged down.

So many others—some whose names I never learned—helped Pete and me along the way. From the depths of our souls, we thank you.

About the Authors

LIZ FORDRED and her husband Pete own Power Center, a small-engine sales and repair business in Fort Lauderdale, Florida. In addition to working full-time, Liz has been her daughter's Girl Scout leader for the past five years. The troop's phenomenal cookie sales have financed many camping trips and one out-of-state trip for the troop. A trip to Europe is in the works. "I'm shameless," she says. "I park my wheelchair in front of the supermarket, and no one dares walk past without buying a few boxes of cookies." Liz continues her two decades of outreach efforts by addressing groups about the abilities of the handicapped. She gets home to Zimbabwe about every three years and wishes she had time to see more of the United States.

SUSIE BLACKMUN has been a freelance nonfiction and medical writer since 1984. She coauthored *For Better or for Worse: A Couple's Guide to Dealing with Chronic Illness* (1989), has contributed to numerous Mayo Clinic publications, and has written articles for *Sail, Grit, American Baby, Dermatology Times, Psychiatric Times,* and other national magazines. Writing is her third career. In her first she was a diving instructor, diving research psychologist, and the first woman certified in scuba by the U.S. Navy. In her second she sailed, logging 50,000 miles and racing with the first all-female team in Asia. Now firmly settled in Orlando, Florida, with her husband, daughter, and way too many animals, Susie hasn't time for enough of the traveling she still craves.

NORTH
AMERICA

NORTH
ATLANTIC
OCEAN

Fortaleza

Natal

W   E

N

S